child
counseling

child
counseling

Kenneth M. Dimick
Vaughn E. Huff

Ball State University

Wm. C. Brown Company Publishers

COUNSELING AND GUIDANCE SERIES

Consulting Editor

JOSEPH C. BENTLEY
The University of Utah

Copyright © 1970 by
Wm. C. Brown Company Publishers

ISBN 0–697–06021–7

Library of Congress Catalog Card Number: 75–114803

Second Printing, 1971

Printed in the United States of America

To our children, Julia, Jeffrey, Christopher, and Jennifer, and to their children, as yet unborn, in the hope that they may have a more humane world in which to live.

Contents

Preface

We have often expressed regret at not having lived during the early pioneer days. What excitement there must have been in pulling up stakes to leave for destinations unknown and areas uncharted. What exhilaration must have prevailed in those moments of exploration and discovery experienced by the early adventurers. What joy and satisfaction in being able to say, "I helped shape the foundations of things to come." Our imaginations become captured by the romance and opportunity of such an era; yet such descriptions pertain in many ways to the current scene.

The pioneering spirit of today can be excited, challenged, and satisfied through space exploration, oceanic study, biochemical research, psychological investigations, and a host of other new frontiers. The key ingredient seems to be courage—courage to take that next step, to move beyond the known, to be open to new experience. We submit that the area of child counseling is a frontier providing opportunity for exploration and discovery. You, the reader, may well help shape the foundations from which this area will evolve.

One task of this volume is to point the reader toward unexplored lands in an attempt to blaze new trails. Most important, however, we would like to convince the reader that he need not be a spectator to the expedition.

Our basic orientation in this book has been founded on humanistic premises. Such concepts as the realization that children are full-fledged people capable of making responsible choices and that man by virtue of being man is worthy of respect and dignity are fundamental to humanistic thought. We have presented concepts and experiences which we ask the reader to judge and filter in the light of his own life experiences. We have attempted to present research evidence and tentative hypotheses regarding those conditions, qualities, processes, techniques, and procedures which transcend theoretical bias and which contribute to the release and development of human potential.

Child Counseling is in some ways a misnomer for this volume since it connotes a narrowed perspective of the counselor's role. We believe that the child counselor's role extends not only to the child but also to those who comprise the child's world. When feasible, then, the most effective counseling approach for promoting the child's well-being is the involvement of his family or other identification groups in the counseling process.

We recognize that much is being done in the name of fostering the healthy development of children. We submit, however, that our current efforts to facilitate the well-being of children are not sufficient to meet the growing demand. A brief essay of unknown origin which we recently ran across seems to capture particularly well our thoughts and feelings regarding the need to do more. We have reprinted it for the reader's consideration.

I TAUGHT THEM ALL

I have taught for ten years. During that time I have given assignments, among others to a murderer, an evangelist, a pugilist, a thief, and an imbecile.

The murderer was a quiet little boy who sat on the front seat and regarded me with pale blue eyes; the evangelist, easily the most popular boy in the school, had the lead in the school play; the pugilist lounged by the window and let loose at intervals with a raucous laugh that startled even the geraniums; the thief was a gay-hearted Lothario with a song on his lips; and the imbecile, a soft-eyed little animal seeking the shadows.

The murderer awaits death in the state penitentiary; the evangelist has lain a year now in the village churchyard; the pugilist lost an eye in a brawl in Hong Kong; the thief, by standing on tip toe, can see the windows of my room from the county jail; and the once gentle-eyed moron beats his head against a padded cell in the state asylum.

All these pupils once sat in my room, sat and looked at me grimly across worn brown desks. I have been a great help to these pupils—I taught them the dates of battles, the boundaries of states and how to find square roots by the algebraic method.

K.M.D.
V.E.H.

Acknowledgments

There are numerous persons who have contributed directly and indirectly to the evolution of this volume. Our students, our clients, our colleagues have all been instrumental in helping us clarify our ideas and beliefs. Most important, however, are our wives and children who have given unstintingly of their time and energies to support this endeavor. We are most grateful for their understanding and patience.

We would be remiss in not giving special acknowledgment to the loyal commitment of three young ladies who aided us in the typing and retyping of the manuscript drafts. We extend our sincere expression of appreciation to Mary Glenn, Pam Flesher, and Debby Decker for their steadfast assistance.

1

Child Counseling:
History and Rationale

Counseling is an age-old process—a process which only in recent years has been formalized for study and practice. Historically, there have always been "helping persons" willing and able to aid the distressed and needy individual in his hour of stress and need. Such persons have been variously called intimate friends, confidants, great teachers, healers, and a host of other names.

More recent times have seen the emergence of professional persons, again with a variety of labels, who have been trained to be "helpful people." Child counseling is no exception. In this area we find child psychiatrists, child psychologists, family therapists, social workers, probation officers, welfare workers, residential treatment-center staffs, clergymen, and most currently, elementary school counselors among those who are assuming responsibility for aiding needy children.

Although we recognize that there is much historical precedence for individual counseling, we believe that child counseling as a process directed only at helping children is unnecessarily narrow and parochial. From our perspective, the child counselor should be a generalist in that he has responsibility in working with parents and other significant persons in the child's world, in addition to the child; hence, our focus in this volume is toward defining the child counselor's role broadly. We shall discuss his role in terms of his work as an effecter of change in the lives of children and adults. Techniques and approaches, including individual interviews, group processes, family counseling, play techniques, as well as environmental approaches, will be presented for the reader's consideration.

For the reader to understand the formalized process of child counseling as it currently exists it is necessary to have a grasp of the historical perspective that has contributed to its present status. Such an understanding seems most easily obtained through a discussion of the evolution and development of counseling as a "helping" process.

1

THE DEVELOPMENT OF COUNSELING

To say that the history of counseling is the combined history of psychology and education is, of course, to say that the history of counseling is the history of man. Hence, to comprehensively trace the development of counseling becomes a monumental task indeed. In lieu of a comprehensive historical development we have chosen to present an overview, beginning our discussion with the emergence of scientific theory. Such a point of departure is not meant to deny or depreciate in any way the importance of earlier contributions. Another beginning point could have been chosen with equal justification.

The Modern Era

With the introduction of humanitarian care of the mentally disturbed in the latter half of the eighteenth century there came a decline in reliance upon primitive explanations of etiology. Through the efforts of Chiarugi (1759–1820) in Italy, Pinel (1745–1826) in France, Tuke (1827–1895) in England, and Dorothea Dix (1802–1887) in the United States, the shackles of patients were removed and hospital surroundings were at least in theory developed for the care and rehabilitation of patients. During this period of time and beyond, nearly all prominent theories dealing with man's deviant behavior were biological and organic in nature. This was undoubtedly a result of the involvement of physicians and other medically trained personnel in this newly developing area of human concern; hence, a medical model for the explanation and treatment of deviant behavior was adopted. Since that time, however, it has become increasingly apparent that biological and physiological explanations are not totally adequate when dealing with the "whole" person; yet the medical model has persisted. Moreover, it would seem that it has become an inhibiting influence to the development of a more appropriate model for dealing with deviant behavior stemming from psychological and sociological causation. This is not to belittle the contributions of medical science, for its contributions have been considerable. It would seem, however, that a new model to complement the existing medical model is essential for the future growth and development of the nonmedical "helping professions."

The late eighteenth century also saw an increase in scientific experimentation. Again, the focus of attention was directed away from primitive, superstitious explanations for the causation of maladaptive behavior. With the advent of controlled experiments, physiological explanations were able to be substituted for disorders previously believed to be the result of demon possession, witchcraft, and sorcery. One of the most noteworthy of these experiments brought about the discovery of *Spirochaeta pallida* and the subsequent tests for syphilis. This discovery by medical science represented a defeat of what had superstitiously been considered a disorder to be treated by exorcism, torture, and/or exclusion from society.

The pioneer works of an Austrian monk, Mendel, and a British scientist, Galton, provided yet another way of considering human behavior. Through controlled observations, each was able to demonstrate the importance of eugenics in determining characteristics of offspring. Galton, after studying approximately 1,000 eminent statesmen, military leaders, and professional persons, concluded that genius was inherited. Encouraged by this finding, he began research into the relationship between heredity and art. His study showed that 64 percent of the children of artistic parents were artistic, as compared to only 21 percent of the children of nonartistic parents; hence, it seemed clear to him that heredity's influence far outweighed that of environment. His conclusion, however, was promptly challenged by De Candolle who pointed out the many environmental factors affecting over 500 European scientists. Since that time much debate has been held relative to the heredity versus environment issue—an issue yet unresolved.

Prior to the establishment of the first experimental psychological laboratory in 1879 by Wilhelm Wundt, a professor at the University of Leipzig, and the publication of *Principles of Psychology* in 1890 by William James, an American psychologist, the discipline of psychology has been regarded as unscientific, if not mystical. These events, however, led to the birth of psychology as a science and the beginning of distinct schools of psychology (*i.e.,* structuralism, functionalism, behaviorism, gestalt psychology, and psychoanalysis).

Shortly before 1900, Hermann Ebbinghaus, a German noted for his work in memory, advanced a theory that intelligence was the ability to combine and integrate. The Frenchman Alfred Binet extended this concept by stating that intelligence could only be estimated by tests of higher faculties such as reasoning, comprehension, judgment, adaptability, persistence, and self-criticism. In 1904, Binet, as an appointed member of a national educator's committee to investigate retardation in French schools, was able to put his ideas into concrete form. In collaboration with Neophile Simon, he published the first intelligence test. It consisted of thirty items arranged in order of increasing difficulty and consisted of such tasks as repeating spoken sentences, recognizing objects in pictures, defining abstract terms, and giving rhymes for a given word. With this scale Binet introduced the concept of mental age, a concept placing emphasis on a dimension of human behavior other than physical development and chronological age. Revised editions of Binet's scales are still regarded as among the most valid individual measures of intelligence.

At the turn of the century, John Dewey, having been influenced by James, had attained prominence among American educators. One of his many significant contributions was his shift in emphasis from the teacher to the individual student as the central figure in the educational process. The ideas proposed by Dewey seem to have given birth to many concepts contained in current psychological theory and most specifically to contemporary counseling theory and practice.

The name Sigmund Freud has come to be almost synonymous with the word psychology, especially to the layman. Even though Freud's name is much maligned in some professional circles, his vast contributions to the understanding of human behavior cannot be ignored. No psychological theory nor psychological practitioner since Freud's time is completely free from the effects of his ideas and works. In the light of new knowledge, it is easy to question and perhaps depreciate the theoretical constructs formulated by Freud. However, his impact at a point in time upon a fledgling discipline was monumental.

Freud, the theorist, Freud, the scientist, and Freud, the practitioner, were all brilliant. However, possibly the greatest contribution to present-day psychology was made by Freud, the teacher. Two of his colleagues, Alfred Adler and Karl Jung, have contributed considerably to the present status of modern psychology. Although both broke away from Freud in 1911 due to theoretical differences, they remained strongly influenced by his teachings, an influence which is reflected in their writings. Their individually unique contributions have helped broaden our understanding of human behavior and the theoretical formulations of Freudian psychology.

Freud's impact on American psychology was slight until 1923 when he gave a series of lectures at Clark University. In these lectures he introduced the idea of mental mechanisms, the childhood determinants of behavior, and exposed sex and religion to scrutiny. This resulted in another dimension being added to the study of psychology in the United States.

The Russian psychologist Ivan Pavlov is also considered to have had a significant influence on modern psychological thought with his discovery of the conditioned reflex. Leaning heavily upon Pavlov's research, the American psychologist J. B. Watson formulated behaviorism from which learning theory has emerged. From Watson's work, still another avenue was opened, leading to a deeper and broader understanding of the human organism and its behavior.

The foregoing, then, represent some of the major historical events which prepared the way for the emergence and development of counseling and guidance in the United States.

The Emergence of Counseling and Guidance

To understand more fully the development of the counseling and guidance movement in the United States, it would seem important to picture briefly the climate of the country prior to and during the early stages of that development.

During the late nineteenth century, a trend away from a rural agrarian economy to that of an industrial economy with growing centers of population began to take shape. With the upsurge in farm mechanization which accompanied industrialization, it became increasingly apparent that additional training was needed in order for workers to most efficiently assemble, operate, and maintain machinery and mechanical devices. In addition, fewer farm laborers were needed for those agricultural jobs where machinery could be used. As a result, numbers of displaced farm laborers migrated to the cities where jobs were available. However, the majority of these jobs demanded different skills than those possessed by the displaced farm laborer; hence, trade schools, where the needed skills could be learned, became a necessity.

Agriculture was not the only area affected by the first labor-saving devices. The home, both rural and urban, also saw many changes as a result of mechanization. It was then rather common to have regular household help in order to carry out the tasks of laundering, food preserving, cooking, cleaning, and so on. However, with the advent of washing machines, irons, canned foods, electric and gas ranges, and the like, such household help no longer was needed. Although these changes were not as dramatic as air and space travel and computerized living, the need for more training and retraining was, at that time, similar to the present-day need for more training and retraining.

At the turn of the twentieth century, many states had just begun to develop secondary schools, although "academies," normal schools, and colleges had been in existence for some time. Prior to this time formal education had not been the distinct asset to individuals which it was to become. It had been customary for doctors' sons to become doctors; blacksmiths' sons to become blacksmiths; farmers' sons, farmers. With the formulation of new jobs by industry, however, it became possible for young people to pursue occupational goals other than those which had fallen their lot by virtue of their birthright. With the economy changing and expanding in new directions, the "younger generation" saw the unfolding of new opportunities. They also recognized that those who had specific training were most employable. As a result, high schools began to develop vocational training as well as college preparatory facilities. The circumstances were right for an effort to be made to steer people toward niches where they would seemingly best fit.

Another development during the late 1800s and early 1900s which had influence on the evolvement of counseling and guidance was the "Child Study" movement. G. Stanley Hall is generally given credit for arousing interest in the study of the child among psychologists and educators. With his baby biographies, educational theories, and observational studies of individual children, Hall emphasized the need to regard the child as an individual person with unique characteristics and attributes. In stressing the child's uniqueness as a person, he pointed up the need for systematic observation of the child. From such observations, data about the child could be organized so that his individual needs could be more readily understood and met. As a result of this new emphasis on individual child study, focus was also directed to the maladjusted and the deficient child.

The individual usually given credit for officially initiating the guidance movement in the United States is Frank Parsons who planned and organized the Vocational Bureau of Boston. Designed to give vocational guidance to out-of-school youth, the bureau, which opened in 1908, became the first organization to attempt to match people with jobs. Parsons proposed a three-step method of counseling clients: (1) know the person, (2) know the world of work, and (3) match the man with the job. However, Parsons found that instruments and techniques needed to "know the person" were virtually non-existent; hence, his process bogged down due to a lack of "trait" measurements. Even so, Parsons advocated the establishment of guidance programs in the public schools, and his book *Choosing A Vocation* became the first guidance book in the country.

Jesse B. Davis, however, had done extensive work in school guidance before the evolution of Parsons' Vocational Bureau. From 1898 to 1907 he spent the majority of his time counseling with more than 500 boys and girls who attended a Detroit high school. Later, after becoming the principal of a high school in Grand Rapids, Michigan, he added a guidance program for all students in the school. Davis was also responsible for the founding in 1913 of the first professional guidance organization, the National Vocational Guidance Association.

At about the same time in history Eli Weaver was introducing a program similar to Davis' in intent and nature in the New York public schools. Teachers served as counselors, and all students were required to formulate a career plan. Although such a procedure met with some opposition from students and teachers, it paved the way for the individualization of counseling. Moreover, the function of job placement came within the jurisdiction of the public school for the first time.

To these three men, Parsons, Davis, and Weaver, goes the title "Fathers of Guidance." The community guidance center and the school program can trace their roots to the inspiration and dedication of these pioneers. However, it should be remembered that the focus and emphasis of the programs developed during this period were primarily of vocational assessment and placement.

Contemporary with the vocational guidance movement was Clifford Beers, a mental patient who rehabilitated himself. He wrote of his rehabilitative process in *A Mind That Found Itself*. Beers was able to interest famous people, such as William James and Theodore Roosevelt, in his plan to reform conditions in mental hospitals, and he became instrumental in the development of the mental health movement in this country. With his efforts, another approach to aid individuals toward the realization of their potentials was begun. The impact of this movement was also to help shape the development of counseling and guidance.

World War I brought about a critical need to sift out from the thousands of draftees those who were "mentally unfit" and, at the other extreme, those men best qualified for officer training. Immediately, the American Psychological Association appointed a committee of experts to draw up tests that could be administered to many persons simultaneously. In devising the new tests, every effort was made to keep them independent from education or other training. As a result, two tests were constructed, the Army Alpha for literates and the Army Beta for illiterates or persons with a meager knowledge of English. More than a million and a half recruits took the Alpha test in 1918, with several thousand taking the Beta. The tests helped considerably in the placement of military personnel in specific jobs. At the same time psychologists were supplied with volumes of data relative to human ability and its measurement. Shortly after the war many other group tests and inventories were designed to measure "traits" for use in schools, business, and industry, with the major emphasis being directed toward screening and placement. Also, with the development of trait assessment Parsons' three-step process was made more feasible.

The early 1900s also saw the emergence of professional interest in the delinquent child. William Healy is given credit for instituting programs designed to administer to the needs of the juvenile offender. In his work at the Chicago Juvenile Psychopathic Institute, which operated in conjunction with the Juvenile Court, Healy emphasized the importance of environmental factors in the etiology of delinquent behavior. As a result, analysis and treatment of the child's environment, or milieu, in addition to or in lieu of treating the child became a significant dimension of the Child Guidance movement. Since no single professional person could be expected to work with the child, his parents, and the larger environment of both, the "clinical team" approach was proposed. This "team" approach, consisting of the combined skills and efforts of a psychiatrist, psychologist, and psychiatric social worker, continues to be the basic *modus operandi* for the majority of modern Child Guidance Clinics.

During the two decades following World War I, problems of industrial turnover became the focus of much concern and study. Considerable effort was expended in order to determine the causal factors behind quitting, sporadic employment, misemployment, and employee morale. The now famous Hawthorne studies were conducted in 1927 and gave emphasis to the idea that people in industry who were treated with consideration became more productive workers. This finding was later reflected in the thinking of theorists primarily concerned with the mental health of the citizenry.

The depression also had a marked effect upon the guidance movement. With unemployment rising as businesses and industries failed, it became increasingly necessary to provide services so that prospective employees could make the best possible use of their skills and aptitudes. Again, the need for trait assessment and placement was underscored. This need was to be recognized and at least partially met by the appointment of guidance directors in nearly every state in the union.

World War II can certainly be considered as having had a significant influence upon the development of counseling and guidance. Recognition of the important contribution to be made by guidance was given by the granting of military commissions to qualified civilian guidance personnel to perform guidance functions for the military. As had been the case in World War I, tests were developed and used in the screening and placement of draftees. As a result of the testing, vast amounts of data were collected regarding the American male's abilities, his aptitudes, and his personality. Testing and being interviewed became rather routine activities for military personnel. Consequently, the interview and tests of various kinds came to be recognized as routine activities for individuals seeking training opportunities and jobs when they returned to civilian life. Moreover, guidance and counseling became an integral part of the readjustment process from military to civilian life. With the passage of the G.I. Bill and through federal support of the Veteran's Administration rehabilitation programs, the guidance movement was assured a place of importance in the American way of life.

The early 1940s also saw a period of significant writing in the field of counseling. Edmund Williamson had begun to publicize the trait-and-factor approach to counseling through the introduction of his book *How to Counsel Students* (1939). Carl Rogers, making a substantial departure from the majority of his contemporary theorists, presented his first statement of the now popular client-centered counseling approach with the publication of *Counseling and Psychotherapy* (1942). Although both authors have evolved from the respective positions discussed in these volumes, the basic concepts presented still provide two major emphases for counselor theory, practice and training.

The 1950s ushered in a greater emphasis in mental health than had yet been seen. Concern for the increasing divorce rate, the incidence of mental disturbances, and other factors led to an increase in marital and pastoral counseling. Group counseling became more popular with professional personnel as the demand for counseling services began to far exceed the supply of qualified counselors. Both the American Personnel and Guidance Association and the Counseling Psychology division of the American Psychological Association were formed in the 1950s so that professional counselors could better organize to meet the needs of the citizenry.

The 1957 launching of the sputnik created an immediate threat to our national security and international prestige. At once, widespread concern was expressed that our public schools were not doing as adequate a job of identifying and encouraging talented youth as was needed to compete with the Soviet Union's scientific advancements. Therefore, as a reply to sputnik, the United States Congress rapidly passed the National Defense Education Act of 1958. Title V of this act made provision for funds to be used to expand and upgrade school guidance programs, facilities, and personnel. Fellowships and institute programs were devised to provide school guidance personnel with the knowledge and skills needed to aid students in taking advantage of their abilities and interests in higher education.

Another significant event in the development of counseling and guidance was the publication of the "Wrenn Report" in 1962. Under the leadership of C. Gilbert Wrenn, the American Personnel and Guidance Association nominated a group of leaders in the field of counseling and guidance to project the future of the profession. The completed work, *The Counselor in a Changing World,* became a guidepost for development. Although when the report was written the commission expressed concern that its predictions might have been too extreme, Wrenn later expressed publicly that they had indeed been too conservative, that is, change was and is taking place at a rate beyond what could be foreseen in the 1962 report.

Other factors have influenced and will continue to influence the directions taken by the evolving profession of counseling and guidance. Such federally-sponsored programs as the Manpower Development and Training Act, Job Corps, Youth Opportunity Centers, and Employment Services have all been encouraged to more extensively involve the counseling process in working with their respective clientele. The direction being taken seems to emphasize the need to involve the total person in the search for the meaning and the purposes of life.

More recently, the United States Office of Education has initiated Project ERIC (Educational Research Information Center) designed to centralize and disseminate research and professional literature to educators throughout the nation. To date ERIC has established twelve external clearinghouses to collect and distribute all available research results and research-related materials pertaining to various areas of education. ERIC's guidance and counseling information, located at the University of Michigan, emphasizes that library research time will be greatly reduced while the amount and comprehensiveness of the information that is available will be increased. In the not too distant future, individuals will be able to obtain inexpensively, easily, and rapidly nearly all of the pertinent research for any given area in the field of counseling and guidance. With this eventuality the ease of conducting research should increase the volume and caliber of research in counseling and guidance which is a much needed development.

The Development of Elementary School Counseling

Elementary school counseling and elementary school guidance are relatively recent terms, yet elementary school counseling programs can be traced to the early 1900s. In 1909 the Boston public schools appointed a counselor-teacher for each of its elementary schools. The failure of this program may have been responsible, at least in part, for the delayed emergence of elementary school counseling programs.

Although little had been written about the functions of counseling and guidance in the elementary school prior to 1960, some mention was given the process more than a decade earlier. Jones (1945) pointed out, "the logical place for beginning organized guidance is the point at which the child enters school." (p. 287) Emphasizing the importance of the need for elementary school guidance programs, Krugman (1954) stated, "to begin guidance at the age of 14, as though life began then, is contrary to all we know about personality formation." (pp. 271-272)

The later 1950s saw a small number of investigators reporting their findings with respect to guidance services existent in elementary schools. By 1960, articles and books began to appear in which varied opinions as to the desirable nature of such services were expressed. It appeared that the evolution of the elementary school counselor had begun.

Hill and Nitzschke (1961) seem to have been instrumental in developing concern with regard to the definition of the guidance function in the elementary school. After surveying persons in charge of 154 preparation programs in elementary school guidance in the United States, they concluded, "Preparation programs for guidance workers in elementary schools are as yet not well defined. Some of these programs make little, if any, differentiation between preparation for elementary school and preparation for secondary school. Very few universities have clearly planned programs for the preparation of guidance workers in the elementary school." (p. 159)

Shortly after Hill and Nitzschke reported their findings, Anna Meeks (1962), writing for the *National Educational Association Journal,* made a plea for a recognition of the differences between the elementary school counselor and the secondary school counselor. Apparently fearing the undefined role of the elementary school counselor, she warned: "I believe that in the next ten years elementary-school guidance will grow rapidly. It is essential, however, that such guidance not be a pale replica of secondary-school guidance. Rather, the two programs must complement each other. . . ." (p. 32)

Nitzschke and Hill's concern for the preparation and function of the elementary school counselor prompted the publication in 1964 of a report dealing with this question. They prefaced their report by saying, "The guidance movement in secondary schools was strongly influenced by pioneers who developed training programs and shaped the emphases of secondary school guidance by these efforts. The same thing is happening in elementary school guidance." (1964, p. 3)

Meanwhile, Arbuckle, Patterson, Tyler, Wrenn, and other leaders in the field were continuing to define the role of the school counselor, making little or no distinction between the secondary and elementary school function of the counselor. This tendency seemed to be encouraged by the passage of the National Defense Education Act of 1958. The Act, as mentioned before, was designed to aid in the identification and encouragement of talented secondary school counselors, but not for the training of elementary school counselors. A direct result of the Act were NDEA Institutes which represented a distinct departure from traditional training programs in counseling and guidance.

As early as the later 1950s, a few elementary schools were beginning to employ elementary school counselors, and universities were developing training programs for counselors at that level; yet as recently as 1964, Oldridge (1964) attempted to determine the role of the elementary school counselor but was unable to obtain a clear definition.

Discussing the emergence of the elementary school counselor, Otto (1964) said:

The concern for guidance services in the elementary school has emerged largely from two sources. First, high school and college personnel with interest in guidance services increasingly became aware that the kinds of guidance offered to children in elementary school influenced the effectiveness of the guidance program for the older pupils. They saw a need for organized guidance efforts throughout the school system. A second source of guidance interests came from within the elementary school itself. This interest grew out of the concern for the "whole" child. The broadened concern for all of the facets of child development required attention to the non-intellectual aspects of development. The attention given to the total organism required understanding of the many influences both inside the school and out which affect the child's behavior.

As the interest of the total development of the child emerged, teachers became concerned with physical and mental health, behavior inside and outside the school, diagnosis of learning problems, and a myriad of other facets which formerly had not been of particular concern. The introduction of these new problems and activities brought about the need for specialists to augment the efforts of classroom teachers. The expansion of visiting teacher, psychological, psychiatric, and social services took place during or about the same time that the *whole child* concept was taking hold in the schools.

Elementary schools were organized for the most part on a single-teacher-per-grade basis, so that the classroom teacher was able to get to know the child well enough to understand him and to be valuable in meeting his needs. Specialists were added to assist the teacher rather than to service the child as a supplement to the contribution of the teacher, as was the case in the secondary schools. This became a basic difference in the guidance programs of secondary and elementary schools. (p. 239)

The 1965 extension of the National Defense Education Act seems to be greatly influencing the growth and development of elementary school guidance programs. With this extension monies became available for the training of elementary school counselors. Discussing the implications of federal legislation for elementary school guidance programs, Wellman (1965) said: "I think we can say without reservation that all of the new legislation, including the revision of the National Defense Act, are people-oriented rather than program-oriented; that the basic purpose of this legislation is to assist people all the way from pre-school age up to adult." (p. 1)

Other recent legislation seems also to be having a direct influence upon elementary school guidance programs. In speaking about the Elementary and Secondary School Education Act of 1965, Wellman (1965) said, "Both Title I and Title III of this act have tremendous potential for the support of elementary school guidance." (p. 3)

Current Status of Elementary School Guidance

Even though federal support and professional encouragement for the development of elementary school guidance programs have markedly increased in recent years, confusion about the nature and extent of the functions performed by the elementary school counselor still exists; yet leaders in the field continue to emphasize the need and potential significance of the elementary school counselor. Nitzschke and Hill (1964) concluded their report by saying, ". . . it is conceivable that the future role of elementary school guidance will be one of greater impact and importance than that at the secondary school level." (p. 20)

In 1965 a committee was established to set up guidelines relating to the role and function of the elementary school counselor. This responsibility was shared jointly by the Association for Counselor Education and Supervision and the American School Counselor Association. The committee prepared a tentative preliminary statement in 1965 for presentation at the American Personnel and Guidance Association Convention. The text of the statement follows:

The purpose of this statement is to identify and provide guidelines for the development of the role of the elementary school counselor as perceived by the membership of the Association for Counselor Education and Supervision and the American School Counselor Association. Guidance for all children is accepted as an integral component of the total educational experience in the elementary school. Guidance is defined as a continuing process concerned with determining and providing for the developmental needs of all pupils. This process is carried out through a systematically planned program of guidance functions which are a vital part of the elementary school's organized effort to provide meaningful educational experiences appropriate to each child's need and level of development.

The teacher's many responsibilities in the guidance process are recognized and respected, but the significant complementary role of personnel in addition to the teacher is also acknowledged. Such additional personnel are essential if the elementary school is to provide the maximum opportunity for learning, enabling each child to learn effectively in terms of his own particular abilities and his own developmental process. The elementary school counselor, one of these additional professional persons, has a significant contribution to make in the cooperative process of identifying and providing for the developmental needs of children. The purpose of the ACES–ASCA Policy Statement is to describe, not what presently exists, but the contributions that a counselor could make in an elementary school program.

The identity of the secondary school counselor has been reasonably well established through the years and has been clearly stated in the ASCA Statement of Policy for Secondary School Counselors, published in 1964. The identity of the elementary school counselor is in the process of developing.

School Counselor in an elementary school is a term used in this policy statement to designate a counselor working as a member of the professional staff of an elementary school; responsible to the principal of that school; concerned with and accepting a responsibility for working with pupils, teachers, and parents; and having as his major concern the developmental needs of all pupils. The counselor is educationally oriented, highly knowledgeable in the area of child growth and development with a broadly based, multidisciplinary background in the behavioral sciences and a high degree of competence in human relations.

Counseling is one of the responsibilities of the counselor. Other responsibilities of the counselor include consultations and coordination. The counselor will counsel and consult with individual pupils and groups of pupils, and with individual teachers and groups of teachers, and with individual parents and groups of parents. He will coordinate the resources of the school and community in meeting the needs of the individual pupil.

Counseling, consultation, and coordination are considered pupil personnel services and the school counselor works within a pupil personnel framework. School counselors have much in common with counselors in non-school settings and with other pupil personnel and instructional staff members. However, significant differences do exist between school counselors and each of these groups in regard to the nature of professional responsibilities, competencies, and preparation. The elementary school counselor claims professional identity in the fields of counseling, education, and the behavioral sciences. (ACES–ASCA Committee, 1966a, pp. 258–259)

A year later, in 1966, the tentative statement was expanded and the same committee published the preliminary statement regarding the elementary school counselor. This statement presently serves as a guideline for the development of elementary school counseling and guidance programs:

We believe that guidance for all children is an essential component of the total educational experience in the elementary school. We recognize the teacher's many responsibilities in the guidance process, but we recognize also the significant complementary role of personnel in addition to the teacher. We believe such additional personnel are essential if the elementary school is to provide the maximum opportunity for learning, enabling each child to learn effectively in terms of his own particular abilities and his own developmental process.

We envision a "counselor" as a member of the staff of each elementary school. The "counselor" will have three major responsibilities: counseling, consultation, and coordination. He will counsel and consult with individual pupils and groups of pupils, with individual teachers and groups of teachers, and with individual parents and groups of parents. He will coordinate the resources of the school and community in meeting the needs of the individual pupil. The "counselor" will work as a member of the local school staff and as a member of the team providing pupil personnel services.

We believe that guidance for all children is an essential component of the total educational experience in the elementary school.

By *guidance* we mean a continuing process concerned with determining and providing for the developmental needs of all pupils. This process is carried out through a systematically planned program of *guidance functions*. These guidance functions are a vital part of the elementary school's organized effort to provide meaningful educational experience appropriate to each child's need and level of development.

We envision a "counselor" as a member of the staff of each elementary school.

By "counselor" we mean a professional person, educationally oriented, highly knowledgeable in the area of child growth and development, with a broadly based multidisciplinary background in the behavioral sciences and a high degree of competence in human relations.

By *educationally oriented* we mean having a knowledge of the elementary school program, including curriculum, the learning process and school organization. We recognize the value of teaching experience in the elementary school but feel that knowledge of the school program and processes can also be gained through a planned program of experiences in the school as a part of the "counselor's" preparation.

By *broadly based, multidisciplinary background* we mean a program of preparation carefully planned to include the contributions of several disciplines —anthropology, economics, education, philosophy, psychology, sociology. The graduate program will, of course, be determined by the undergraduate program, but we would like to see the graduate program be multidisciplinary in approach from the very beginning. There will be a need for cooperative efforts by all universities and college departments concerned to provide appropriate programs designed specifically for elementary school "counselors." We are not thinking of combining the traditional programs of preparation for secondary school counselors, social workers, or clinical psychologists to make a "multidisciplinary program."

We recognize the value of different types of experiences in the "counselor's" background, especially in the development of skill in human relations, and would encourage experiences in addition to those directly related to education.

We realize that this long-range goal of a "counselor" in each elementary school will not be immediately possible for many individual schools. The size of the school, community resources, and the nature of pupil needs will determine the number of professional personnel and the organizational pattern required to provide a continuous, systematic approach in meeting the developmental needs of all pupils.

We also recognize that there will be varying levels of responsibility in such a program and that contributions to the total guidance process may be made by persons less highly prepared professionally than the "counselor" we have described. We definitely need to explore the specific functions which may be performed by such personnel.

We would emphasize, however, our belief in the importance of first having a "counselor" such as we have described as a member of the individual school staff.

The "counselor" will have three major responsibilities: counseling, consultation, and coordination.

The "counselor" will perform a counseling function with pupils as well as with parents and teachers.

The "counselor" will perform a consultative function with parents and with other school community personnel. One significant area of consultation in the school will be as a participant in the development of curriculum and in making decisions about the use of curriculum. The "counselor's" point of emphasis will be to include experiences that will be meaningful to the child and will help him to develop a realistic self-concept. The more closely an individual can be identified with a particular school the more effective he can become in this phase of the consultant role.

The "counselor" will perform a coordinating function in integrating the resources of the school and community-ideas, things, and people—to meet the developmental needs of the individual. Many persons through many different programs are working in separate ways to affect the child's concept of himself.

The "counselor" in the school integrates these many individual efforts into a meaningful pattern. As elementary schools change their organization and teaching procedures, this integrated support for the individual pupil will become increasingly important.

The "counselor" must also see himself and the school as an integral part of a total community effort. There will be a need for clearly perceived relationship and definition of functions in working with community personnel. The strength of community resources should be recognized and the efforts of the community should be closely related to those of the school. We see the "counselor" with other personnel in the school and community as colleagues willing to explore together new ways of achieving mutual goals. (ACES–ASCA Committee, 1966b, pp. 259–261)

In an address at the 1965 national convention of the American Personnel and Guidance Association, Meeks attempted to synthesize thinking with regard to elementary school guidance. Pointing out the dilemma that must be recognized with such a consensus, she said:

First, a great many people are attempting to find their way through this whole question of elementary school guidance, and we must face the fact that the people who are reacting—all bring tremendously different backgrounds of experiences, and I think we have to be able to sift out the things which are said which represent a lack of first-hand knowledge in some of this, because if we try to speak from lack of experience, we have to be very careful in studying what we say.

She concluded her discussion by saying:

If the youngster is going to learn about himself, he's got to start early. I like to think of this as counseling, in which he has a chance to discover himself, and then emerge as that adult that we so desperately need in great numbers. I like to think of him using the counseling, especially in groups, to learn to listen to other people as a counselor does. I believe that we can actually teach youngsters to listen with the counselor's ear, and mind, and heart. I think we could change the face of human relations in this great country of ours with two generations of helping youngsters through counseling to become the kind of person who tries to understand what the other fellow is saying. So, today, I make a plea to you. Let's not freeze at any level of development of this elementary school guidance program. Let's get it based in hard rock, and then let's grow as this program grows, and as the ideas and concepts become more and more clear. Let's be able to say, "I helped to move it along," not "I held the fort for something I wanted." (1965)

Underscoring the importance of child counseling in the schools was the introduction in 1967 of *Elementary School Guidance and Counseling*, a professional journal. Since that time much has been written attempting to clarify the role and function of the child counselor in the school setting.

Most recently, the Education Professions Development Act (EPDA) of 1968 has broadened the scope of federal support for the training and utilization of educational personnel. It is expected that the Act will provide additional impetus for the development of counseling personnel to serve school children.

PSYCHOLOGY, EDUCATION, COUNSELING: A FAMILY

Certainly the history of elementary school counseling is a brief one if, in fact, it has a history at all. The major developments in the past decade have indicated a rapid growth in this area, but rather an uncertain direction. Perhaps a helpful way to understand the development of elementary school counseling is to view it as analogous to the development of the elementary-school-aged child. This becomes evident as one pictures a wide-eyed but bewildered first grader who is new to the educational scene, but who is a youngster from whom much is expected. His father, psychology, has had a long and dignified past, yet few people know his father well. Father is respected and admired in the community but is also somewhat mystical and feared. Naturally, father would like to have a significant influence on his son's growth and development. He would like to see young elementary school counseling fulfill his parental expectations. As elementary school counseling views father's family tree, he is awed. He is also aware that his father shows less love and acceptance toward him than toward some of his older brothers and sisters; hence, he turns to mother in hope of more fully gratifying his needs.

Mother, public education, is known to almost everyone. She is a well-accepted and respected member of the community. Although not as mystical and feared as her husband, she, too, has rather rigid expectations for her son. If elementary school counseling is going to live in her house, then he is bound to some degree by her philosophy. He must adhere, as have her other children, to her rules and regulations. In order to avoid the possibility of being functionally orphaned, elementary school counseling strives hard to please his mother for it is from her that he gets his bed to sleep in and his food to eat. He hopes to grow to maturity and independence, but it will only be with the blessing of his mother and his older siblings that he will reach fruitful adulthood.

Probably the biggest influence in elementary school counseling's family has been his big brother, secondary school counseling. Although a relative newcomer to school himself, older brother has gained acceptance from his classmates and has already become one of the high school's star pupils with money and attention being showered upon him. He has left some big shoes to fill and some ill-fitting hand-me-downs. Some rivalry exists, and elementary school counseling is aware that it is going to be difficult for him to meet his family's expectations. At the same time he is seeking to establish his own identity, father is pushing in one direction, mother in another, and big brother in a third. How can he please them all? He wants to learn to read and write as his brother did and as his parents have done; yet, he is not certain of what is to be done or how to do it. He, like most school beginners, is eager to begin, but he is awed by the tasks and challenges which confront him.

RATIONALES FOR CHILD COUNSELING

There are a number of rationales and justifications for the development of child counseling. Generally, these rationales can be broken down into functions which pertain to the prevention and remediation of maladjustment and to the release and development of human potentials.

Prevention of Maladjustment

Pages could be filled with citations of statements by "experts" supporting the need for counseling in the elementary school. Probably all of us could, with but a little reflection, think of individual children in our environments who we thought needed "help," but who, all too often, had nobody to "help" them. We could also think of children whose behavior we wished would change; yet, no change occurred. It is impossible to read a newspaper without reading about antisocial acts that have been committed, some by young people of elementary school age. It is further sobering to realize that our prisons and mental hospitals are filled with ex-elementary school children. Why? What went wrong? How can we remedy the situation? How can we prevent its reoccurrence?

In addition to crime, other forms of social maladjustment not so frequently read about, such as alcoholism, drug addiction, and sexual perversion, are becoming more prevalent. Alcoholics, drug addicts, and sex perverts, of course, are people, and nearly all of these people were elementary school pupils at some point in time. The above comments refer to the "more serious" maladjustments. However, they say nothing of the countless people who lead unhappy and/or unproductive lives, but who never become classified as maladjusted.

It has been said that we live in an age of anxiety. Americans spend over $10 billion a year on liquor. In some circles tranquilizers and pep pills are becoming nearly as commonplace as chewing gum. Suicide is topped only by accidents as the leading killer of young adults. Gurin, Veroff, and Feld (1960) reported that one out of five people interviewed, in a representative sample of Americans, had at one time or another felt that he was going to have a nervous breakdown. Furthermore, it is estimated by the National Institute of Mental Health that mental disorders will continue to increase most dramatically in young people below the age of twenty-one.

Statistics reported in terms of *millions of Americans* or in *percent of the population* are often easy to depreciate or to keep from having much personal meaning. Let us look at maladjustment in this country in a slightly different way. Let us suppose that things do not get any better or any worse but remain just as they are for the next twenty years. (All available evidence would indicate that if the present trend continues, psychological disturbance will be much more prevalent in twenty years than it is now.) Let us also assume that you are viewing the "average American elementary school classroom" of about thirty students. On the basis of our best predictions and judgments, this is what we will see. One or two of these students are or will become seriously neurotic. Four of them already have emotional and behavioral problems. Seven of their marriages will end in divorce. One will become a problem drinker or alcoholic, and if the present trend continues, three of them will be hospitalized at some time for mental illness. As we view this group of faces and attempt to determine which of the children will be high school dropouts, who will go to college, and who will graduate from college, we must also look at who among the group will be victims of suicide. How many of these children will have opportunity to grow to be happy, productive adults?

Mental disturbances incapacitate more people than all other health problems combined, and mental patients occupy more than half of the country's hospital beds. Possibly the most bothersome of all the data, however, is the fact that for each of those currently hospitalized for mental illness there are at *least* twenty more who are in need of psychiatric or psychological aid (Coleman, 1964). Couple these figures with the ever-increasing crime rate and the reason for needed change in the present trend becomes all too obvious.

When one reads in the paper of the hideous crimes, such as mass murder, committed by children and young adults, he can often read of a reporter's probe into the "why" of the crime. Such probes may contain interviews with the past teachers of the individual. Sometimes the teachers report absolute amazement and paint a rather glowing picture of the individual as he was remembered in schools. Sometimes, however, they comment that they could have predicted such an outcome for "that troublesome kid." Perhaps something could have been done to turn the tide of events that prompted the destructive behavior of the individual if there had been a trained person to aid in his early development. To date we seem to have ignored the evidence of investigators such as Gluck and Gluck (1950) in discovering the potentially maladjusted or potentially delinquent child. We certainly can do more to identify and aid such children toward a more satisfying way of meeting their needs.

We do not begin to propose that elementary school counseling will wipe clean this blackened slate. Instead, we propose that effective, new, and creative programs of counseling in the elementary school and elsewhere could have a widespread effect in deterring the current trend.

Development of Human Potential

There is, of course, a completely different form of rationale for elementary school counseling. Counseling may help that minority of maladjusted and potentially maladjusted to become better adjusted and more productive. And yet, can not everyone gain from being "better adjusted"? Adjustment is not the same for each individual and must be thought of in terms of individuals, not groups.

Maslow (1954) has written of the idea of the self-actualizing person— the person who is more fully functioning and lives a more enriched life than does the average person. He has also emphasized that an individual's movement *toward* self-actualization leads to not only a happier but a more productive individual. Maslow (1962), Rogers (1961), Brammer and Shostrom (1968), and others strongly suggest that self-actualization may be the end product of psychotherapy or counseling. According to Maslow, an elementary school child would be incapable of attaining self-actualization since the condition of being actualized is an end product of the growth process. He would not object, it would seem, to a process that would facilitate growth *toward* self-actualization which can be set as a goal of the elementary school counselor.

The adjustment-maladjustment dichotomy or the self-actualizing non-self-actualizing dichotomy are like all other dichotomies; they do not exist in fact. Adjustment lies along a continuum, and each individual has a continuum of adjustment unique to him. The role of the elementary school counselor can be an opportunity to aid each individual child in moving along *his* continuum of adjustment *toward* optimal functioning.

Still another aspect of the rationale for child counseling is "freeing the child to learn." As a child becomes less threatened and more able to perceive his environment accurately, as he learns to know and understand himself and accordingly seeks experiences that promote personalized and meaningful learning, and as he frees himself of internal concerns that preoccupy his being, he is more open to learning.

The child counselor has a twofold responsibility in facilitating this freedom: (1) He has the responsibility of helping the individual child attain a direction toward personal freedom. (2) He has the responsibility of promoting the development of an optimal learning atmosphere.

Freeing the child to learn has specific implications for the child counselor in the elementary school setting. The fundamental purpose of the school is the education of the child. All programs that exist within the school do so directly or indirectly toward this fundamental purpose.

It should be obvious to the reader that these rationales are not discrete, but rather that they overlap and intermingle. If elementary school counseling can help meet these needs, its relevance and impact in the lives of children can be significant.

COMMENT

In this chapter we have presented a discussion of the historical evolution of child counseling. We have emphasized the interrelationship of education and psychology in this evolution and have stressed the necessity for child counseling to develop its own unique identity. The impact of federal legislation and professional advisement have been cited as primary determinants of child counseling, especially as it has evolved in the public schools. Rationales supporting the developmental and/or remedial approach to child behavior have been presented. The suggestion has also been made that the child counselor has responsibilities beyond those of working with children. He must also be capable of working with parents and other significant persons in the child's world.

REFERENCES

ACES–ASCA COMMITTEE ON THE ELEMENTARY SCHOOL COUNSELOR. Tentative Statement. *Personnel and Guidance Journal* 44 (1966*a*):658–659.

———. Preliminary Statement. *Personnel and Guidance Journal* 44 (1966*b*): 659–661.

BRAMMER, L., AND SHOSTROM, E. *Therapeutic Psychology*. Englewood Cliffs, N.J.: Prentice-Hall, Inc., 1968.

COLEMAN, J. *Abnormal Psychology and Modern Life*. Chicago: Scott, Foresman and Company, 1964.

GLUCK, S., AND GLUCK, E. T. *Unraveling Juvenile Delinquency*. New York: Commonwealth Fund, 1950.

GURIN, G.; VEROFF, J.; AND FELD, SHEILA. *Americans View Their Mental Health: A Nationwide Survey*. Joint Commission on Mental Illness and Health, Monograph Series No. 4. New York: Basic Books, Inc., Publishers, 1960.

HILL, G. E., AND NITZSCHKE, D. F. "Preparation Programs in Elementary School Guidance." *Personnel and Guidance Journal* 40 (1961):155–159.

JONES, A. J. *Principles of Guidance*. New York: McGraw-Hill, 1945.

KRUGMAN, M. "Why Guidance in the Elementary School?" *Personnel and Guidance Journal* 32 (1954):270–273.

MASLOW, A. H. *Motivation and Personality*. New York: Harper and Row, Publishers, 1954.

———. *Toward a Psychology of Being*. Princeton, N.J.: D. Van Nostrand Co., Inc., 1962.

MEEKS, ANNA R. "Consensus of Thinking in Elementary School Guidance." Paper read at American Personnel Guidance Association, Minneapolis, 1965.

————. "Guidance in the Elementary School." *National Education Association Journal* 51 (1962):30–33.

NITZSCHKE, D. F., AND HILL, G. E. *The Elementary School Counselor.* Athens, Ohio: Ohio University Press, 1964.

OLDRIDGE, B. "Two Roles for Elementary School Guidance Personnel." *Personnel and Guidance Journal* 43 (1964):367–370.

OTTO, H. J. *Elementary School Organization and Administration.* New York: Appleton-Century-Crofts, 1964.

ROGERS, C. R. *On Becoming A Person.* Boston: Houghton Mifflin Company, 1961.

WELLMAN, F. Implications for Federal Assistance in Elementary School Guidance. Paper read at American Personnel Guidance Association, Minneapolis, 1965.

SELECTED ADDITIONAL READINGS

BEERS, C. *A Mind That Found Itself.* New York: Doubleday, 1921.

DEWEY, J. *Democracy and Education.* New York: Macmillan, 1916.

FAUST, V. *History of Elementary School Counseling.* Boston: Houghton Mifflin Company, 1968.

FREUD, S. *Autobiography.* London: Hogarth Press, 1946.

JAMES, W. *Principles of Psychology.* New York: Holt, 1890.

PARSONS, F. *Choosing a Vocation.* Boston: Houghton Mifflin, 1909.

ROGERS, C. R. *Counseling and Psychotherapy.* Boston: Houghton Mifflin, 1942.

WILLIAMSON, E. G. *How to Counsel Students.* New York: McGraw-Hill, Inc., 1939.

WRENN, C. G. *The Counselor in a Changing World.* Washington: American Personnel and Guidance Association, 1962.

2

Rationale for Definitions

DEFINITIONS: A POINT OF DEPARTURE

The purpose we have in writing this book is to in some way affect in a positive manner the development of children. We shall never see, much less get to know, our end product. We are depending on these written pages to communicate our ideas to the reader who, acting as the middleman, will positively influence the behavior of children.

We realize that we are putting a considerable amount of faith in printed words. Words, it seems, are not wholly adequate for expressing ideas when they are compared to human encounters. One of the principal difficulties is that the word on the printed page allows for no feedback, hence there is no opportunity for the writer to clarify his intended meaning for the reader. Words are, however, all that we have to use, so we are going to spend the majority of this chapter explaining, as best we can, what certain words and concepts mean to us. We are not attempting to tell the reader that this is what they should mean to him. In order that we may effectively communicate our ideas, we feel it is necessary to give the reader a guide to our language.

One of the major fallacies of which most of us are guilty in writing, teaching, counseling, or other less formal methods of communicating is to assume that the spoken word means the same thing to the "hearer" as it does to the "sayer." However, often it does not.

Simple words such as "house" create thirty different pictures in thirty different minds when spoken to a classroom of thirty children; and yet the speaker hurries on to his next word seemingly assuming that his picture of "house" is the picture that has been communicated to all. The example of the word "house" deals with a concrete word. The process becomes even more complex and confusing with the usage of abstract words and concepts, such as justice, trust, compassion, and a host of others.

Words, then, which are one of the tools we have to work with in communicating, mean different things to different people. The extent of communication, therefore, becomes dependent upon the degree to which individuals who are trying to communicate have meanings that are common; that is, when people share concepts which have similarity in meaning for each other, they will be able to communicate and understand each other better. When, however, people have less and less in common in the meaning of the concepts shared, communication is less and less possible.

Moreover, certain problems arise in attempting to make clear-cut distinctions in definition and role between and among concepts. In order to communicate, man has been forced to make up dichotomies that do not truly exist. It is the author's belief that *there are no true dichotomies.* In other words, our worlds are not black or white, true or false, good or bad, right or wrong. They are comprised of many shades of gray and of relative "truths," "goods," and "rights." We tend, because of our language, not to recognize that distinctions which we make fall along a continuum. Instead we come to believe in those dichotomies which we make up for purposes of communication when in fact no such real dichotomies are justifiable. Similarly, we are proposing distinctions between guidance, counseling, and therapy, but we recognize that clear-cut distinctions are impossible. Such distinctions only represent arbitrary points bisecting a continuum. This being the case, a certain amount of overlap between these functions is obvious.

GUIDANCE AND/OR COUNSELING—A DILEMMA

In the main, we subscribe to the point of view which distinguishes guidance and counseling as separate functions. The major emphasis of this book is one of *counseling* with children rather than *guiding* them.

Traditionally, counseling has been viewed as one of the services of the total guidance program. In other words, counseling has been only one of the things a counselor does. He has combined counseling with his other duties, including the organization, collection, and dissemination of information; the conducting of relevant research; the testing and placement of students; and other duties, to form the total guidance service. Counseling, then, has been viewed as a subdivision of the broader concept, guidance. If this is the case, then it would seem confusing, if not absurd, to speak of counseling *and* guidance. One does not generally refer to one's family as "my son and my family."

Even though quantitative differences between the terms *counseling* and *guidance* are suggested, more often than not the words are used synonymously and interchangeably. If counseling *is* guidance and the two terms can be used interchangeably, it becomes redundant to speak of counseling *and* guidance. To use an analogy similar to the one above, one does not speak of "my family and my family."

This leads to a third distinction that is made regarding the terms *counseling* and *guidance*. From this point of view the two terms are made to complement each other and also to be completely distinct. Advocates of this position call for separate functions and separate functionaries. Schools would then have counselors and guidance workers. Both occupations would be part of the total pupil personnel program. However, even though the roles would complement each other, they would be separate and distinct.

This latter approach would seem to be gaining support not only by counselors and counselor educators but also by administrators and other workers closely connected to the field. McCleary and Hencley in their book *Secondary School Administration* (1965) have made such a distinction by saying:

> Throughout the field of student personnel there is considerable interest in developing a distinction between the terms "guidance" and "counseling." "Guidance" connotes some positive external direction. The student is guided when he is told about the rules of the school and that he is expected to obey them, or when he is directed to take certain tests. These and a host of other requirements and expectations are established "in the student's interest." At base, however, "guidance" seems to be concerned with action considered necessary in order that the school fulfill its responsibility to society. Thus, when such actions are prescribed the individual is being guided, even though he may be permitted a choice of when and how he will satisfy them.
>
> "Counseling," on the other hand, refers to those activities that are conducted only in terms of the individual's interest, and *he* decides what action, if any, is to be taken. There is abundant evidence to indicate that attitudes and values are not likely to be changed by exhortation or even by objective, intellectual analysis. What the individual student needs is a confidential, accepting relationship with someone who understands and with whom he can review his problems, express emotions, and puzzle out solutions. Under these conditions the counselor can suggest; but, if he is to maintain the counseling relationship, he must always communicate to the student that the decisions are his own. (pp. 250–251)

The above point of view would seem to allow for a clear differentiation between the roles of counselor and guidance worker. Furthermore, it would raise a serious question with respect to the meaningful use of the term *guidance counselor*. (We hope that this term is conspicuous by its absence in our writings.)

We are aware, however, that to suggest that elementary schools should have both counselors and guidance workers is impractical and perhaps even inadvisable at this time. We feel that many of the traditional guidance services can be carried on best by the teacher, particularly the teacher in the self-contained classroom. Such functions as providing needed information and aid to children regarding socialization processes, achievement, study skills and habits, educational and career opportunities, and others, can be successfully carried out by the qualified and willing teacher. This does not, of course, rule out the involvement of the counselor in guidance activities when they are relevant and important for the well-being of the child. We submit, however, that the major function of the counselor is counseling.

GUIDANCE—COUNSELING—THERAPY: DEFINED

Guidance from our point of view is largely a cognitive process designed to provide the individual with data external to himself—such as test data. This informative data hopefully will be assimilated by the client and made personally relevant so that the individual will be able to make the most appropriate choices for himself. Due to the specific problem-orientedness of the guidance function, it tends to be short-term in duration and relatively counselor-structured. The degree of counselor-client involvement is also minimal when compared to counseling and therapy. Such functions as advising, collecting and disseminating information, placement and follow-up, are typically considered guidance functions.

Counseling has often been characterized as a process relationship between two people where one, a trained person, helps the other to change aspects of himself or his environment which trouble him. Gustad (1953) in an attempt to comprehensively define the counseling process says:

> Counseling is a learning-oriented process, carried on in a simple, one-to-one social environment, in which a counselor, professionally competent in relevant psychological skills and knowledge, seeks to assist the client by methods appropriate to the latter's needs and within the context of the total personnel program, to learn more about himself, to learn how to put such understanding into effect in relation to more clearly perceived, realistically defined goals to the end that the client may become a happier and more productive member of his society. (p. 17)

Although both definitions emphasize the traditional one-to-one relationship, it should be noted that a current, strong trend is emerging which would include the application of these therapeutic principles to groups as well as individuals.

Therapy has been judged by some to be qualitatively different from guidance and/or counseling. Although we are able to see such a distinction between guidance and therapy, we are unable to so differentiate counseling from therapy. At best, we regard as quantitative differences—differences of degree—whatever differences that are generally held. Semantics problems, job settings, and status needs on the part of the practitioner seem to account for much of the argument which surrounds the proposed differentiations. The reader is referred to Brammer and Shostrom (1968) for a more thorough discussion of traditional differentiations.

It is our experience and belief that the work of a competent counselor, whether he is called social worker, psychiatrist, therapist, or what-not, cuts across whatever qualitative and quantitative differences that exist between and among guidance, counseling, and therapy. In the final analysis, the "helping person" is helpful because of what he is as a person and what he is able to communicate of his person to the "needy person." What he calls himself or what he calls what he does is of little real consequence.

One additional comment seems important to make at this point: We see counseling as a way-of-life, not as a "thing" to be done in an office, nor as a service to be provided to needy people in their time of need. Counseling is undergirded by an attitude about people, an attitude which in its essence affirms that personhood is good and should be cherished, respected, and enhanced. We submit that such an attitude or operational philosophy about people is one which must pervade the existence of the effective counselor. It is not one which can be "turned on" when the counselor enters the interview or playroom.

BEHAVIOR DEFINED

It is obvious from the preceding discussion regarding counseling that behavior change is one desired outcome of counseling. The meaning of *behavior,* however, is an issue surrounded by controversy.

Definitions of *behavior* have their origin in differing philosophical bases. The meaning of the word seems to vary greatly with the theoretical constructs of the user.

From one position, counseling outcome must be determined in terms of behaviors which are observable and quantifiable in some systematic way. This means that abstract feelings such as love can only be defined in terms of visceral reactions, hugs per minute, blood pressure, heartbeat, and so on. We contend that such a definition of behavior is too limited. Our own personal experiences suggest that there is something more to human experience than observable behaviors which lend themselves to "scientific analysis."

Perhaps the confusion can be traced to J. B. Watson who formulated the behaviorist school of psychology. He explicitly stated that only "observable behavior" was the province of psychology, thus the adherents to Watsonian behaviorism required operational, scientific, objective evidence before admitting a concept to their system. Such constructs as "feelings of love" in the absence of observable manifestations of those feelings were not admissible to the "behavioral" system.

At the other end of the continuum is the concept that any action or reaction—a feeling, a thought, an understanding—whether observable or not is behavior. To accept a definition of this nature rules out rigorous measurement of all behavior and eliminates, in part, "behavioral" outcome as a potential method of evaluating the counseling process.

It would seem that we are dealing with a number of concepts, sometimes almost unrelated, but all called by the same name. "How did John behave?" This is a very different question when asked by a parent of a teacher, a physician of a nurse, a psychologist of a social worker, and a minister of a Sunday school teacher. The meaning comes from the frame of reference within which each of these persons works. The struggle between and within disciplines to have their own personal definitions approved does nothing to facilitate communication nor advance knowledge.

One way of attacking the problem would be to invent unique words or phrases that would represent the thought intended rather than lumping many diverse concepts under the general heading of behavior. Thus, observed behavior, clinical observations, change in feelings, thoughts, and so on, would each hold its own unique meaning which seemingly would reduce the confusion which exists.

Our inclination is to view behavior (as most constructs) as falling along a continuum. At one extreme are the most objective behaviors, the most observable, the most easily measureable. At the other extreme are the most subjective behaviors which give little possibility of outside observance or measurement. Behavior encompasses the entire continuum from one extreme to the other. For the sake of communication, however, and within the confines of language, that line has been arbitrarily divided at the point where behavior can no longer be observed or measured. All behaviors to one side of the line are regarded as objective behaviors, and all behaviors to the other side are regarded as subjective behaviors.

We are able to deal only with the objective behaviors in terms of measurement, but we realize the importance of other behaviors that are not presently measurable, behaviors which do exist within the individual.

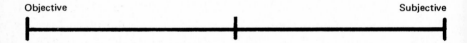

Objective   Subjective

Scientific experimentation, then, must at this stage in our development be done in terms of objective behaviors, but human beings are more than purely objective beings. The goal of counseling toward changing behavior refers both to subjective and objective behavior, hence we must continue to evolve methods for submitting subjective as well as objective behavior to experimentation and measurement.

LEARNING

If behavioral change takes place on the part of the client, it is assumed that learning has also taken place. That is to say, one's definition of learning closely parallels one's view of behavior. By expanding the definition of behavior, we must also deal with learning in a broader way.

The phenomenological approach to learning seems to most closely meet this need for an expanded way of looking at learning. Phenomenology as a theory of learning states as its basic postulate that reality is what the individual perceives it to be. If a mother loves her child but the child perceives his mother's behavior as dislike, then, for the child, his reality is that the mother dislikes him. The inverse of this is also true. If the mother dislikes the child but the child views her behavior as love, she does, in fact, in the child's phenomenological world, love the child.

Learning is a subjective experience. What is learned is not necessarily what is taught objectively by the teacher but what is perceived subjectively by the learner.

Stimuli are perceived from the frame of reference of the learner. To the extent that meaning is derived by the learner, to that extent he has learned. When a stimulus is presented to fifty different people, fifty different sorts of learning take place in fifty different phenomenological worlds and fifty different "things" are learned, all somewhat different from what the "teacher" or stimulus presenter has intended.

Since only the individual knows what he perceives, learning is a very private affair. The learner's personalized meaning is not readily subject to comparison, observation, or rigorous quantification. A major way to know what he has learned or what he has perceived is to rely on what he says.

In contrast to the phenomenological approach which views learning as the development of subjective meaning for the individual is the behavioral point of view emphasizing objective and normative meaning. This latter approach assumes general laws and principles underlying human behavior, that is, the specific behaviors have common meanings. It has been demonstrated that individuals can be "taught" to overtly behave in a way that the "teacher" desires. It has not been demonstrated, however, that the learner's personalized meaning (covert behavior) is one and the same with the "teacher's" desired outcome. Most often it is assumed that the observed behavior fits into a class of behaviors which have a common meaning. Such an assumption can lead the observer to misinterpret the "real" meaning which has been gained.

Seemingly these two systems of learning conflict with each other. They may. Our frame of reference, however, allows for both. Reality is what the individual perceives reality to be *and* objective behavior can be learned so that the learner demonstrates a particular behavior that is desired. This does not guarantee that the child's subjective experience can be accurately inferred from his overt behavior.

These are not the only systems of learning. Hull, Spence, and others have attempted to reduce learning to mathematics. Some interesting new evidence in the physiology of learning has suggested that learning may be transferred by transplanting ribonucleic acid (RNA) from the brain cells of one individual into another individual. These experiments have been conducted with planaria and rats (Hyden, 1962; Thompson and McConnell, 1955). The implications for human learning are not as yet clear.

It is our contention that *the* theory of learning has not yet been completely evolved. It may be helpful to the reader to realize that most scientific and psychological research comes from the sort of model which follows.

Several suppositions are made: (1) The universe is lawful. (2) Man is capable of discovering these laws. (3) There is a law of learning. People experiment and philosophize, and to the degree they can prove their hypotheses, to that degree they have tapped the "real" law. Each new theory that adds a new dimension gives us a little more information regarding the law which is evolving. The illustration which appears below graphically represents our position with respect to the current status of learning.

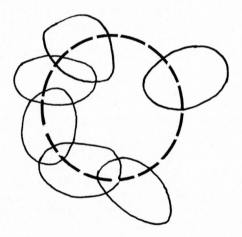

We contend that the existing theories are not in conflict. Instead, there is an overarching system into which all that is currently "known" can eventually be integrated. At this point in time, however, our knowledge is fragmented and incomplete. Until such an overarching system is developed to our satisfaction, we feel we must hold to several theories of learning that sometimes appear to be in conflict.

VIEWS OF MAN

Man can be viewed from many different frames of reference. At first glance it appears to make little difference how we view man. Allport's article

"Psychological Models for Guidance" (1962), however, makes a second glance imperative.

He explores the nature of man from three basic points of view: (1) Man: A Reactive Being; (2) Man: A Reactive Being in Depth; and (3) Man: Being in the Process of Becoming.

Man as a Reactive Being

Allport (1962) discusses this construct by saying:

> Seen through this lens man is no different in kind from any other living reactor; and therefore, like the paramecium or pigeon, may be studied biologically, behaviorally, mathematically. To be sure a few special concepts need to be devised to take care of the vast complexity of human behavior, but all these concepts—among them habit hierarchy, secondary reinforcement, input and output of information, and the like—are consistent with the postulates of physicalism and naturalism. (p. 374)

Man is reduced to his simplest terms, but the allowance of such things as subjective behaviors is not provided for. From such a view of man comes the stimulus-response model of behavior which emphasizes that man's essential nature is neutral and that he learns to be what he is.

Man: A Reactive Being in Depth

Psychoanalysis has its roots in this construct. Once again referring to Allport's discussion (1962), he speaks of man as a reactive being in depth by saying:

> Central to depth psychology and important for guidance is the doctrine of recall and recovery. Therapy, and presumably guidance, proceeds by disclosing to the client some buried motive, or a troublesome and repressed psychic trauma. The client's solution, if indeed he has any, lies in this vital recall. . . . Freud never allows for the individual's capacity to disregard his past or to reshape it freely. Indeed, since the structure of the Id never changes, the future can at best be a redirection, never a transformation, of one's purposes. What one becomes is essentially what one is, and what one was. (p. 376)

Such a view of man is pessimistic and leaves little room for the things that seem to be of greatest importance to us, such as the transcendence of one's past and the release of unrealized human potentials. Most central to this belief is the lack of action or movement available to man. These static concepts defeat the purposes of counseling as we see them, that is, if man is a prisoner of his past, he has no real freedom to choose alternative ways of living. It may seem unreasonable to dismiss this view because it does not fit what we personally believe about man; yet it seems that if man is not free to choose and change, he would not be able to think about or demonstrate choice and change. At any rate, if this view truly represents the nature of man, we may as well abandon our efforts to change man. If man's nature is determined, there is no efficacy in counseling.

Man: Being in the Process of Becoming

Allport has proposed an alternative that seems to fit our viewpoint. As he suggests, this view initially asks the question, "Who am I?" Such a view of man denotes movement toward a fuller existence and offers hope to the searcher.

This viewpoint seems to fit well into the existentialist viewpoint. However, in attempting to clarify their beliefs, it has been our experience that many existentialists seem to have a particular talent for writing in a way that makes it very difficult to know if we understand what they are saying. This, of course, is consistent with the theory that each man is unique and so existentialism is something different to everyone. As a result, each discussion of the theory reflects a personally meaningful understanding, and the communication of this meaning becomes obscured due to the uniqueness of that meaning.

Allport (1962) discusses the concept of existentialism when he says, "We have the freedom to commit ourselves to great causes with courage, even though we lack certainty. We can be at one time half-sure and whole-hearted." (p. 378) Comprehensive discussions of existentialism have been advanced by Van Kaam (1962, 1966). The reader is referred to these sources for a more thorough presentation of existential philosophy.

Man would seem to us to be in the process of "becoming." Man can be viewed as good, as bad, or as neutral. The importance of such thought, however, seems to be more of an academic nature than a practical issue. We cannot recall sitting in our offices working with a child and thinking, "There is a child in the process of becoming." By the same token we do not tend to view clients as good, bad, and so on. Such categorizations fail to contribute to the outcomes of counseling.

Man is what he is. From our viewpoint he has the potential to be something more. It is from this frame of reference that we view our clients. Furthermore, *children are people,* and for this reason we view children as being what they are. They have the potential and are in the process of becoming something more than what they are at any given moment. In viewing children in this way, it seems necessary to see them as having more rights than they are often afforded and accordingly being required to assume more responsibility than they are often afforded.

COMMENT

We hope that by now the reader knows us and our beliefs a little better. We have tried to discuss definitions of importance, some basic concepts, and our personal points of view. We want to reemphasize that we are not trying to superimpose our thoughts upon the reader. It is, however, our intention that the reader understand more fully what we mean as we attempt to integrate these and other concepts into the remainder of our text.

Perhaps all the discussion seems academic and without relevance to child counseling. We hope not. We hope instead that it has laid a foundation and a point of reference that will make our ideas more understandable to the reader who in turn will help to positively influence children.

With this thought in mind we hope we have successfully presented a point of departure which can act as a bridge from what has happened in the field of child counseling toward what the field may become.

REFERENCES

ALLPORT, G. W. "Psychological Models for Guidance." *Harvard Educational Review* 32 (1962):373–381.

BRAMMER, L., AND SHOSTROM, E. L. *Therapeutic Psychology.* Englewood Cliffs, N.J.: Prentice-Hall, Inc., 1968.

GUSTAD, J. W. In *Roles and Relationships in Counseling,* edited by R. F. Berdie. Minneapolis: University of Minnesota Press, 1953.

HYDEN, H. "Satellite Cells in the Nervous System." *Scientific American* 205 (1961):62–83.

MCCLEARY, L. E., AND HENCLEY, S. P. *Secondary School Administration.* New York: Dodd, Mead & Co. 1965.

THOMPSON, R., AND MCCONNELL, J. R. "Classical Conditioning in the Planarian, Dugesia dorotocephala." *Journal of Comparative Physiological Psychology* 48 (1955): 65–68.

VAN KAAM, A. "Counseling From the Viewpoint of Existential Psychology." *Harvard Educational Review* 32 (1962): 403-415.

———. *The Art of Existential Counseling: A New Perspective in Psychotherapy.* New York: Dimension Books, Inc., 1966.

3

The Child

The world of the child is a most difficult world for the adult to understand. In a sense we all consider ourselves to be experts in knowing and understanding children and child development because we have all been children. To recapture significant childhood events is not too difficult. To recapture our feelings as children, however, is difficult but necessary if we are to at least begin to understand the child's world.

What is it like to feel the feelings which are so characteristic of childhood? Of course, children are unique beings, and consequently their feelings cannot be lumped together and understood in categories. There is, however, an area of commonality which cuts across childhood feelings and behaviors which could be more fully understood by adults. The commentary following is meant to help the reader grasp more fully an understanding of the child's world as he may perceive it.

As a child you are physically smaller than those giants who rule you, and you are forced to look up to your rulers while they look down upon you. You are punished for your mistakes as you experiment with ideas and things in your attempts to learn. The punishment usually takes the form of your either being physically overpowered and hurt or being verbally insulted without chance for rebuttal.

The Constitution of our country and the Bill of Rights, together with the laws of city, state, and nation, do not apply to you for you are legally assumed to be irresponsible regardless of the degree of responsibility that you may demonstrate.

You must ask permission for almost all that you do. This permission can be refused without reasons being given. Your food is selected for you and you are told how to eat, how much you are to eat, and when you are to eat. You are rarely praised because when you do something well, that is only what is expected of you. Sometimes if you do something particularly well, you are set apart and embarrassed by being put on display and made to perform this same task over and over for the pleasure of visiting giants. These same visiting giants often ask you simple questions to which they already know the answers in order to test your knowledge and your willingness to perform. However, you are usually made painfully aware that all giants would rather that you act like a trained pet and let the giants alone, perhaps being seen but not heard, except when the giants want to be entertained.

Your feelings are often disregarded, or you are told directly or indirectly, "Don't feel that way!" Your most treasured possessions (old machine parts, ragged and dismembered dolls, scraps of paper, etc.) and exciting fantasies are considered to be worthless junk or stupid nonsense by your rulers. These possessions are confiscated and destroyed at any time upon the whims of these rulers.

After having served this home imprisonment fairly well, you are transferred, at about age six, to another kind of prison that you might enjoy were it not for the overwhelming number of restrictions which are imposed upon you. This new stockade is generally made of brick and cement and tends to be much larger than the prison from which you have been transferred.

The building is divided into cell blocks called classrooms. About thirty other children your same size are put into one of the cell blocks with one teacher giant who commands you from 9:00 A.M. to 3:00 P.M. five days a week. At first you are rather excited about being with thirty others your own size and of your own plight, but that excitement is soon lost, for one of the rules you learn is that only under special circumstances and in special ways are you allowed to talk and interact with your friends.

In this new environment you are told what to do, how to do it, and when to do it. If you resist you are likely to be labelled immature, unready, emotionally disturbed, a trouble-maker, a potential dropout, a bad influence, and a host of other terms which connote social disapproval. With such labels in hand, the giants meet together and believe they understand why you resist and set about trying to get you to not resist so that you can be called mature and ready.

If you do something wrong ("Grade F") or if you do not do as well as the others ("below average"), you are told that YOU are wrong ("failure"). Then, as if you didn't feel bad enough, a letter is sent to the pair of giants who are your home rulers. As a result, they too can tell you that YOU are wrong.

You are called "nice" if you don't talk, but rejection and ridicule may result from telling or showing how you feel. Sometimes you are told you did not do your job well enough last year, so you are not going to advance with your cell mates. Instead, you are informed that you will be required to go into a cell block with a group of smaller midgets and do it all over again.

You are continuously being warned about showing proper respect to the giants in your world, yet little respect comes your way. Even though you are shown often that you are resented, you are accused of not being appreciative of all that the giants do for you. To top it off, if you should mention not loving these giants, you are severely punished, for you are supposed to love them no matter what. Similarly, you are supposed to interpret all of their behavior toward you as evidence of their love for you.

We, the parent giants and the teacher giants, do in fact say that we love these small child creatures. Sometimes we pay lip service to the fact that they are full-fledged people, yet we very rarely treat them as such. We scarcely show them any true respect. We seldom do for them or with them what we might do for one of our friends or associates. What we do in essence is a fairly effective job of showing children that they are unimportant.

By this point in our discussion we expect that you, the reader, have had some sort of reaction to what we have said. You may have been angered by our "attack." You may have found yourself defending parents, teachers, and others. You may have thought, "What tripe! Who do these guys think they are. What gives them the right to judge?" If these have been some of your reactions, we are not surprised. We recognize that our statements are extreme. They are meant to be, primarily for the purpose of provoking the reader to look again at his beliefs about children and his behavior with them. The kernel of meaning that pervades the "attack," however, has to do with how well adults understand the phenomenological world of the child. Trying to understand a child's world as it appears to the child may cause the reader to pause and reflect again on that kernel of meaning.

One final comment must be made. A common expression of indignation among adults is summed up in, "Don't treat me like a child!" A meaning inherent in that statement is that being treated like a child is degrading, demeaning, and insulting because children are inferior and helpless. If this is a general connotation of childhood, then our plea is, "Don't treat a child like a child!" Children are not inferior human beings. They are not pawns to be manipulated and controlled by the adults in their world. They do deserve to be treated with respect if for no other reason than their humanness.

Similarly, it should be emphasized that the child must learn to treat adults with respect and dignity. Neither children nor adults have the right to usurp the human rights of each other.

CHILD DEVELOPMENT: OUR POINT OF VIEW

Child development has primarily been approached in a way which involves systematic observations of children of different age levels. From these observations, general classes of behaviors have been defined as characteristic of children of specific chronological age groupings. Such classification of behaviors is based on the concept of normal distribution, that is, the most frequently occurring behavior is "normal" and exceptional behavior in either direction is "abnormal." This notion that certain behaviors are characteristic of certain age groupings of children may lead teachers and others involved in the development of the child to "wait" for such characteristics as interest and readiness to emerge.

In the nineteenth century, baby biographies and clinical child studies became popularized, as the thrust to understand the process of human development intensified. Piaget is probably the best known contemporary child psychologist who is a proponent of this "observe, describe, and classify" approach to the study of child development. We consider the work that has been done using this approach as important. However, in the discussion which follows we have chosen to consider child development in a somewhat different light. Rather than discussing what is "normal" and "abnormal" from a normative point of view, we shall look at child development as existing along a continuum from "optimal" to "deficient" functioning. Moreover, our discussion will hopefully increase the reader's awareness of the impact and the potential impact of specialists (teachers, counselors, etc.) on the development process toward the full realization of human potential.

Harry Stack Sullivan (1953) coined the term *participant-observer* in referring to the function of the counselor. Believing that a person's behavior was a function of interpersonal events, he advocated the avoidance of analyzing the individual's behavior apart from interpersonal transaction; hence, in the counseling relationship, he held that the counselor was an analyst of the client's total behavior at the same time as he was an active participant in the social exchange between counselor and client.

Similarly, child development is not a process that the practicing counselor can sit back and simply observe. Rather, it is one in which the counselor has an active, direct, and determining part to play. For the counselor as a scientist, it is conceivable that a somewhat detached posture for the purpose of "objective" observation is tenable. It is not conceivable, however, that the counselor as practitioner can allow himself to be a spectator of child development. Counseling is a child development process. Its major purpose is to foster child growth. Effective counseling precludes detachment. It involves intense counselor participation simultaneously with an awareness of the meaning of that participation for both the child client and the counselor.

CHILD DEVELOPMENT AND SCHOOLS

In one of the final issues published by *The Saturday Evening Post* (January 8, 1969), John Holt states:

Almost every child, on the first day he sets foot in a school building, is smarter, more curious, less afraid of what he doesn't know, better at finding and figuring things out, more confident, resourceful, persistent and independent than he will ever be again in his schooling—or unless he is very lucky, for the rest of his life. (p. 12)

George Leonard begins his thought-provoking book, *Education and Ecstasy* (1968), by saying:

Teachers are overworked and underpaid. True. It is an exacting and exhausting business, this damning up the flood of human potentialities. What energy it takes to make a torrent into a trickle, to train that trickle along narrow, well-marked channels! (p. 1)

The indictments of Holt and Leonard are ones that we in education can reject, ignore, defend, or do something constructive about. The development of children is the reason for the existence of schools and the personnel who staff the schools. The time has come to do more than recognize that we have not done a very good job in fulfilling that purpose. It would seem wise to decrease the expenditure of our time and effort in devising and developing new knowledge, but at the same time we need to increase our efforts to more productively do something with the knowledge we already have—knowledge relative to child development that in large part has been ignored. The work of Gluck and Gluck (1950) related to the prediction of juvenile delinquency behaviors illustrates this need. Basically, they have devised a system for predicting the potential of a child to become a juvenile offender. This is done through the use of environmental data. The process, however, has been little used in attempting to control the development of delinquent children.

HUMAN POTENTIAL

As we have stated and implied, much of what has gone on in the name of educating a "fully functioning" citizen has not been successful. Education, psychology, and most other disciplines have tended to focus on what is "normal," "modal," "characteristic," "typical," "average," "expected," "acceptable," and "conforming." This in large measure precludes the discovery, study, and facilitation of man's highest potentials. There are encouraging signs, however, that a new thrust is evolving which can reshape education at all levels, in all directions, and ultimately reshape our very lives.

Many serious students of the human animal agree that less than ten percent of man's potential abilities are typically used; some even put the estimate as low as one percent. Many marvel at what "released" man could be. The exciting questions facing all of us have to do with what and how man can become what he is.

Leonard (1968) has discussed some of the most recent findings relating to man's unfathomed potentials. From the laboratories of biochemistry, evidence is accumulating that seemingly confirms the hypothesis that RNA (ribonucleic acid) molecules in brain cells act as miniature storehouses of all information and experiences that the human organism is exposed to. From this step, it may be but one creative leap to the means of discovering how to retrieve such material to consciousness. The findings of other researchers seem to suggest that the brain may have infinite creative capacity. The *how* of tapping these capacities and potentials, however, still remains to be discovered.

HOW CHILDREN LEARN

If we are to be instrumental in the development of children, it is essential that we have some understanding of how they learn. As we develop our discussion in the following paragraphs, we encourage the reader to again evaluate our comments against his own experience. Only in so doing can what we have to say become meaningful and relevant.

It is doubtful that there is a teacher of the twentieth century who has not at least heard of John Dewey's philosophy of "learning by doing." Since his early focus on the experiential aspect of learning, there have been numerous interpretations and misinterpretations of Dewey's philosophy. Most recently, Holt (1967), in recounting his own clinical experiences as a teacher, has stressed the importance of "learning by doing." But what is implied in the expression?

From our experience, effective learning is an active self-initiated process, one which requires personal involvement and investment by the learner. It is a highly personal process since it entails the exploration and development of personalized and relevant meaning. Although the content of what is presented to various learners may be identical from the point of view of the presenter, that which is learned and integrated into the understandings of the learner is a function of that learner's perceptions. Certainly, a "kind" of learning can be accomplished through intimidation ("these facts must be learned before you can pass on to the third grade"), manipulation ("if you learn these words, I'll give you a quarter"), and force ("you must learn the rules of the game today"). We contend, however, that significant learning that changes behavior is not acquired most effectively through such methods. The child as passive recipient may "learn about" many ideas but not learn to invest these ideas with personally relevant meanings. To do the latter he must become actively involved in his own learning process.

The responsibility, then, of one who seeks to foster learning in a child is not one of telling the child things. Rather, it is one of providing experiences for the child and helping the child find his own personal meanings from these experiences.

Self-Other Learning Experiences

Learning experiences exist along a continuum from self-provided to other-provided. Although some learning experiences emphasize one or the other ends of that continuum, most learning combines these polar positions.

DIRECT EXPERIENCE

At the one extreme is the kind of learning that results from the direct experiences of the learner. A clear example is the "touch the hot stove" example. The process involved might go something like this: "The stove felt warm when I was near it. I liked the warmth. I touched the stove. I got burned. I won't touch it again." The child has learned to respond through his own experiences with the stove. Moreover, the chances are good that other objects which radiate warmth will also be avoided by the child as he learns to generalize his experience to other similar situations.

CREATIVITY

Another learning process which is largely self-provided is that which could be called creative interpretation. Some theories of creativity insist that being creative is largely a matter of associating a response to a stimulus with which it is not usually paired. In other words, the child may learn something new by taking his past learnings and experiences and perceiving and/or applying them in a new or different way. An example might be the child who, when asked by the teacher to explain why horses swish their tails, said, "They do it to wave to children when they are happy." This is certainly not an anticipated response to the given stimulus, but who can say it is invalid?

MODELING

In the opposite direction on the continuum are learnings derived from observations of others. Much of the learning of children is a result of modeling and imitation. The child observes behavior in others and either unconsciously or incidentally, or by conscious plan, may adopt the behaviors of the models in his environment. The intent of the modeling, whether incidental or planned, is the same, that is, to do what someone else does or to be like someone else is. Whether the modeling process succeeds is clearly dependent upon the meanings which are attached to the acquisition of new behaviors by the child. However, behaviors which have lost their original reason for existing can be learned through modeling.

As an example, one of our students tells the story of his daughter learning to cook. The girl's mother was instructing her in preparation of a ham. "The first thing you do is cut off the end," her mother said. And as little girls will, the child asked, "Why?" "Because that is what my mother taught me, and besides, that's the way you do it," said the mother.

The little girl, still persisting, went to her grandmother and asked why the end of the ham was always cut off before the ham was cooked. "That is the way my mother taught me, the way I taught your mother, and that is the way I have always done it," the grandmother said.

It so happened that the little girl's great grandmother was still living, so the child asked the same question of her mother's mother's mother. "Oh," said the old lady, "that is because when I was learning to cook, I didn't have a pan large enough to cook the whole ham in, so I cut off the end to make it fit."

Vicarious Learning

Somewhat different from modeled learning is vicarious learning which can result from one person having direct observations and/or information about another person. All of us have at some time gained joy or satisfaction from seeing or hearing about the good fortune of another person. The experience of the observer or hearer has been a result of substitutional participation in the experience of the other person.

Television, movies, and the theater provide the clearest examples of this type of learning. As a consequence of the feelings displayed by the players, the audience is able to develop feelings similar to those displayed. In such ways, the audience can "learn how it feels" through indirect participation.

The classroom also provides much opportunity for this type of learning. When a child is encouraged for what he does, it makes a difference to him, but it also makes a difference to those who observe him being encouraged. Conversely, when a child is discouraged (ignored, scolded, ridiculed, physically punished, etc.) for his behavior, the other children also readily learn to avoid and control for fear of being treated in a similar way.

Threat and Competition

Threat and competition are both very much a part of our everyday lives, whether we are teachers, students, patients, or professional "helping persons." But what do threat and competition do to our behavior? How do they affect our relationships with others? What are their impacts on optimal human development?

Rogers (1969) has explained in some detail the consequences of threat on learning. He illustrates these consequences by describing the experience of the poor reader. "When he is called upon to recite in class the internal panic takes over and the words on the page become less intelligible symbols than they were when he was sitting in his seat before he was called upon." (p. 161)

Is this not the experience of us all? Remember that last time when you were singled out and asked to perform? Remember the churning in your stomach, the sweaty palms, the dry mouth, the blocking of thoughts, the general anxiousness? Were you able to use your potentials to their best advantage in this circumstance? If you are anything like us, you are answering "NO!" Threat, then, diminishes one's ability to be open to the potential of one's experience. When threat is reduced to a minimal level, one is able to perceive the field of experience more accurately and in a differentiated fashion. One is free to recognize differing elements for their differences and to assimilate the meanings of these differences.

Competition very often blocks effective learning. All of us at one time or another have undoubtedly watched children working with puzzles. As they develop and become more group-oriented, they often become tearful and angry when they are unable to put the pieces together. Why does this happen? We suspect that one explanation is because children even as early as nursery school are already caught up in a very competitive, status-conscious way of life where approval of the teacher, parent, and each other is of paramount importance. The child who is unable to do the task may feel that he is expected to be able to perform and consequently suffers depression in self-esteem and worth. How tragic that competition and threat may keep him from experimenting and discovering in his own time and in his own way.

For an example closer to home, let us consider the issue of merit pay for teachers. One argument against such an idea is that in such a system a teacher would be afraid to share ideas and methods with others for fear that he would not get proper credit for the ideas; hence, it is feared that classrooms and teachers would be isolated and insulated from each other. Competition for approval between and among teachers could promote such an unhealthy learning environment.

We hasten to add that we are not against all competition. We do, however, advocate that learning can be more effectively accomplished through a combination of group cooperation and the individual's competition with himself. Competition where the child has to "measure up" to some external criterion for acceptance and approval prevents him from "measuring up" to his own internal unique potentials.

Learning Summarized

Children learn most effectively when the *why* and the *what* of learning have relevance for the individual child as a total being (thinking, feeling, behaving). It is self-initiated and necessitates the child's personal involvement in the commitment to the learning event, whether direct or vicarious. Central to significant learning is the ability to derive personalized meaning from experiences. Threat and competition should be minimized for effective learning to happen.

If the preceding discussion is valid, then our homes, our schools, and our society at large rarely provide satisfactory conditions for the child's optimal development.

BEHAVIOR CONTINUA

Conforming–Nonconforming Continuum

Farson (1967) points out the effect of school by saying, "Indeed, if one were to design an educational system for the express purpose of stifling creativity in students, it would differ very little from our present system." (p. 8) The spoken goal in education has for some years been one of fostering creativity or nonconformity. The practiced goal has been one of fostering conformity.

Are we implying that all nonconforming behavior is good and all conforming behavior is bad? Not at all. There is danger in categorically viewing nonconformity as good and conformity as bad just as there is danger in much of "black and white" thinking. Conformity, like most of the other constructs which we have discussed, lies along a continuum extending from the extreme in conforming behavior to the extreme in nonconforming behavior.

All of us as teachers and parents have, to varying degrees, rewarded conforming behaviors and punished nonconforming behaviors. This has been largely true because we have been raised in environments where rewards for nonconforming behaviors were scarce; hence, we have come to be suspicious and untrusting of our own nonconforming potentials and to pass on our suspicions and distrust of self to others. Only inasmuch as we can learn to be spontaneously ourselves will we be able to foster spontaneous nonconforming behavior in those children who are our sons, daughters, and students.

Deficient–Optimal Continuum

For us, behavior falls along the value dimension of deficient to optimal as well as falling along the nonvalue dimension of conforming to nonconforming. That is, all behaviors exist along a continuum from those which fail miserably to fulfill the needs of the individual to those which meet those needs well. The grid on page 44 is meant to graphically represent our total view of behavior. It is our attempt to present the reader with the way of conceptualizing and understanding behavior which has meaning for us.

The Behavior Grid

All behavior falls loosely into one of the four quadrants of the grid presented below. In order to better understand children's behavior and development, we shall discuss these four quadrants separately.

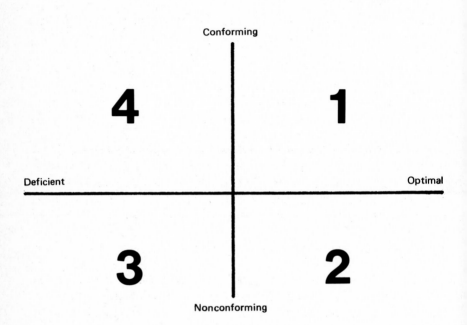

OPTIMAL CONFORMING BEHAVIORS

These are the behaviors that would be represented in quadrant one. They are behaviors which are "good for" the child in terms of being toward the peak of his potentials. Moreover, such behaviors are generally approved of and rewarded by parents and teachers since they tend to conform to expectations. For most children quadrant-one behaviors are the only optimal behaviors which are fostered and encouraged to develop by the school.

For the few persons who are prone to regard any kind of conformity as bad, and who are proponents of change for the sake of change, quadrant-one behaviors are regarded as "bad." Such behaviors are, however, potentially creative and actualizing behaviors for the individual involved, in spite of their external evaluation.

A very simple example might be tooth-brushing. It is a "good" behavior for the child's health and is seen by parents as a good behavior for the child. The behavior is thus fostered because it is seen by adults as being good for the child and is in fact good for the child.

OPTIMAL NONCONFORMING BEHAVIORS

From a brief inspection of the grid, page 44, it is obvious that many behaviors which may be considered optimal are found in the second quadrant. These are behaviors which, if allowed to actualize, would promote the creative realization of the individual child's potentials—potentials which would enhance his personal existence and ultimately the culture at large. Unfortunately, the behaviors which occur in the quadrant are frequently ignored, unrewarded, or punished by teacher and parent alike; hence, the child's potential for optimal development goes unrealized.

If we are to be instrumental in providing opportunity and encouragements for the development of "whole," fully-functioning, creative citizens, we must do more to encourage children to explore their own unique ways of being and behaving, that is, quadrant-two behaviors. The home, the school, and the community must assume such responsibilities if we are to become more than a "nation of sheep."

The child who asks *why* when told to do things, not to be obnoxious, but because he wants to learn *why,* can be a thorn in the side of a teacher who has not himself thought out *why.* Such a behavior is usually nonconforming, but may well be toward the optimal development of the child. Such behavior may be seen by adults as "talking back" or acting "smart" and is therefore often punished.

DEFICIENT NONCONFORMING BEHAVIORS

These behaviors are not to the child's best interest in his development as a human being, nor are they readily acceptable to those who comprise the child's environment. Consequently, they receive little reward, support, or reinforcement, and are infrequent in occurrence. There are fewer behaviors occurring in quadrant three than in any of the other quadrants.

Quadrant-three behaviors are generally extinguished for their nonconforming quality rather than from the perspective of being detrimental to the child. The end result, however, is the same. The child's behavior through a variety of methods is "shaped up" so that the resulting behavior patterns occur in one of the other three quadrants.

The belligerent child who attempts to resolve all conflicts with fighting, and by so doing has isolated himself from his peer group, might serve as an example of deficient nonconforming behavior. Such a child is shunned by adults and peers because he acts in an unacceptable way.

DEFICIENT CONFORMING BEHAVIORS

Behaviors occurring in quadrant four tend to be rewarded for their conforming nature even though they are detrimental to the optimal functioning and development of the child. To "fit in" is important for children and adults. However, "fitting in" at the expense of developing one's own unique and creative self is destructive. Much criticism leveled at education is legitimate when one considers the frequency with which quadrant-four behaviors are encouraged and rewarded in schools.

Again, the emphasis of our schools must be reassessed. The reward for quadrant-four behaviors must be challenged and quadrant-two behaviors must be fostered if we are to provide an environment in which optimal child development can occur.

Optimal–Deficient, Conforming–Nonconforming Behaviors Defined

To this point we have talked about optimal-deficient and conforming-nonconforming behaviors as though the reader were fully apprised of our definitions. Since this is not so, we shall attempt to clarify our meanings for these concepts.

From what we have already said or implied, we see the majority of adults regarding conforming behaviors as optimal and normal, and nonconforming behaviors as deficient and abnormal. The problem, however, is that behaviors are not optimal or deficient merely because someone thinks they are, wants them to be, or says that they are.

"Normal" has traditionally meant usual or conforming; hence, by definition, all behaviors in quadrants one and four are "normal" and all behaviors in quadrants two and three are "abnormal." Most child development study has identified the usual, or "normal," and in so doing has inferentially defined unusual, or "abnormal," behavior. From our standpoint such research has helped perpetuate deficient child development by the consideration of quadrant-two behavior as "abnormal." In other words, to consider behaviors which do not conform, behaviors which are creative ways of experiencing the world, as behaviors with little or no value inhibits the child's realization of his potentials. To know, then, what is "normal" and what is "abnormal" serves little purpose in attempting to provide optimal developmental conditions for the child. We contend that students of human behavior have unduly narrowed their vision of human potential. We must redirect our attention and efforts to the study of optimal and actualizing behaviors, to the study of what each individual person can become.

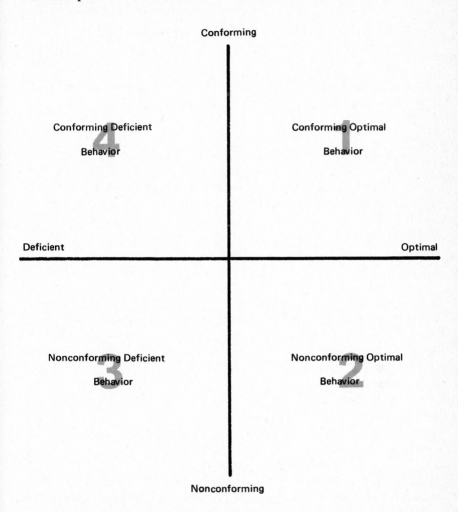

If investigation and past experience do not help us define optimal behavior, how then can we determine what is optimal development for the child? First, it appears that there is no universal optimal development for all children. Children have been divided for study into groups by sex, age, race, religion, nationality, wealth, intelligence, and a host of other considerations. The overwhelming conclusion that is arrived at from such studies is that there are greater differences within the groups than there are between the groups.

For example, if we consider the normal distribution of height for boys and girls of the same age, we find that there is greater range of heights from shortest to tallest of either group than there is between the average heights of the two groups.

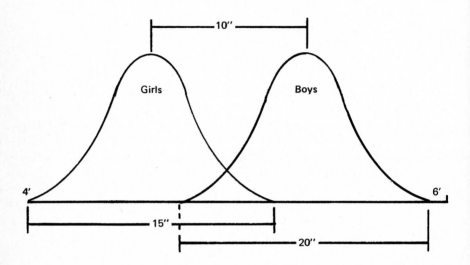

Perhaps the most important aid in discovering optimal behavior patterns for individual children is the ability to honestly ask the question, Why? "Why would piano lessons be a good thing for Harry?" "Why isn't it wise to have Mary continue her study of ballet?" In order to justly answer such questions, one must be aware of the needs of the child and be able to understand how things seem to him. We submit that the question *why* ought to be answerable before a child is encouraged or discouraged in some area of development. Furthermore, answers such as "because I told you so," "that is the way it is done," "because I know best" are unsatisfactory and irrelevant to the fostering of behavior in the child which will tap his highest unique potentials.

Much misinformation surrounds the area of child development. This misinformation leads people to misconstrue the meaning of optimal–deficient, conforming–nonconforming behavior in children. The topic of masturbation in preadolescence and adolescence serves as a good example of how misinformation affects attitudes. Even though there is increasing evidence that masturbation at this age is a common practice and that for most children it is of no greater significance than nail-biting (Kanner, 1957), many adults in the child's world regard such behavior as bad, deficient, abnormal, immoral, deviant, and so forth. Often these adults try to control this practice through severe reprimand and intimidation. Falsehoods such as telling the child that he will weaken himself physically, intellectually, morally, and emotionally, or even that he will drive himself insane by masturbation, are perpetuated by misinformation.

So masturbation is in fact common (normal) and is not harmful, but is it optimal behavior for children? In other words, where does masturbation fall along the continuum of deficient to optimal behaviors? We contend that it falls at different places for different children. However, we also believe that it will fall more toward the optimal end of the continuum if the child is not made to feel guilty for participation in masturbation. Again we suggest the honest pursuit of answers to questions such as "Why does Mary masturbate?" "Why shouldn't she?" will be helpful in resolving the deficient-optimal issue as it pertains to Mary.

Another common example of child behavior that is often misinterpreted is daydreaming. "John, stop staring out the window and do your math problems" is certainly not an unusual teacher response to a daydreaming John. But why is John daydreaming? Why shouldn't he be daydreaming? Obviously, there are a myriad of reasons why John daydreams. Let us suppose in the above instance, however, that John is toying in his mind with an alternative way to solve the math problems in question. Is daydreaming now a deficient behavior? The point we want to stress here is that daydreaming for children per se does not fall along a continuum ranging from deficient to optimal. Rather, daydreaming for John falls along such a continuum. It is important to understand what the behavior in question means to the child before one assesses whether such behavior is nurturing development or not.

ASSESSING THE MEANING OF BEHAVIOR

For the most part, the meaning of behavior has been determined through the application of external standards; that is, the behavior of the child has been understood and explained from the perspective of the observer, rather than that of the child. Consequently, many child behaviors seem to the observer to have no purpose, no rationale, no justification. However, all behavior is purposeful and meaningful. It has purpose and has meaning for the behaver.

How, then, does one go about understanding the purpose and meaning of behavior? Certainly there is no magic formula which can be applied. Understanding the private logic of the child is a learned skill, a skill which can be developed and sharpened through guided instruction. A first step seems to involve the observer's making the assumption that he is more like other people than he is different from them.

We have a colleague who talks about the "little man who lives behind his belly-button." This little man has a "guess" regarding the purpose and meaning of particular observed behaviors. Surely there are times when the little man's guesses are wrong, but a key to understanding the other person is observer-willingness to "check out" these guesses with the behaver. It is our contention that as a person "trains" himself to listen, to trust, and share his little man's guesses, he becomes increasingly able to understand the other person from that person's own personal frame of reference. Dreikurs (Ford and Urban, 1963) has called this ability "intuitive guessing."

Another reliable source for understanding the behavior of the other person is through what has been labeled empathetic understanding. A comprehensive discussion of this ability can be found in chapter 5.

To facilitate optimal development in a child, then, it is necessary to understand the purposes and meaning of the child's behavior from the child's perspective. Using some sort of external standard to assess behaviors often precludes the discovery of the private logic which causes and maintains the behavior in question. The following personal experience of one of the authors may serve to illustrate the importance of understanding from the perspective of the behaver.

John was a big boy for his twelve years. He was popular with the children who were his peers but a thorn in the side of the majority of his teachers; hence, it was not unusual to see John sitting outside the principal's office awaiting discipline.

On the day in question, John seemed to be particularly upset. He was crying, and when invited by the counselor to come to his office, John accepted. John was crying because he had just been expelled from school for "smart talkin' my teacher." In the few minutes that John and the counselor talked, the following situation was described.

All of the students in class had been asked to turn to a particular page in their geography books where a map representing a region of South America was located. Having done so, John was asked by the teacher to read the names of the countries in that region. John replied belligerently, "You have the book, why don't you read them?" John had been warned on other occasions about such behaviors and so was immediately taken to the principal's office.

Why had John acted this way? Through his tears he provided the private logic behind his behavior. "Did you expect me to say I couldn't read those countries?"

Neither teachers nor students had realized that John could scarcely read. John, a bright boy indeed, had successfully fooled his teachers and classmates for years. Until John confided in the counselor, no one had understood John's behavior.

Not all real examples have happy endings. This was a real example, and that was the last day that John ever spent in school.

DEFICIENT CHILDHOOD BEHAVIORS

It would not be responsible of us to leave the reader with the notion that there are no child behaviors that are in and of themselves deficient. Because of our commitments to life and the fulfillment of life, we categorically reject as deficient behaviors which cause severe problems of adjustment to society for the child. Often such behavior adjustment problems result in separation from society until a "reasonable adjustment" can be made to the society at large. Most basically, it is our personal system of values which dictates what sort of behavior is deficient and what is not. Moreover, we suggest that the reader's decisions relative to unacceptable and deficient behaviors are arrived at in a like manner. Our real values are reflected in our behaviors. Yours are too.

Earlier in our discussion we suggested that we have difficulty using the "normal-abnormal," "sick-well," "good-bad" schemes for classifying behavior. We have attempted to state our reasons for this difficulty; yet, we fully recognize the usefulness of some types of classifications in helping the observer understand the behavior of children. Before proceeding with our discussion of such classification systems, it should be emphasized again that classification schemes have at least two serious liabilities. First, they tend to be self-fulfilling. Consider the "normal" child who, for whatever reason, becomes labeled "mentally retarded" in his early school experience. By being so treated, he learns to behave in the expected way. Second, they tend to be dichotomous. By saying "mentally retarded," we conjure up a whole set of stereotypes fitting that definition. At the same time, the stereotypes for "non-mentally retarded" are implicitly defined. We must continually recognize and remind ourselves that most human qualities are not dichotomous. They occur along continua, the poles of which are identified by our labels.

And now to some classifications which are meaningful to us.

Brain Disorders

Some children behave as they do because their brain is impaired and is incapable of functioning in the way that the brain normally functions. Many disorders of this kind occur before and during birth, and most commonly are the result of some chemical and/or genetic imbalance or birth trauma. Often brain damage is the result of the brain being deprived of adequate oxygen for an extended period of time, resulting in damage or death to brain cells.

Although the detection of brain damage and disorder is traditionally the province of the neurologist, the psychiatrist, or the clinical psychologist, it behooves the child counselor to have some expertise in the detection of symptoms indicative of brain dysfunction so that adequate referral can be made. Coleman (1956) lists the following five major symptoms of potential brain disorder: (1) impairment of orientation, (2) impairment of memory, (3) impairment of intellectual functioning, (4) impairment of judgment, and (5) lability and shallowness of affect. (p. 427)

Suicide Potential

Self-destructive behavior may seem far removed from the world of the child counselor. It is, however, an increasingly prevalent behavior among children and adolescents. One situation, moreover, can make it only too real.

Children sometimes threaten to kill themselves for effect; that is, they primarily want to see what reaction adults will give to such threats. Sometimes a suicidal threat is intended to let the teacher, parent, or counselor know that things are very rough and that the child is in need of help. At other times the suicidal threat is very real. The difficulty is in knowing or having some assurance of the meaning of the child's threat.

Symptoms of potential suicide victims vary so greatly that to write definitively about the suicidal individual is very difficult indeed. This is especially true of children, since very little literature exists with respect to the suicidal child. Generally, however, the potential suicide victim can be characterized by one or more of the following: periods of deep depression, low self-regard, intolerable physical or psychic pain, fear of discovery of disgraceful acts, overwhelming discouragement, extreme hostility, and the desire to punish significant people in the child's life, as well as grandiose ideas about joining a dear departed friend (person, dog, etc.).

On occasion, counselors of children will be called upon to make judgments relative to the self-destructive potential of the child. This is risky business and at best is an educated guess. Some general guidelines that may make such judgments easier are (1) Past behavior is the best predictor of future behavior; (2) Most children who "act out" have an unusually high frequency and intensity of negative feelings. However, these feelings can be afforded acceptable means of expression. It is the shy, withdrawn, pent-up child who is more likely to be self-destructive, for no acceptable avenue of expression is seen as available for the release of inner, troublesome feelings.

Aberrant Childhood Behavior Patterns

Childhood schizophrenia, infantile autism, and other classifications seem like such unreal ways of talking about real children. Nevertheless, terms themselves do serve a somewhat useful purpose in that they help one professional person communicate with another.

For our purposes, however, it seems more useful to discuss behavioral symptoms which forewarn us of psychologically deficient child behavior.

Some of the more extreme deficient childhood behaviors that child counselors ought to be aware of are deep and frequently occurring depression, seclusiveness and withdrawal from reality, excessive anxiety, delusions and hallucinations, excessive daydreaming and preoccupation, obsessive and phobic reactions, hypersensitivity to comment and criticism, bizarre behaviors, extreme mood fluctuations, ignoring of other children, perfectionist tendencies, tics, and rejection by peers, teachers, and others.

We realize that this presentation is far from comprehensive, and we are concerned that our scant discussion may be of greater detriment to the child counselor than it is of service to him. We would like to stress again that these behavior patterns exist in varying degrees. Normality is only distinguishable from abnormality in terms of degree. We recommend that the counselor familiarize himself with the excellent discussions of the more extremely deficient child behaviors that have been authored by Coleman (1964), Kessler (1966), and Verville (1967).

COMMENT

Adults often express a desire to return to childhood again, but it seems that all too often they have forgotten those feelings that they possessed as children. They have forgotten the feelings of being treated like a pet or even, in some instances, like a prisoner. They have forgotten the pressures, the competing forces, the discrepancies between adult verbalizations and deeds, the constrictions, the turmoils, the uncertainties and the ambivalences of childhood. Indeed, they have forgotten what it means to a child to be a child.

School quite often has had a detrimental effect upon the child's development. Behaviors which have been externally classified as conforming have been rewarded at the expense of behaviors which might reflect a more optimal development for the individual child. Child-study measures have tended to reinforce such concepts, and hence "normal" has come to be regarded as good and "abnormal" as bad.

We have tried to present an alternative way of conceptualizing child behaviors—a way which has meaning to us. Basically, we have advocated an individualistic approach which considers the purposes and meanings of the individual child's behavior. Moreover, we have suggested the need for questioning traditional beliefs so that our behavior as facilitators of child development is grounded in other than whimsy and personal prejudice.

Finally, we have provided some of our ideas about deficient childhood behaviors and have supplemented these ideas with references to comprehensive works by other authors.

REFERENCES

COLEMAN, J. C. *Abnormal Psychology and Modern Life.* 2nd ed. Chicago: Scott, Foresman and Company, 1956.

———. *Abnormal Psychology and Modern Life.* 3rd ed. Chicago: Scott, Foresman and Company, 1964.

FARSON, R. E. "The Education of Jeremy Farson." Paper read at California State Committee on Public Education, March, 1967.

FORD, D. H., AND URBAN, H. B. *Systems of Psychotherapy: A Comparative Study.* New York: John Wiley & Sons, Inc., 1963.

GLUCK, S., AND GLUCK, E. T. *Unraveling Juvenile Delinquency.* New York: Commonwealth Fund, 1950.

HOLT, J. *How Children Learn.* New York: Pitman Publishing Corp., 1967.

———. Speaking Out. *The Saturday Evening Post,* 242 January 8, 1969, p. 12.

KANNER, L. *Child Psychiatry.* 3rd ed. Springfield, Ill.: Charles C Thomas, Publisher, 1957.

KESSLER, JANE W. *Psychopathology of Childhood.* Englewood Cliffs, N.J.: Prentice-Hall, Inc., 1966.

LEONARD, G. B. *Education and Ecstasy.* New York: The Delacorte Press, 1968.

ROGERS, C. R. *Freedom To Learn.* Columbus, O.: Charles E. Merrill Publishing Co., 1969.

SULLIVAN, H. S. *The Interpersonal Theory of Psychiatry.* New York: W. W. Norton & Company, Inc., 1953.

VERVILLE, ELINOR. *Behavior Problems of Children.* Philadelphia: W. B. Saunders Company, 1967.

SELECTED ADDITIONAL READINGS

BARUCH, DOROTHY. *New Ways in Discipline.* New York: Basic Books, Inc., Publishers, 1949.

BERKOWITZ, PEARL, AND ROTHMAN, ESTHER. *The Disturbed Child: Recognition and Psycho-educational Therapy in the Classroom.* New York: New York University Press, 1960.

BIJOU, S. W., AND BAER, D. M. *Child Development: Volume One.* New York: Appleton-Century-Crofts, 1961.

COOPERSMITH, S. *The Antecedents of Self-esteem.* San Francisco: W. H. Freeman and Co. Publishers, 1967.

DINKMEYER, D. C. *Child Development: The Emerging Self.* Englewood Cliffs, N.J.: Prentice-Hall, Inc., 1965.

ERIKSON, E. H. *Childhood and Society.* New York: W. W. Norton & Company, Inc., 1950.

GALE, R. F. *Developmental Behavior.* New York: The Macmillan Company, 1969.

GINOTT, H. G. *Between Parent and Child.* New York: The Macmillan Company, 1965.

GORDON, I. J. *Human Development.* Chicago: Scott, Foresman and Company, 1965.

HAMMER, M., AND KAPLAN, A. M. *The Practice of Psychotherapy With Children.* Homewood, Ill.: Dorsey Press, 1967.

JENKINS, GLADYS G.; SHACTER, HELEN S.; AND BAUER, W. W. *These Are Your Children*. 3rd ed. Chicago: Scott, Foresman and Company, 1966.

NEILL, A. S. *Freedom Not License*. New York: Hart Publishing Co., Inc., 1966.

———. *Summerhill*. New York: Hart Publishing Co., Inc., 1960.

OSBORN, A. F. *Applied Imagination*. New York: Charles Scribner's Sons, 1953.

PHILLIPS, B. "Problem Behavior in the Elementary School." *Child Development* 39 (1968): 895–903.

REDL, F., AND WINEMAN, D. *Children Who Hate*. New York: The Free Press, 1951.

———. *Controls From Within: Techniques for the Treatment of the Aggressive Child*. New York: The Free Press, 1952.

SCOTT, L. H. *Child Development*. New York: Holt, Rinehart and Winston, 1967.

SLAWSON, S. R. *Child-centered Group Guidance of Parents*. New York: International Universities Press, 1958.

TORRANCE, E. P. *Guiding Creative Talent*. Englewood Cliffs, N.J.: Prentice-Hall, Inc., 1963.

WICKES, FRANCIS G. *The Inner World of Childhood*. New York: Signet, 1955.

4

Theories of
Counseling with Children

Two basic questions would seem to require discussion before various counseling theories can be meaningfully surveyed, that is, What is a theory? and Why is a theory? We shall attempt to provide clarification of these questions before discussing specific theories.

WHAT IS A THEORY?

As graduate students we were once given an assignment to answer this question, "What is a theory?" To determine the nature of a theory seemed a fairly simple task, and armed with dictionaries and a mountain of psychology and counseling books, a group of us sat down to complete the assignment. As we searched and discussed, it became increasingly apparent that there were a number of different definitions of theory—a discovery that complicated the assignment considerably. Our dilemma was now to make some sense of the diversity. Could all of these definitions have merit? Were certain ones more valid than others? How did one determine the relative validity of each?

Stefflre (1965) has drawn an analogy that not only makes clearer the meaning of theory but also emphasizes that theory is only a temporary set of postulates, hopefully to be proven true or to be disregarded in light of new evidence. He says, "A theory is a map on which a few points are known, and a road between them is inferred. Good maps can be filled in as we learn more about the world, and poor ones will need to be thrown away as we find out they are leading us astray." (p. 2)

Perhaps the most concise definition of theory is offered by Hall and Lindzey (1957) when they state, "A theory is an unsubstantiated hypothesis or speculation concerning reality which is not yet definitely known to be so." They continue by pointing out, ". . . when the theory is confirmed it becomes a fact." (p. 10)

Blocher (1966) defines counseling theory as "a way of organizing relevant, available knowledge about human nature in a way that enables the user to be helpful to other people within the framework of a counseling relationship." (p. 25)

There are, of course, numbers of people who have formulated theories of counseling. Many of these theories have been publicly stated and discussed and have to varying degrees aided in organizing our observations and in our understanding of the counseling process. As Patterson (1966) has pointed out, however, there is probably no theoretical model which has yet been formulated which reflects the explicitness and comprehensiveness necessary to legitimately qualify as a well-defined, formalized theory of counseling.

WHY IS A THEORY?

"You pays your money and you takes your choice," one of our professors used to say quite regularly. The suggestion contained in that statement was that no one theoretical formulation is any more valid than any other. Although such a statement is often questioned and many theorists and practitioners contend that one or another of the existing theoretical positions is most valid, the evidence does not support such contentions. Even so, one of our concerns in writing this chapter is that readers will take a look at the various materials surveyed and will decide to become a "this" or a "that." It may well be essential at this point to remind the reader that Sigmund Freud never heard of Freudian theory, and Carl Rogers did not have a professor in graduate school who espoused client-centered therapy.

The Pepinskys (1954) mention the dual roles of the counselor as scientist and practitioner. They propose that the use of theory may be different depending upon the role assumed by the counselor. As a scientist, the counselor has an obligation to help expand and refine knowledge and understanding as much as he can. Theory to the counselor as scientist is therefore global, a means of searching for answers to human behavior in general. On the other hand, theory to the counselor as practitioner has a different emphasis. It takes on a more personalized, everyday client-counselor (when the counselor is me) sort of flavor. The best way that *I* can work with and help clients becomes the search for theory by the counselor practitioner.

From our frame of reference, each person operates from a theory, his own, although he may not have it well defined or be able to verbalize it. Nevertheless, some sort of theory is implied by his beliefs and behaviors. It is also our belief that the task of the counselor is made more complicated and his potential for effectiveness reduced when his theory has not been made explicit. Often, implicit and unexamined theories contain incongruities which may result in inconsistent and unpredictable counselor behavior. From evidence that is available, inconsistency may be the single, most frustrating factor that an individual can bring to a relationship. If this is true, it would seem essential that the counselor develop for himself a personalized theory with which his behavior can be consistent. The more thoroughly he can test his theory against reality, the more consistently he can behave.

If it were possible for us to organize and retain in our mind the knowledges we have accumulated, the need for delineating a theory of our own might not be as necessary. Since such a task is well-nigh impossible, it makes of utmost importance the evolution of a theory which has relevance and meaning for the individual. It is a much more difficult job, but perhaps a more rewarding one, to develop one's own theory than it is to buy one lock, stock, and barrel from another.

WHAT IS AN ECLECTIC?

Eclectic, like so many other words, communicates different things to different people. In some circles, to call a counselor an eclectic is much the same as calling Hitler a saint. In one sense of the word, we are all—and to be effective must be—eclectic. In another sense of the word, we cannot be eclectic and be effective.

The trouble seems to come from the borrowing of techniques from theories without first examining the foundations of the theories from which the techniques have grown. There are very basic differences in theories of counseling. Because of these differences, different methodologies are employed by the practitioners of these theories.

The counselor who borrows methodology developed from theories and places them within a rational, theoretical framework of his own is a most legitimate eclectic. If his own personal theory is developed from knowledges of other theories, there can certainly be no serious objections.

If, however, aspects of an individual's own theory are developed by helter-skelter selection from the individual theories and methodologies of others with no systematic and theoretic foundations, an inconsistent theory from which the individual operates is obtained. Such an eclectic approach can hardly be helpful to the counseling process or to the evolution of a more meaningful, global theory of counseling.

Brammer and Shostrom (1960) treat the question of eclecticism in a similar manner by saying:

> There are many practitioners who decline to identify themselves with a current theoretical system or "school" and who use the identifying label "eclectic" since they either de-emphasize theory or feel that it is too premature to identify too closely with a current position. Some eclectics take their position out of a feeling of defeatism or inertia so as to avoid rigorous exercise of scientific thinking. Their views are based on a process of picking and choosing between the many theories, relying on a superficial knowledge of them, to suit their needs and fancies of the moment.

Other eclectic counselors realize fully the current limitations of systematic theory, so they struggle to integrate and rationalize the elements and conflicts among several theories of personality. They try assiduously to organize their observations and hypotheses into a flexible but workable and consistent position. They prefer to keep their opinions open and to struggle creatively and honestly toward a more highly developed theory. This view represents our position and is most descriptive of therapeutic psychology.

We believe that no counselor or therapist at this early stage of our science can afford to be too parochial in his views. From the latest research and theories he must continue to evolve new positions which have meaning for him. Furthermore, he must be willing to revise his present practices in light of the new data. We have come to call this position "evolving eclectism." (p. 26)

EVOLVEMENT OF A THEORY

As we have tried to emphasize, we believe that the evolution of an individual's own theory is an essential aspect of becoming a counselor. Not only is the development of a well-thought-out, individual theory practical in systematically observing behavior, but without theory from which to operate the counselor is at a loss in knowing how to operate most effectively.

May we also here reemphasize the necessity of developing one's own theory! A useful theory is molded for the individual and is well thought out, practical, and consistent with the behavior of the individual counselor. At the same time it is flexible enough to incorporate change by the individual counselor. The necessity that is so often felt to align oneself with one of the "camps" is not only not a necessity but is, rather, a deterrent to the individual counselor's development. The counselor should evolve a theory that helps him explain his own beliefs and behaviors. Theory evolvement should help free the individual rather than constrict him.

These statements are not made to detract from the many widely accepted theories nor to discourage the individual's study of these and other theories. It is with the knowledge of existing theories that we can most effectively grow and expand our own personal theories so that our counseling efforts make a positive difference to our clients.

SPECIFIC THEORIES OF COUNSELING

We have chosen to review the basic theoretical constructs, principles, and methodologies of counseling within five theories of counseling having current support as being effective in working with children of elementary school age. It is an impossibility to cover each of these theories in depth in the confines of a single chapter. We prefer to call our presentation a survey or overview of major counseling theories for counseling with elementary-school-aged children.

Each of these theories has changed and been adapted to individuals and situations. The basic foundations and principles, however, as we present them, remain to a large degree constant.

The Theory of Psychoanalytic Counseling

Although psychoanalytic counseling has traditionally been thought of as the approach of the psychoanalyst, the psychiatrist, and the social worker, and therefore the preferred approach of child guidance clinics operated under the guidance of psychiatrists and social workers, its concepts and principles are not reserved for the professionals in such a setting.

Few, if any, trained counselors in any setting are completely free of psychoanalytic theory in their own practices. For that matter, psychoanalytic theory is reflected in many of our everyday cultural practices, such as child rearing.

Classical psychoanalytic theory is difficult for the individual, particularly the layman, to accept. A reason for this would seem to be that it presents man as basically evil. The best we can hope for is to tolerate life and the social pressures that are in conflict with our basic "base" nature. Carkhuff and Berenson (1967) describe this aspect of Freudian thought by saying, "To understand and accept fully the validity of the psychoanalytic stances promotes a passive acceptance of life as a series of painful episodes with infrequent periods of balance and no real joy." (p. 117)

No matter what the orientation of the counselor, it is impossible to deny the influence of psychoanalytic theory on all psychological systems. Freud's influence becomes even more evident when one becomes aware of the multitude of everyday concepts which have their origin in psychoanalytic theory. Such concepts as the unconscious; free association; the id, ego and superego; defense mechanisms; and psychosexual stages of development all trace to Freud's psychoanalytic theory. These concepts have been modified and in some cases rejected, yet the fact remains that they have had an impact on current psychological thought. The discussion which follows focuses on these concepts from psychoanalytic theory which seem to have the greatest relevance for the child counselor.

THE STRUCTURE OF PERSONALITY

Freud postulated that personality is made up of three major systems: the id, the ego, and the superego. Although he conceived of these systems as separate entities, he emphasized their interrelatedness and recognized that it is impossible to disentangle their relative individual contributions to man's behavior. He likened the personality to an iceberg which was largely submerged, with the part showing above the water surface as the region of consciousness and the submerged portion as the region of unconsciousness. With this new emphasis on man's unconscious mind, an added dimension for understanding man's behavior was introduced.

The Id

The id is the basic and original system of the personality. It is present at birth and consists of a reservoir of chaotic instinctual impulses which constantly are seeking expression. If allowed to go unchecked, the unrestrained id would produce people who would be pleasure-oriented, selfish, and base.

The Ego

The ego is an acquired system which has an integrating function. Hall and Lindzey (1957) suggest that the ego "comes into existence because the needs of the organism require appropriate transactions with the objective world of reality." (pp. 33–34) That is to say, the ego coordinates the base id impulses with external reality and acts as the executor of the total personality system. The ego is the most flexible part of the mind system. It is continually engaged in harmonizing and reconciling the differences between the inner world of id demands and that which is socially acceptable in the external world. Under severe and continued stress, the ego may break down resulting in id impulse expression and maladaptive behavior.

The Superego

Simply stated, the superego embodies the code of society. This system is the third and last personality system to develop and represents "the traditional values and ideals of society as interpreted to the child by his parents, and enforced by means of a system of rewards and punishments imposed upon the child." (Hall and Lindzey, 1957, p. 35) The superego is popularly called conscience. However, conscience is only one of the two subsystems of the superego.

Conscience represents the introjected values of society and is established by the individual incorporating what is regarded by others as being improper and subject to punishment as his own personal belief. The other subsystem of the superego is the ego-ideal which incorporates what is regarded by others as good and worthy of reward. The conscience controls the individual's behavior by making him feel guilty while the ego-ideal rewards the person by making him feel proud of himself. Through the process of superego development, self-regulation is substituted for parental regulation.

The Total System

As a dynamic system, the id represents base impulses which seek expression and pleasure. As the ego develops, it acts as a controlling agent on the id, allowing expression of these impulses which are acceptable in the external world of reality. The superego, however, actively suppresses id impulses and attempts to persuade the ego to substitute moralistic goals for realistic ones. In other words, the superego opposes both the id and the ego in an attempt to structure the world in its own image. It is, however, similar to the id in that it is nonrational and similar to the ego in that it attempts to exercise control over instincts and id impulses. It may seem that such competing forces would operate at cross-purposes. This, however, is not the case. On the contrary, they work cooperatively as a team under the administrative leadership of the ego. For example, an individual sees an attractive watch in a store window. The id selfishly says, "I'd like to have that watch," and if it were allowed to gratify itself without control, it would stoop to any means to get the watch. At the same time, however, the superego moralistically says, "Thou shalt not steal!" which represents a conflict between the systems. Realizing the conflict, the compromising agent (ego) makes suggestions for appeasing both systems—suggestions such as "If you work ten hours overtime next week, you will be able to buy the watch."

Personality Development

According to Freud, the basic characteristic structure of the person is laid down in the early years of infancy and childhood. He felt that personality was pretty well formed by the end of the fifth year, and that subsequent development was largely an elaboration of the basic formulation. He postulated that personality developed "in response to four major sources of tension: (1) physiological growth processes, (2) frustrations, (3) conflicts, and (4) threats." (Hall and Lindzey, 1957, p. 46) As these tensions are experienced, the person is forced to learn ways of reducing tension. This learning is personality development.

Freud further postulated various mental mechanisms by which this tension was dealt with. Some are considered healthy mechanisms while others are less healthy. It should be emphasized, however, that the chief criterion in determining the degree of healthiness related to a particular mechanism is dependent in large part upon the individual's degree of dependence upon that mechanism and the flexibility of such mechanisms. Any mechanism that becomes a crutch to the individual is less to be desired than one which is used and controlled by the individual to bring about an effective adaptation to life.

It should be recognized that all of us make continual use of mental mechanisms in order to protect our egos. Life would be unbearable without resort to rationalization and similar psychic reactions. It should be recognized that these mediating mechanisms of control are largely unconsciously selected and operate automatically. The discussion of various mechanisms which follows has been developed in a reasonably comprehensive manner due to the widespread use of these constructs in describing behavior motives regardless of theoretical allegiances.

Identification

Identification is the most significant of the mental mechanisms for determining the growth of the ego. The child takes on selected characteristics of significant others in his environment in an attempt to emulate those significant others. This identification is seldom complete since the personality of the emulated person is seldom perceived in its totality. Although very often this produces a constructive influence on personality growth, it depends upon the personality of those to whom the child is exposed. A child may take on socially undesirable characteristics of significant others if these appear to provide some strength or merit.

Displacement

Displacement is another mental mechanism which is useful to effective adaptation to one's environment. By this mechanism an emotional feeling is transferred from its actual object to a substitute. Feelings and attitudes such as love and hate are particularly apt to be displaced from one person to someone else or to some thing. For example, the child who comes home from a fight with his teacher at school and kicks the dog without the dog provoking such a kick is engaging in displacement. The anger he feels cannot be directed toward his teacher, the object of anger, without potential negative consequences, so the dog catches it.

Sublimation

A displacement of feelings and attitudes which produces a higher cultural achievement is called sublimation. When unacceptable urges are channeled and given expression in socially acceptable ways, the tension is reduced and the individual is able to make a satisfactory adjustment. For example, aggressive impulses which cannot be expressed directly toward the sources of those impulses can be channeled into physical activities which give sanction to aggressive behavior such as football.

Rationalization

Probably none of us realizes the extent to which rationalization is a part of our everyday lives. This self-deception mechanism consists of giving plausible and favorable explanations for our behavior rather than real explanations. We prefer to believe that our behavior is the result of thoughtful deliberation, unbiased judgment, and full awareness of all of the motives prompting it; hence we formulate presentable reasons which we believe determine our conduct, when in actuality our reasons are *ex post facto* justifications for real desires and attitudes which remain disguised or concealed. The philanthropist who gives away a large sum of money to a charitable organization may tell himself and others that he is doing so out of a deep concern for the less fortunate. His real motivation, however, may be to gain esteem from others by making such a contribution. The real philanthropic person may be more prone to remain anonymous.

Projection

This mechanism is in many respects a form of displacement. Acting as a defense mechanism against anxiety, projection is directed outward, and one's objectionable character traits, attitudes, and feelings are attributed to others. One constantly meets people who severely criticize in other persons the very same faults and shortcomings which are their own weak points. In the process, they utterly fail to recognize that they themselves possess these despised characteristics. Such a defensive posture on the part of the counselor may be particularly disruptive to the establishment and maintenance of an effective client–counselor relationship.

Repression

One of the common mental mechanisms used in dealing with conflict is that of repression. Through this mechanism, desires, thoughts, impulses, and feelings which are incompatible with, or disturbing to, the individual's conscious self-requirements and motives are excluded from awareness and pushed down into the unconscious; hence, these incompatible thoughts, and so on, remain inaccessible to recall so that they do not produce unbearable anxiety. Repression is an involuntary repudiation of those experiences which particularly involve guilt, shame, and the reduction of self-regard. Even though such experiences remain out of awareness, they do not lose their dynamic drive and tension. They continue to lead a subterranean life covered up by a socially acceptable and appropriate surface.

It should not be concluded that repression is always undesirable. It is a mechanism which may result in a well-adjusted life. It is in the extreme that repression may become pathological.

Compensation

Physical and psychological compensations are phenomena that are familiar to all of us. The average athlete who by dint of hard work becomes an outstanding athlete, the diminutive and frail youngster who becomes his class president, both may be evidencing compensatory behavior. Self-esteem seems to be at the base of compensation. By compensating for perceived or real inadequacies and imperfections, the individual attempts to enhance his self in his own eyes and in the eyes of others.

Unfortunately, this mechanism may easily become exaggerated, and overcompensations may occur. The small person who becomes aggressive and domineering is an example of overcompensation which is familar to all.

Reaction Formation

This mental mechanism involves the replacement in consciouness of an anxiety-producing impulse or feeling by its opposite. The original impulse still exists but is disguised by an impulse that does not produce anxiety and internal conflict. Perfectionistic and uncompromising characteristics are often reaction formations against forbidden tendencies, desires, or feelings. Scrupulous politeness and excessive expressions of gratitude may be disguising feeling of rejection and hostility just as overt aggressiveness may be a cover for deep feelings of insecurity.

Fixation

In the course of normal development, an individual passes through various development stages. Each new step has the potential for producing anxiety, and if this becomes too great, normal growth may be temporarily or permanently halted. Such a cessation of the normal development process is known as fixation. Just as the child may continue his baby talk and his dependence on mother beyond the period when such behavior is expected, so phases of his personality development may be arrested. The arrest, however, is not in the intellectual but in the emotional and dispositional realm of personality maturation.

Regression

Closely related to fixation is the mechanism of regression. In this instance, an individual who encounters a traumatic and anxiety-arousing situation retreats to an earlier stage of development, a lower level of integration. For example, a child who is toilet trained may revert to wetting the bed upon the birth of a sibling who infringes on the maternal attention for him. He seeks by his regression to regain the gratifications of an earlier period in life. Even though regression is adjustive, it tends to be disruptive and does not promote a desirable adaptation to conflict.

PSYCHOANALYTIC ASSUMPTIONS

Carkhuff and Berenson (1967) have summarized four basic assumptions underlying psychoanalytic theory: (1) Man is essentially base and governed by rudimentary instincts which destine him to become a victim of the interaction and conflict between these instincts and social forces; (2)

Man's only real hope is to achieve and then diligently maintain a balance between his internal impulses and life's external demands. In this way he may be able to tolerate life and living; (3) Man can accomplish this balance through a deep understanding of what makes him weak; and (4) An essentially base person (counselor) who has achieved some reasonable balance between inner and outer forces can help other essentially base persons (clients) achieve such a balance. (pp. 118–119)

Life is really presented as an endless series of basic conflicts (ego versus id, rational versus irrational, conscious versus unconscious, reality versus wish, individual versus society, life versus death, and so on) against which man must struggle. Such a struggle maintains homeostasis but fails to provide an opportunity for man to transcend.

Sex plays a major role in classical Freudian thought. Man is viewed as developing through a series of psychosexual stages as he moves through childhood to adulthood. The five basic stages (oral, anal, phallic, latency, and genital) represent modes of reaction of particular erogenous zones of the body (Hall and Lindzey, 1957). The oral phase which lasts about the first year of life involves gratification derived from sucking, eating, and biting which constitutes the infant's chief source of pleasure. The second stage (anal) which lasts during the second year involves pleasure associated with the eliminative functions. Stage three (phallic) follows the anal stage and focuses on the sex organs as the chief source of pleasure. Autoerotic activity which is accompanied by the child's fantasy sets the stage for the appearance of the Oedipus complex. Briefly stated, this complex consists of a sexual impulse to possess the parent of the opposite sex and to reject the same-sex parent. Resolution of this complex is necessary for healthy emergence into the postphallic stages. Stage four (latency) is, as the name suggests, a dormant stage preceding pubescence. The child during this prolonged period remains immune from the impulse of the pregenital stages. However, with the onset of the genital stage, the dynamic emergence of adolescence reactivates the pregenital impulses which must be successfully displaced and sublimated in order for the person to pass into the final stage of maturity (Hall and Lindzey, 1957).

Many people have rejected Freudian thought because of these concepts regarding sex. If they were not in part true, we might not have the need to so quickly reject them. We do not like to look at ourselves as animals, much less frustrated animals. We deny such thoughts as the Oedipal complex in ourselves and even find Freudian theory distasteful. Perhaps Freudian theory is self-defeating in that Freud provides a better explanation for our denial than is offered by other theories of counseling. It is much more pleasant for us to assume Freud was wrong than it is to closely inspect what he was saying in reference to ourselves.

IMPLICATIONS OF PSYCHOANALYTIC THEORY FOR COUNSELING

The analytically oriented counselor assumes the existence of unconscious as well as conscious processes which determine behavior. He tends to concentrate on the conflicts between id impulses and ego defenses and on the relationship of such conflicts to anxiety. If in the face of ego threat the ego defenses are unable to bind or discharge the threat, anxiety results—anxiety which can incapacitate. It is with such anxiety-producing conflicts that the counselor aids the client toward resolution of the conflict. The chief task of the client in counseling is to respond to the counselor, verbally or nonverbally. Without client response, the resolution of emotional conflicts is impossible, and the work of the counselor is thwarted. The assumption is made that talking (through the use of language or play) progressively desensitizes the client to internal elements which previously had been threatening. By the desensitization, less energy is used by the ego to maintain its defenses, and more energy is available for the rational processes of ego to grapple with reality and the demands of the id.

The counselor is responsible for creating an atmosphere of trust and security in which the client is able to reveal his most intimate thoughts and feelings. As King has stated (Stefflre, 1965), the task of the analytically oriented counselor is ". . . to keep the client on the job producing material and actively attempting to uncover repressed or conflictful content." (p. 106)

The major technique used by the counselor is explanation or interpretation. In effect, the counselor makes statements in response to the client which provide the client with different ways of thinking about his behavior. Although such a process sounds simple, it is not what it sounds. The factors of knowing what kinds of thoughts to provide and when to provide them are complex and crucial.

Transference is considered to be an essential aspect of psychoanalytic counseling. The responses the client makes toward the counselor and the quality of their relationship largely determine the outcome of counseling. Such responses are grouped into three classes: (1) the simple friendly feelings of the client for the therapist, (2) strong affectionate feelings with sexual overtones (positive transference), and (3) hostile feelings (negative transference). The assumption is that "transferred" feelings can be expressed by the client in the safety of the counseling relationship because the counselor has done nothing to foster them. They are really feelings held about parents and/or significant others. These responses toward the counselor represent basic inner conflict and present the child's ambivalent responses of love and hate toward the parent. Since in the counseling relationship these responses can occur under different circumstances and can elicit different responses from the counselor, the client is provided with the opportunity of learning different ways of coping with the conflicted feelings (Ford and Urban, 1963).

Countertransference, which refers to the counselor's "transferred" feelings toward the client, also should be considered in a discussion of psychoanalytically oriented counseling. Again, these transferred feelings can be healthy to the relationship when they represent objective and honest feelings of respect and acceptance of the client. They can, however, be deleterious when they stem from the counselor's own subjective unresolved conflicts. Countertransference would seem to be particularly important in working with children since the child's relative dependence on adults could encourage the counselor to "mother," coddle, or react negatively toward the child as a result of past negative experiences with children. For a comprehensive discussion of countertransference the reader is referred to Brammer and Shostrom (1960).

Individual Psychology

Most discussions of psychological theories place the work of Alfred Adler (1870–1937) with the psychoanalytic schools. In one sense, this seems justifiable in that Adler was a student of Freud and was more than a little influenced by his teacher. Even so, many of Adler's theoretical constructs developed in directions which differed significantly from the classical Freudian stance. In light of modern theoretical models for psychology and counseling, one might be as justified in associating Adler's Individual Psychology with phenomenological thought as in linking it to psychoanalytic theory. (Phenomenology postulates among other things that reality is what the individual perceives it to be. A more complete discussion of phenomenology can be found later in this chapter.)

Individual Psychology, the identifying name given to Adler's system, emphasizes the individual and his uniqueness. At first glance at the current practice of Individual Psychology in working with children, one is struck by what appears to be a basic contradiction. That is, the name Individual Psychology seems not to be a fitting one since most work done with children is done in groups, both peer and family. Popularly, this school of thought has come to be known as Adlerian counseling with its practitioners calling themselves Adlerians.

The basic postulates of Adler's theory are quite simply stated: (1) Man is inherently a social being and is motivated by social rather than sexual urges. He places social welfare above selfish interest; (2) Man is a creative being seeking experiences that will enhance his own unique life style; (3) Man is primarily a social creature; (4) The personality of each individual is unique; and (5) Consciousness is the center of personality. (Dreikurs, 1957)

Had these basic postulates been the only contribution of Adler, a discussion would seem hardly necessary. Adler, however, did far more than state his basic view of man. He was a prolific writer and published literally hundreds of books and articles.

Although Adler lived the last two years of his life as a practitioner in the United States, the major credit for the adaptation of Adlerian theory to this country, and more precisely to elementary-school-aged children in this country, must be given to Rudolph Dreikurs, presently a professor of psychiatry at the University of Chicago Medical School.

Dreikurs, like his predecessor Adler, is a prolific writer. The basic principles as discussed here, applying the theory of Individual Psychology to work with elementary school children, might be called Dreikurian rather than Adlerian.

Some Basic Concepts

The heredity-environment argument is of little importance in that it seems a child's environment and his perception of his environment are the factors that cause a child to behave as he does, and they most certainly are the only factors with which we can deal in changing a child's behavior.

By the same token, if we remove a child from his environment to counsel with him, and if that environment and/or his perception of the environment are causing him to behave in the manner in which he does, we can talk until we are blue in the face; but if neither of these factors is changed and we return him to the same environment, his behaviors will be as they were before the counseling.

It is then only logical to bring the significant aspects of the child's environment to the counseling session. In the case of elementary-school-aged children, the basic desire to become an accepted member of the group is most usually directed at the family group. For this reason, Adlerian counseling involves not just the child but the child and his family members. It should be pointed out that as the child grows older, acceptance by the peer group becomes more important than acceptance by the family group. Hence, Individual Psychology counseling with adolescents and upper-elementary-aged children normally is done with groups of students.

As a child attempts to become a member of his family group, he meets a number of situations that, if not provided for, can easily cause *discouragement*. To start with, he is physically the smallest and least adequate member of the group. He lives in a world of capable giants. These basic frustrations, combined with the other normal setbacks the child experiences in attempting to become a member of the family group, tend to discourage the child. Only when a child becomes discouraged will he misbehave (Dinkmeyer and Dreikurs, 1963).

The treatment for this situation is easily derived but not always so easily administered. The antonym for discouragement is *encouragement,* and that encouragement becomes one of the major roles of the Adlerian counselor.

Teachers adhering to the Adlerian point of view often mark students' tests by giving recognition to correct items rather than checking incorrect answers. Recognition of what children are doing well rather than punishment of what children are doing poorly encourages the child.

The formation of a child's *life style* is a basic element in this theory. Life style, or life pattern, is basically an individual's attitude toward life. As a child attempts to become an accepted part of the group, he learns that certain behaviors have not helped him or have hindered him in seeking this goal. He learns to avoid these behaviors. Out of fear and a recollection of disappointments, he avoids hindering behaviors and develops at a very early age his own unique life style.

The child's life style is usually well formed by the age of four or five. He operates after this age with well-established, basic premises and no longer encounters new situations from a trial-and-error basis.

The *family constellation,* or more precisely the position of the child in the family, is of great importance. Observers of children's behavior often are amazed at the differences in behavior of children from the same home. The environment, these observers contend, is the same, or at least very nearly the same, for all children in a given home. However, such is not the case. The family constellation, and thus the environment, is very different for each child.

The first child, for instance, has no older siblings after whom to model his behavior. He was, at least for nine months, an only child. Therefore, he presents much of the behavior of the only-child syndrome. He is, as soon as a sibling is born, dethroned, and his environment is often more radically changed by the addition of siblings than are the environments of subsequent children. He does, however, have a wider range of choice in deciding what manner he will attempt to attain acceptance and recognition or to find his place in the group.

Subsequent children are more limited in this choice. If they were to choose the same method of attaining success as did the older sibling, the rivalry would be a frustrating war that most likely could not be won by the younger child as he would always be a step behind the older child. If a younger child does the things his older sibling(s) does, he has done only what his environment (his family) is expecting of him—nothing more. This factor, coupled with the skills and experiences obtained by the older sibling, forces most children with older brothers and/or sisters to choose a way other than the way chosen by their sibling(s) to "make their marks."

Athletics, school achievement, particular skill in crafts and hobbies, and others are all positive directions that children may take. However, negative directions of achievement may also be taken by children. When positive roads are blocked, or if parents, teachers, counselors, and others are unaware of a child's need for unique achievement and direct him into an unwanted and frustrating competition with his siblings by encouraging him to take the same path as a brother or sister, negative results may occur. The child may rebel or decide to do the best job of being the "bad guy" in the family. It may be for this reason that fewer first-born children are delinquent than are last-born children.

The Adlerian counselor, working through the family, helps to discover positive directions of achievement for the child. He also helps the parents to understand the private logic or the rationale for the child's behavior.

Adler coined the phrase *inferiority complex*. This phrase, however, is much misused from the manner in which Adler intended. The most painful experience for anyone is the feeling they are inferior to others. Once again, referring to the phenomenological point of view, the deterring factor is feeling inferior, not necessarily being inferior. One may, in actuality, be inferior, but if he does not feel he is, this has little psychological effect upon him. On the other hand, he may not actually be inferior; but if he feels he is, his development is restricted.

The display of these real or imagined inferiorities as an excuse or a mechanism of escape constitutes the inferiority complex. An individual demonstrating behavior connected with this syndrome may not compensate for his inferior feelings and is able to achieve nothing. Growth is impossible when the individual is in this state.

THE MEANING OF THE CHILD'S BEHAVIOR

There are four goals of the child's disturbing behavior: (1) *Attention-getting*—This is a normal way of a child attempting to attain social status. It may take a "positive" (doing nice things) or a "negative" (doing not such nice things) direction. (2) *Power*—If the attention-getting stage is thwarted by adults, a *power struggle* between child and adult occurs. This struggle is predominant in most homes and is the style of life in the classrooms of most schools. Often neither adult nor child wins the *power struggle*. (3) *Revenge*—This involves a battle between child and adult. The child no longer is merely seeking acceptance but is out to "get" the adult. Children displaying this step are usually disliked by all with whom they come into contact. (4) *Assumed disability* (or withdrawal)—The child has given up and does nothing or next to nothing. He sees himself, as do others around him, as defeated and hopeless (Dreikurs, 1957).

These steps, or labels, are useful for several purposes: (1) They help to describe and conceptualize about behavior and (2) They provide a system for observing behavior. Just as the child must go through the stages of atten-

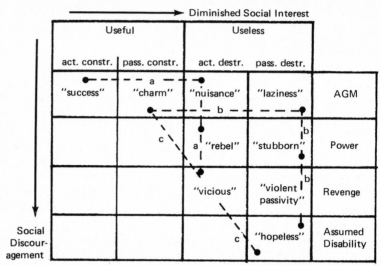

From Dreikurs, *Psychology in the Classroom*, Chart I, p. 15

tion, power, and revenge to arrive at assumed disability, when he "improves" he must retrace his steps through these stages. Hence, the observer has reference points to observe if the child is improving.

This particular point has more than once been a bone of contention between Adlerian counselors and teachers. Such comments as "I just had the kid squared away—didn't bug anyone—just sat there—now you have him in counseling and he is ripping the room apart—Thanks a lot!" are not unique in what Adlerians see as the beginning of a successful case.

It is not important that a child be rigidly placed in a category or even that mistakes in diagnosis are made. What is important is that direction of a child's behavior (negative *toward* positive or positive *toward* negative) be recognized. These directions are indicated by the dotted lines in the diagram above.

THE COUNSELING APPROACH

Adlerian family counseling interviews are often held in front of an audience. A counselor, a co-counselor, and a recorder question the entire family, observing the behavior of the family as to interactions, lines of communication, and so on. The children then are sent to a playroom while the parents are interviewed and the parents' perception of the situation is obtained. Such things as the differences in parent behavior with and without the children present are observed. The children return and the parents leave, and the children's perception of the situation is discussed while their behavior is being closely observed.

During the session with the children, such techniques as confrontation are often employed by the counselor. An example may clarify the technique. In a particularly argumentative family, a six-year-old boy discovered that when his parents became angry with each other, they didn't yell and scream at him. He also discovered that one of the things which made his mother the angriest was when his father couldn't find his car keys in the morning before leaving for work. "Why are you so disorganized? Why don't you find a place to always keep them?" she would yell, much to the delight of the young boy who knew no yelling was coming his way for awhile. He then discovered that by moving his father's car keys he could cause the scene, and he began to do so with regularity. When the counselor realized during a counseling session what the child had been doing, the counselor confronted the child with this knowledge. The mere fact that somebody else knew what he was doing ruined the game for the child and the behavior ceased.

When the interview with the children is completed, they are dismissed from the room. Reports from the playroom worker, children's teachers, and others are made. With the help of the recorder and the co-counselor, recommendations to the family, consistent with Adlerian principles, are discussed by the counselor. When specific recommendations are decided upon, the entire family is recalled and the recommendations are explained to the family. Such principles as punishment by *logical consequences* are often recommended (Dreikurs and Grey, 1968). Ideas for the development of mutual respect are often explored with the family members.

Logical consequences as a form of punishment may be made clearer with the use of another example. A mother came to counseling complaining that she was sick and tired of fixing dinner at 6:00 and again at 6:30 and usually again at 7:00 as the children staggered in to be fed whenever it was convenient for them. She felt that her children should be made to be at dinner on time. She had spanked, yelled at, and threatened, all to no avail. "Why should they be there on time?" asked the therapist. "Because," replied the mother, "I spend my whole evening fixing dinner and cleaning up after them. Even when the kids fix their own dinner if they come in late, they make a bigger mess to clean up than I do. Besides that, they seem to invariably eat something I was saving for the next day and that hurts our budget." Those all seemed like legitimate reasons to the therapist so he pointed out the logical consequences position to the mother.

The logical consequence of being late for dinner is, of course, no dinner. He suggested that the mother friendly but firmly adopt the policy: "We eat dinner at our house at 6:00. If you are there and ready to eat, we would be glad to have you eat with us. If not, try us for breakfast which is served at 7:00 in the morning." Getting angry, preaching, and yelling served no purpose. The practice of logical consequences did.

Control of behavior through logical consequences, except when the consequence is one that would be extremely harmful, has proved a successful process in many homes and classrooms.

Mutual respect emphasizes the need for all members of the family constellation to be respected by all other members. Very often parents demand respect and obedience from their children but do not in turn feel any obligation to respect the rights and feelings of the child. All family members have individual rights and responsibilities. No family member, whether child or parent, should be forced to behave in a particular way without a reason.

Communication and understanding between children and adults, as facilitated by the methods of Adlerian counseling discussed here, is improved. Often misperceptions of the demands of adults or children can be clarified by this approach to the counseling process. The result is often a home that is a happier place for the entire family.

Parent study groups and teacher study groups teaching the basic Adlerian principles are other methods Adlerian counselors have employed with success in helping people to work and/or live with a better understanding of children.

Behavioral Counseling

Behavioral counseling, like other theories of counseling, is known by a variety of names. Learning theory, desensitization, and operant conditioning (a major aspect of behavioral counseling) are but a few of the terms often used synonymously, albeit inappropriately, for behavioral counseling. Practitioners of behavioral counseling or those adhering to a behavioral viewpoint are most commonly referred to as behaviorists.

The equation $B=f(S)$, meaning behavior is some function of stimulus, is the basic construct of behavioral psychology (Bijou and Baer, 1961). From this construct an empirical theory of counseling is developed.

The purpose of counseling is to change behavior. The only real disagreement that seems to arise from this statement is in a definition of behavior. No matter how behavior is defined it would seem logical that it could be more easily changed in the desired direction by a systematic approach rather than a helter-skelter "let's see what happens" approach.

The child's environment must, it would seem, constitute the child's stimulus. His behavior is then some function of his environment. Some behaviors (responses) are controlled by *preceding* stimulation and some responses are controlled by *consequent* stimulation. Respondent, or reflex, behavior is a response controlled by a preceding stimulation. This has long been characterized by the equation $S \rightarrow R$, meaning stimulus yields response. The equation has been expanded in terms of Skinner's "Black box" concept to read S-O-R, indicating that a stimulus comes into the organism and a response comes out of the organism. In other words, the organism mediates the response.

Pavlov demonstrated that respondent behavior can be attached to a new stimulus in terms of a conditioned stimulus. The response to a conditioned stimulus can also be extinguished or deconditioned. When, however, the response becomes binding with the conditioned stimulus, as was the case with Pavlov's dogs, the response is referred to as a conditioned response.

The major focus of the behavioral counselor, however, is operant conditioning, where the response is controlled by a consequent stimulation. Once again looking at what is being said in terms of a formula we have: S→R→R+, meaning that a stimulus elicits a response which must be positively reinforced in order for the response to continue or increase in frequency. With operant, as contrasted to respondent, conditioning, the respondent (the organism) has the control over what, if any, response will be elicited from a given stimulus. If the response given when a stimulus occurs is positively reinforced, the next time the same or a similar stimulus is presented a like response will occur. This is *not* because of the stimulus but because of the anticipation of the reinforcer, for example, "Have some candy" (Stimulus). Puts candy in mouth (Response). Candy tastes good (Positive reinforcer). The next time the individual is offered candy he will put it in his mouth, not because it is offered, but because he anticipates its tasting good.

Reinforcers can also be negative, causing responses to stimuli to be terminated, decreased, or modified, for example, "Have some candy" (Stimulus). Puts candy in mouth (Response). Tastes very bad (Negative Reinforcer). The next time somebody says, "Have some candy," and if the candy looks like the candy of the negative experience, the response is not apt to be putting the candy in the mouth—not because of the stimulus, but because of the anticipation of the negative reinforcer.

The process to strengthen a response (to assure specific behavior when a given stimulus occurs) is relatively simple. A reinforcer is given immediately after appropriate behavior occurs in the presence of a given stimulus. Food, approval, money, or some other reinforcer is given to the respondent when the response to a given stimulus is desired. When this S→R bond is strengthened, the reinforcer need not be applied each and every time. Intermittent reinforcement may maintain the response.

When a stimulus elicits an undesired behavior, the counselor must first determine what the maintaining reinforcer is (the reinforcer that causes the child to behave as he does when confronted with the specific stimulus). The reinforcer is then removed and the behavior is extinguished. Such things as teacher's or parent's smiles may be the maintaining reinforcer for an undesirable behavior, even though the teacher or parent may be unaware of his participation in the behavior maintenance.

A child is incapable of giving responses that are not in his repertoire of behaviors. In order to increase his repertoire, the obtaining and subsequent retaining of behaviors that the child has not previously had, two primary techniques are employed: modeling and shaping.

Modeling is a process which attempts to increase an individual's response repertoire through demonstration. The model, sometimes the counselor, responds to a given stimulus in a particular way. The child observes the model's response, sees the consequences of the response, and adopts the response of the model. For example, eight-year-old Jimmy is continually in academic troubles because he is unable to organize his work in such a way that he can get it all done. By being provided the opportunity to observe the way others organize their work, Jimmy may be able to acquire ways that will be helpful to him as he attempts to organize more effectively. It should be noted that modeling is most successful when the model and the child have a positive mutual relationship. Such a relationship provides the incentive for the child to expand his repertoire of behaviors.

The second of these techniques is *shaping*. Basically, shaping involves the production of increasingly complex forms of behavior by small increments from a preceding simpler form. The counselor is in the position to shape behavior in the child by beginning with a behavior that is already in the child's repertoire and by exposing him to a progression of experiences designed to augment his repertoire. To produce new behaviors, differential reinforcement must occur. That is, the counselor must positively reinforce those behaviors which move the child's behavior in the desired direction. To illustrate, Mary, a very shy and passive child, is referred for play therapy. From his observations of Mary in the classroom and on the playground, the therapist establishes specific goals for the therapy experience. Namely, he wants her to become more expressive, aggressive, and self-initiating. At the beginning of therapy he plots Mary's behaviors on a chart. As the therapy experience unfolds, he systematically reinforces all of those behaviors which evidence movement on Mary's part toward the realization of those goals. Consequently, as therapy progresses, Mary does in fact become expressive, aggressive, and self-initiating. Mary's original "normal curve of behavior expectancy" has been shifted toward more adaptive behaviors by the shaping process of selected reinforcement. (See diagram, p. 77.)

Another aspect of behavioral counseling involves the process of *extinction*. Essentially, extinction is the weakening of a response by consistently not reinforcing it until that response fails to occur. This process is most often used in the reduction of tantrum behavior in children. When the child who is "throwing a temper tantrum" gets a parental response (the parent tries to

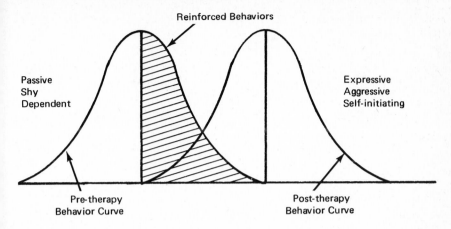

comfort the child), there is an increased probability that the child's incidence of tantrum behavior will increase. If such behavior is ignored (the parent walks off and lets the child throw his tantrum by himself), the incidence of tantrums will decrease.

The process of desensitization is also a method of extinguishing maladaptive behaviors. Fundamental to this process is the postulate that no human being is capable of entertaining two antagonistic feelings at the same time, that is, one cannot feel anxious and relaxed simultaneously.

A typical situation where desensitization procedures might be employed is with the child who is frightened to speak in front of a group. In order to extinguish this fear response, the counselor might set up a series of experiences for the child which would be presented to him in a hierarchical order from least fright-provoking to most fright-provoking. For example, such a series might include watching someone speak to an audience, waiting to speak to a group, speaking informally to a small group of close friends, speaking formally to a small group of strangers, speaking formally to a large group.

The procedure involves having the child move through this sequence of fear-producing stimuli in such a way that his fear at each level is minimized before moving to the next level of stimulation. Ultimately, he will be able to accomplish the most difficult task without experiencing overwhelming anxiety. Wolpe and Lazarus (1966) have refined this process by adding systematic relaxation procedures to help accelerate desensitization to anxiety-producing stimuli.

One final concept that should be briefly explained is that of stimulus generalization. It is highly unlikely that any two stimuli are ever exactly the same. The child, however, learns to view similar stimuli as being appropriately responded to by the response that is conditioned to a similar stimulus. For example, the child may develop prejudiced attitudes by saying to himself, "Bill smells bad. Bill lives on the other side of the tracks. Therefore, people who live on the other side of the tracks smell bad."

From the standpoint of the behavioral counselor, children are much like machines. Counseling is a process providing major overhauls, minor tune-ups, and preventive maintenance for children. The counselor is a behavioral engineer who, through the scientific application of empirically validated principles, brings about behavior modification in children. He not only fixes poorly functioning machines but also helps provide environment conditions in which the machine can optimally function.

Schwitzgebel (1968) has reported the development of a variety of devices currently being used experimentally to promote behavior modification by behavioral engineers. For instance, the "Mowler sheets" have become a common apparatus for attempting to eliminate enuretic behavior in children. Basically, this devise is an electric pad which, when activated by a small amount of urine, starts a tape recording which tells the child to get up. Approximately a minute after this initial warning, a buzzer or mild shock begins and continues until it is shut off. The reader will find descriptions of this device in the Sears Roebuck catalog.

Although many of these techniques and devices do not now directly relate to the range of human problems commonly thought of as the province of counseling, it should be recognized that there is currently a vast movement to make application of scientific behavioral principles to all walks of life. Whether or not one accepts the behavioral approach to counseling, one must consider that all counseling can be analyzed and reduced to behavioral constructs. Moreover, it has been empirically demonstrated that behavior is in fact changed by adherents to this approach. Is it the counselor, his technique, or some combination of the two? That answer is still pending.

Client-Centered Counseling

Client-centered counseling is often referred to as Rogerian, self-theory, nondirective, phenomenological, relationship, and at least to some degree, existential counseling.

If asked to specify or label the single theory of counseling to which they adhere, most counselors would probably call themselves client-centered. (This excludes eclecticism as a theory of counseling.) The client-centered approach is undoubtedly the predominant one for several reasons. First, it is the theoretical training model espoused by most training institutions. Second, it is believed by many (professionals and laymen) that it is an easy technique to learn. Third, it tends to reflect a sort of "ideal democratic philosophy"— a philosophy which is, at least in theory, attractive.

The overall theory is derived from the work of Taft (1933), Rogers (1939), Allen (1942), Rank (1945), Axline (1947), and others. The primary spokesman, however, has been Carl Rogers who, although in his sixties, is still extremely active and professionally productive. The formulation of his revolutionary approach to counseling was first published in 1942. Since that time he has taught at numerous universities, published voluminously, and offered his leadership to the counseling movement both here and abroad. Rogers and his associates have also been pioneers in researching the effects of counseling (Rogers and Dymond, 1954).

Client-centered theory is based upon a number of fundamental premises, the most central of which is that man is basically good, and if allowed to freely do so, he will choose wisely and will do good things. When confronted with choices, he will choose that which he perceives to be the best for him. This will also be for the ultimate good of society since man's natural motives are moral and humane.

In building upon these fundamental assumptions, Boy and Pine (1963) have listed eight basic principles of client-centered counseling which have direct application to counseling with children. It should be noted that these principles and the discussion which follows represent a rather classical client-centered philosophy. This classical theory has undergone numerous interpretations, modifications, and developments. It is fair to say, however, that its essence is stated in the following principles:

(1) The individual and not the problem is the focus; (2) It places greater stress on the immediate situation than upon the individual's past; (3) It places greater stress on the emotional elements, the feeling aspects of the situation, than upon intellectual aspects; (4) The counselor operates on the principle that the client is basically responsible for himself and that he must retain this responsibility; (5) The counselor makes no attempt to evaluate the person's complaint or to probe into it. Diagnosis is not essential to effective counseling; (6) This approach lays stress upon the counseling relationship itself as a growth experience. It is not a preparation for change, it is change; (7) The counselor has respect for the integrity of the counselee. The counselor accepts the counselee's right to be different and strives to help him understand and accept himself; and (8) There is a genuine recognition of the right of the individual to agree or disagree, to be friendly or to be unfriendly, to give information or to withhold, to act or not to act. (p. 14)

Self-actualization has been discussed as the goal of client-centered counseling. If acceptance and respect are perceived by the client in his relationship with the counselor, this will allow the client to be free enough to move toward self-actualization. The process is not one of specific problem-solving, but rather one that has effect upon the total person. A search to know oneself and to find acceptance of that self by another individual characterizes the client-centered counseling process. To the degree that the child accomplishes increased self-respect, self-awareness, and self-acceptance (which are enhanced by the self-respect, self-awareness, and self-acceptance of the counselor and that counselor's respect and acceptance of the child), to this degree he is able to move in a direction toward self-actualization.

The total individual is emphasized here. The direction for growth must come from within (the client) not from without (the counselor) in order that it be meaningful. The client-centered counselor does not make decisions for or about the child in that he does not know as well as the child what the child should or should not do or feel. The child is responsible for himself, and the counselor does not assume nor usurp this responsibility for him.

Rogers (1961) has spoken at length about acceptance and positive regard. From this framework, acceptance and regard do not denote reward or approval any more than they do punishment or disapproval. We do not have the right, much less the obligation, to force our own values upon other people. Acceptance means acceptance of the individual as a worthwhile person, not in terms of how well he fits into our own, or for that matter society's, value structure. It is certainly not the old cliché "There is some good in each person," which really means everybody does something that I think he should do. Rather, each human is a unique person worthy of respect and acceptance. Such behaviors as sympathy in no way demonstrate acceptance, but rather really say, "I am better than you are." Value-oriented words such as "good" and "bad" are often conspicuously missing from the classical client-oriented counselor's vocabulary.

Naïve adherents to client-centered counseling often act and sometimes feel as though they have found a "cookbook" of techniques for applying their philosophy. As Grummon (Stefflre, 1965) points out, however, "The very nature of the theory prohibits learning a set of rules and procedures and then applying these mechanically and objectively in the counseling interview." (p. 31)

Client-centered counseling has also been characterized by the techniques that some of its practitioners rely upon. *Reflection* is probably the best known and least understood of these techniques. From the outside looking in, it might appear that the reflecting client-centered counselor is doing nothing more than repeating what the child has just said. The counselor is, however, integrating the meaning of what has just been said and returning to the child the counselor's perception of the meaning expressed by the child. This, of course, does several things. It allows the child to see how what he is communicating is perceived by another. It helps the child to look more closely at what he is feeling. It allows the child to express feelings without being condemned. It directs the interaction to a feeling level.

Rogers (1951) describes the client-centered counseling process by saying:

> . . . it would appear that for me, as counselor, to focus my whole attention and effort upon understanding and perceiving as the client perceives and understands, is a striking operational demonstration of the belief I have in the worth and significance of this individual and client. Clearly, the most important value which I hold is, as indicated by my attitudes and my verbal behavior, the client himself. (p. 35)

A permissive atmosphere characterizes the classical client-centered counseling which allows a great deal of seemingly extraneous conversation. Long periods of silence may be noted by the observer. This may happen because the child has the right to be silent as well as the right to say and feel what he pleases. It is also recognized that silence does not necessarily mean a lack of productivity. During periods of silence much may be taking place internally without the distraction of the client having to verbalize what is being thought. The assumption here is that the free atmosphere provides an opportunity for the client to "own" his feelings and behaviors without being subjected to censure. Being presented such an opportunity permits the client to examine his thoughts and feelings nondefensively. This in turn can lead to changed perceptions and changed behaviors (Axline, 1964).

Adults have often learned to communicate at a more intellectual or cognitive level than have children. For this reason the client-centered process which relies upon feeling-level interaction between the child and the counselor is often less threatening to a child than the same process is to an adult. Few adults, however, show true respect for children nor do they truly pay attention to the feelings of children without inserting their own values of what the child should be feeling or how he should be behaving. Client-centered counseling relationships are, therefore, usually unique relationships for children.

In that the focus of client-centered counseling is the child not the counselor, not society, and not the child's problems, the process is well adapted to developmental as well as remedial counseling.

As the child learns that another person (the counselor) sees true worth in him as an individual and that the counselor respects and accepts him for what he is, the child in turn starts respecting and accepting himself and begins to see a true worth in himself as an individual.

Perhaps the words of one of Rogers' most prolific students Dugald Arbuckle (1965) best summarizes the client-centered counseling process. "The term 'client-centered counseling' is not a description of a method of counseling, but it refers, literally, to what it says—it is a human relationship

between two people, and it is centered on one of the two people involved."
(pp. 41–42)

A Directive Approach to Counseling

Directive counseling is not in itself a theory of counseling; it is rather a
category into which portions of many theories, some similar and some very dis-
similar, are lumped together; hence, it is the most difficult of the approaches
of counseling with children to present. So many varied and different things are
done in the name of directive counseling, and similarities in theory of these
approaches are often most difficult to recognize.

Woolf and Woolf (1953) list three assumptions basic to directive
counseling:

(1) It is essentially an intellectual process; (2) Maladjustments in normal
persons leave a large percentage of the mind intact and therefore the mind can
be used in learning or relearning; (3) The counselor has superior information and
experience and is competent to give advice about how a problem can be solved.
(p. 22)

We would like to add to these three a fourth assumption, namely that
the advice given by the counselor can and will be integrated by the client to
effectively change the behavior of the client.

Diagnosis and prescription have traditionally been major factors in
directive counseling. Without knowing what is "wrong with" the client, it is
most difficult to know what to do to remedy the behavior.

E. G. Williamson (1942), regarded as one of the chief spokesmen for
the directive school of counseling, states that directive counseling may be
placed into five categories:

(1) *forcing conformity*—designed to force the individual to conform to his
environment; (2) *changing the environment*—attempts to change those parts of
the student's environment which cause difficulties, actual or potential; (3) *selecting the appropriate environment*—involves aiding the student to select from his
environment those elements which are most appropriate to his personality; (4)
learning needed skills—involves assisting the client to overcome those deficiencies
which produce his difficulty; (5) *changing attitudes*—involves bringing about
changes in the individual's attitude in such a manner as to facilitate a harmonious
balance between his needs and the demands of the environment. (p. 215)

The methods of directive counseling appear to be similar to current
methods of teaching elementary school children, and practitioners of the
directive methods of counseling often make no distinction between counseling
and teaching.

The directive counselor must have a clear view of what is right and
wrong for other people to do. Such views vary from the directive "pastoral

counseling," drawing its guidelines from religious dogma, to views of Albert Ellis, founder of rational therapy (described by Ellis as a directive counseling approach).

Ellis believes that the negative aspects of a behavior are the guilt that one feels for having participated or not participated in the behavior. Decisions, he insists, of whether or not to do the socially and religiously approved thing should be based upon whether or not the client will feel guilty afterwards. In a very directive manner, he attempts to have clients look at what they want to do or what they are doing as contrasted with what they have been taught to do or what others think they should do. The intent of the counselor then becomes one of challenging the individual's "stupid" beliefs and substituting "rational" beliefs for them. Such techniques as persuasion, exhortation, and coercion are commonly used by the directive counselor to bring about the desired change in client behavior. Glicken (1968) has discussed this rational counseling approach as it relates to children—an approach which is seeking increased recognition and acceptance among child counselors.

A stronger case has been made for directive counseling with children than with other individuals. By virtue of our adult status (teachers, counselors, and others), we assume the role of being more knowledgeable about life, its complexities, and its problems. To do things *for* children instead of merely with them is the role entrusted to us by society. In order to meet our obligations, it is easy for us to direct and guide children in the way we feel they should be, without paying much heed to their individual uniqueness, their rights, their feelings, or their capacities for self-direction. Children are most certainly human beings who do have rights. They are not, however, miniature adults. They are not given the full rights of the adult in our society. Neither are they made responsible for their actions. We assume that if they are left entirely upon their own to make decisions, they do not possess the experience or congruent philosophy of their counselor to be aware of, to explore, or in the final analysis, to choose the alternative that would be most wise for them. Experiments such as Summerhill (Neill, 1961), however, would seem to seriously challenge such an assumption.

Judgments most certainly play a critical role in directive counseling. Whether these judgments about the client are made by testing or some other form of diagnosis, they are the best that is available and must be followed until better evidence is obtained to modify the judgments made. Other models of counseling often pretend that judgments need not be made, or in fact are not made, by the counselor. Such a thought is nonsense. Judgments by the counselor about the client are always made. If, as in directive counseling, these judgments are made in terms of a consistent philosophy, they are more meaningful than if they are inconsistent and/or ignored by the counselor.

COMMENT

If the reader has not become aware of basic inconsistencies and contradictions in the contrasting theories as we have presented them, then we have failed our purpose. We have tried to present with some degree of objectivity and support those theories that appear to us to have major usefulness as models of counseling with elementary-school-aged children.

If their presentation has done nothing more than whet the reader's appetite toward developing a fuller awareness of these and other counseling theories, the chapter has been a success. If the reader has become able to incorporate into his own theory basic principles with consistency from these presentations, we have been most successful. If, on the other hand, the reader decides he must become one of these types or must strictly adhere to the basic principles of one of these approaches, then we have indeed been dismal failures in our purpose. Our intent has been to imply the need for the development of a personalized counseling theory unique to each counselor. The concepts and techniques discussed would seem to have their maximum usefulness when the individual counselor is able to select and reject them on the basis of the enhancement of his own effectiveness as a counselor. They should be used to aid the counselor in realizing and extending his unique "self" to children.

REFERENCES

ALLEN, F. H. *Psychotherapy With Children.* New York: W. W. Norton & Company, Inc., 1942.

ARBUCKLE, D. S. *Counseling: Philosophy, Theory, and Practice.* Boston: Allyn & Bacon, Inc., 1965.

AXLINE, VIRGINIA M. *Play Therapy.* Boston: Houghton Mifflin Company, 1947.

————. *Dibs: In Search of Self.* Boston: Houghton Mifflin Company, 1964.

BIJOU, S. W., AND BAER, D.M. *Child Development: Volume One.* New York: Appleton-Century-Crofts, 1961.

BLOCHER, D. H. *Developmental Counseling.* New York: The Ronald Press Company, 1966.

BOY, A. V., AND PINE, G. J. *Client-centered Counseling in the Secondary School.* Boston: Houghton Mifflin Company, 1963.

BRAMMER, L. M., AND SHOSTROM, E. L. *Therapeutic Psychology.* Englewood Cliffs, N.J.: Prentice-Hall, Inc., 1960.

CARKHUFF, R. R., AND BERENSON, B. G. *Beyond Counseling and Therapy.* New York: Holt, Rinehart & Winston, Inc., 1967.

DREIKURS, R. *Psychology in the Classroom.* New York: Harper and Bros., 1957.

————, AND DINKMEYER, D. *Encouraging Children To Learn: The Encouragement Process.* Englewood Cliffs, N.J.: Prentice-Hall, Inc., 1963.

————, AND GREY, L. *Logical Consequences.* New York: Meredith Corporation, 1968.

FORD, D. H., AND URBAN, H. B. *Systems of Psychotherapy.* New York: John Wiley & Sons, Inc., 1963.

GLICKEN, M. D. "Rational Counseling: A Dynamic Approach To Children." *Elementary School Guidance and Counseling* 2 (1968):261–267.

HALL, C. S., AND LINDZEY, G. *Theories of Personality*. New York: John Wiley & Sons, Inc., 1957.

NEILL, A. S. *Summerhill*. New York: Hart Publishing Co., Inc., 1960.

PATTERSON, C. H. *Theories of Counseling and Psychotherapy*. New York: Harper & Row, Publishers, 1966.

PEPINSKY, H. B., AND PEPINSKY, PAULINE. *Counseling—Theory and Practice*. New York: The Ronald Press Company, 1954.

RANK, O. *Will Therapy; and Truth and Reality*. New York: Alfred A. Knopf, Inc., 1945.

ROGERS, C. R. *Clinical Treatment of the Problem Child*. New York: Houghton Mifflin Company, 1939.

———. *Client-centered Therapy*. Boston: Houghton Mifflin Company, 1951.

———. *On Becoming A Person*. Boston: Houghton Mifflin Company, 1961.

———, AND DYMOND, ROSALIND F. *Psychotherapy and Personality Change*. Chicago: University of Chicago Press, 1954.

SCHWITZGEBEL, R. L. "Survey of Electromechanical Devices for Behavior Modification." *Psychological Bulletin* 70 (1968):444–459.

STEFFLRE, B., ed. *Theories of Counseling*. New York: McGraw-Hill, Inc., 1965.

TAFT, JESSIE. *The Dynamics of Therapy in a Controlled Relationship*. New York: The Macmillan Company, 1933.

WILLIAMSON, E. G. *Counseling Adolescents*. New York: McGraw-Hill, Inc., 1950.

WOLPE, J., AND LAZARUS, A. A. *Behavior Therapy Techniques*. New York: Pergamon Press, Inc., 1966.

WOOLF, M. D., AND WOOLF, JEANNE A. *Student Personnel Program*. New York: McGraw-Hill, Inc., 1953.

SELECTED ADDITIONAL READINGS

ADLER, A. *Understanding Human Behavior*. New York: Greenberg, 1927.

———, AND DEUTSCH, DANICA, eds. *Essays in Individual Psychology*. New York: Grove Press, Inc., 1959.

ANSBACHER, ROWENA. *The Individual Psychology of Alfred Adler*. New York: Basic Books, Inc., Publishers, 1956.

BERNE, E. *Transactional Analysis*. New York: Grove Press, Inc., 1961.

BETTLEHEIM, B. *Love Is Not Enough*. New York: Collier Books, 1965.

BORDIN, E. S. *Psychological Counseling*. New York: Appleton-Century-Crofts, 1968.

BURTON, A. *Modern Humanistic Psychotherapy*. San Francisco: Jossey-Bass, Inc., Publishers, 1967.

CORLIS, R. B., AND RABE, P. *Psychotherapy From the Center*. Scranton, Pa.: International Textbook Co., 1969.

DOLLARD, J., AND MILLER, N. E. *Personality and Psychotherapy*. New York: McGraw-Hill, Inc., 1950.

ELLIS, A. *Reason and Emotion in Psychotherapy*. New York: Lyle Stuart, Inc., 1962.

FORD, D. H., AND URBAN, H. B. *Systems of Psychotherapy*. New York: John Wiley & Sons, Inc., 1963.

FRANKL, V. E. *Man's Search for Meaning*. Boston: Beacon Press, 1962.

————. *The Doctor and the Soul*. New York: Alfred A. Knopf, Inc., 1965.

FREUD, S. *A General Introduction to Psychoanalysis*. New York: Liveright Publishing Corp., 1935.

FROMM–REICHMANN, FRIEDA. *Principles of Intensive Psychotherapy*. Chicago: University of Chicago Press, 1950.

HAMMER, M., AND KAPLAN, A. M. *The Practice of Psychotherapy With Children*. Homewood, Ill.: Dorsey Press, 1967.

JUNG, C. G. *Collected Works, Vol. 16, The Practice of Psychotherapy*. New York: Pantheon Books, Inc., 1954.

KRUMBOLTZ, J. D., ed. *Revolution in Counseling*. Boston: Houghton Mifflin Company, 1966.

MOUSTAKAS, C. E. *Psychotherapy With Children*. New York: Harper & Row, Publishers, 1959.

————, ed. *Existential Child Therapy*. New York: Basic Books, Inc., Publishers, 1966.

PATTERSON, C. H. *Theories of Counseling and Psychotherapy*. New York: Harper & Row, Publishers, 1966.

PAUL, G. L. *Insight vs. Desensitization in Psychotherapy*. Stanford: Stanford University Press, 1966.

PERLS, F.; HEFFERLINE, R. F.; AND GOODMAN, P. *Gestalt Therapy*. New York: Delta Books, 1951.

SALTER, A. *Conditioned Reflex Therapy*. New York: Creative Age Press, 1949.

SHERTZER, B., AND STONE, S. C. *Foundations of Counseling*. Boston: Houghton Mifflin Company, 1968.

SULLIVAN, H. S. *The Interpersonal Theory of Psychiatry*. New York: W. W. Norton Company, Inc., 1953.

THORNE, F. C. *The Principles of Personal Counseling*. Brandon, Vt.: Journal of Clinical Psychology Press, 1950.

TRUAX, C. B., AND CARKHUFF, R. R. *Toward Effective Counseling and Psychotherapy*. Chicago: Aldine Publishing Company, 1967.

TYLER, LEONA E. *The Work of the Counselor*. 3rd ed. New York: Appleton-Century-Crofts, 1969.

WOLBERG, L. R., ed. *Short-term Psychotherapy*. New York: Grune and Stratton, Inc., 1965.

5

Qualities of Effective Counseling

The preceding chapter has provided the reader with a brief discussion of five theoretical approaches having application to counseling with children and adults. In this chapter we focus on those conditions and qualities which are common to the various theoretical systems. That is to say, our intent is to develop the commonalities in the differing approaches presented—commonalities which characterize effective counseling. We believe that the days of rigid adherence to a "school" or "cult" of counseling are rapidly coming to an end. Furthermore, we believe that continued learnings from experience and research will lead to a transcendent and overarching system of counseling which will preclude theoretical allegiance. The beginnings of such a system are discussed in this chapter.

FOR BETTER OR FOR WORSE

Is counseling effective in promoting change in the client? This question has been seriously asked only in recent times. Extensive reviews of literature having to do with the outcomes of counseling have resulted in considerable controversy with regard to the efficacy of counseling as an approach to the promotion of client change (Eysenck, 1952, 1960, 1965; Levitt, 1957, 1963). The assertion that counseling does not result in average client improvement greater than that which is experienced in clients who do not receive counseling seems to be strongly supported by the research evidence of Eysenck and Levitt. If such an assertion is true, then there appears to be no reason for counseling to continue to evolve and grow. Why do people such as ourselves persist in working as counselors and in writing about our experiences and beliefs? Are we simply deluding ourselves? Are we so ego-involved in our work that we must reject the evidence which challenges our very existence? Perhaps so, but we think not. We believe that there is another and a legitimate way to construe the existing evidence—a way which hinges on the "averaging" of counseling outcomes.

Persons from all walks of life recognize that there are "good" plumbers and "poor" plumbers, "good" salesmen and "poor" salesmen, "good" TV repairmen and "poor" TV repairmen, "good" teachers and "poor" teachers, and so forth. Even though it would seem evident that there would also be "good" counselors and "poor" counselors, such an inference has long been avoided when considering counseling outcome studies. Bergin (1963), Truax and Carkhuff (1967), Carkhuff and Berenson (1967), and others have, after reexamining the data, advanced the interpretation that some counselors produce negative change, some produce no change, and some produce positive change in clients with whom they work. In other words, counseling can be "for better or for worse." In the light of such an interpretation, it would seem inappropriate to lump all counseling outcomes together as though the effect of counseling could only be unidirectional. To indict counseling as ineffective by averaging positive and negative outcomes is to further confuse the problem and to make impossible the important task of determining those practices and characteristics which identify the "good" counselor.

We believe this point to be a crucial one. It suggests that counseling outcomes must be considered on other than the "averaging of outcomes" basis. Moreover, we must determine the counselor, client, and counselor-client interaction variables which produce positive client outcomes. In the following paragraphs we develop what we believe to be common variables and ingredients in the various systems of counseling which contribute to positive client outcomes. Research evidence is cited in support of our contentions when it is available. Tentative speculations based on our own experiences and those of others are also included.

COUNSELING IS LEARNING

Regardless of the theoretical orientation from which the counselor functions, the counseling process is considered a learning and relearning process. The disordered or maladaptive behavior of the child has been learned through the life experiences of that child; hence, in order to help the child behave in more ordered and adaptive ways, he must have life experiences where more ordered and adaptive patterns of behavior can be learned. Counseling provides such a setting.

Theorists generally agree that counseling involves the application of a systematic set of beliefs and principles to the client's life difficulties. There is, however, wide divergence in counseling practice due to the divergent specific beliefs and principles held by individual practitioners. Such differences stem from the assumptions that are made by the individual practitioner regarding the nature of man, the nature of learning, and the development of personality.

(A discussion of these assumptions and their implications can be found in chapter 2.)

Once again we presume that the reader is wondering if there is anything that is "known" or definite in this field. Can all of the differing points of view have merit? If not, which one is right? And yet, how can one be right when counselors who hold such seemingly divergent belief systems as behaviorism and existentialism are both able to promote effective learning and/or relearning in the counseling process? How, you ask, can this be?

We submit that there are at least several possible explanations for this apparent dilemma. (1) It may be that all of the beliefs which seem to differ so markedly are really only part of some larger whole. We are reminded of the story of the blind men and the elephant. One man after having felt the leg of the elephant concluded that the elephant was like a tree. Another concluded that the elephant was like a rope after having touched its tail. Yet another concluded that the elephant must be like a wall subsequent to touching its side. And so it went with none of them being able to realize the true nature of the elephant. Similarly in counseling, it is conceivable that each theorist is justified in his beliefs on the basis of his own experiences. It is also conceivable that these beliefs are only a portion of the "truth." (2) It may be that theoretical suppositions regarding such issues as man's basic nature, the laws of learning, and the development of personality have little to do with the outcomes of counseling.

We are inclined to believe that both of these explanations are valid. We are encouraged by the current trend in counseling toward the unification of constructs and theoretical views. Common elements which make a difference must be identified and freed to become a part of the overarching system. We encourage you, the reader, to examine your own experiences related to learning and behavior change toward the end of aiding in the development of a more comprehensive and unified theory.

COUNSELING IS COMMUNICATION

Not only is counseling a learning–relearning process, it is also a process in which communication must occur in order for the desired learning to take place. That is, there must be *sending* and *receiving* between the child and the counselor in the counseling process.

It is generally held by counselors of differing orientations that some sort of verbal interchange must transpire between the child and the counselor. It is also conceded that nonverbal communication between the child and the counselor can be crucial to the counseling process. But what does *sending* and *receiving* and verbal and nonverbal interchange involve?

From the perspective of the child, *sending* involves transmitting thoughts, perceptions, and feelings either through talking about them or through behaviors from which his thoughts, perceptions, and feelings can be deduced by the counselor. The child may be trying to communicate or not. Due to the child's relative lack of language skill and sophistication, emphasis is often directed toward the behavioral, or nonverbal, medium of communication by the child counselor. Communication has not been accomplished, however, when the messages have been *sent*. They must be *received* by the counselor before the process is complete. *Received* in this context suggests that the intended meaning of the child's message has been made sense of or understood by the counselor.

Similarly, *sending* by the counselor involves the conveyance of thoughts, perceptions, and feelings by word of mouth and through other modes of behavior to the child. *Receiving* involves the child's decoding of the messages *sent* and an understanding of their intended meaning.

Communication, then, is a two-way street between the child and the counselor—it is dialogue. It involves the sending and receiving of messages in both verbal and nonverbal ways. It suggests the need for sensitive listening for meanings by the counselor. Communication is critical to the development and maintenance of an effective counseling relationship. Such a skill is dependent upon the counselor's openness to *hear,* and to interpret accurately what is heard, and upon experience in listening for the essence of the child's communication.

COUNSELING IS TECHNIQUE

All systems of counseling direct some attention to the issue of *what* the counselor says and does, *when* he says and does it, and *how* it is said and done. Considerations such as these are ones of counselor-response technique. Terms such as clarification, leading, restatement, advisement, approval, interpretation, reassurance, reflection, waiting, systematic desensitization, suggestion, modeling, encounter, sharing, structuring, reinforcement, explanation, shaping, silence, confrontation, encouragement, and others have been coined to differentially identify the variety of techniques employed by counselors in their efforts to effect positive changes in their clients.

Even though the general goal of all such techniques is enhanced client well-being through the modification of client thinking, feeling, and behaving, it is apparent that certain techniques evolve most naturally and legitimately out of specified counseling goals and basic counselor attitudes. Moreover, techniques become personal as the counselor evolves his own personalized counseling style of meeting client needs. They become tools by and through which the counselor is able to extend and use his unique self in the most effective way possible to benefit the client.

A concern we have about the misuse of technique prompts us to present a word of caution to the reader. As has been implied, the effective use of techniques by the counselor in the counseling process is based on certain counselor understandings, that is, his understanding of the client's unique needs, his understanding of the therapeutic goals that he has for the client, and his understanding of his "self" and of those techniques which complement that "self" as it engages in the therapeutic dialogue. Without these understandings, the counselor runs the danger of becoming a technician rather than child-centered. Brammer and Shostrom (1968) note: ". . . blind adherence to pat technique applied indiscriminately and invalidly to all clients" is characteristic of the charlatan (p. 191).

COUNSELING IS RELATIONSHIP

The client-counselor relationship constitutes the principal medium for dealing with significant thoughts, perceptions, and feelings which contribute to client disability and lack of personal fulfillment. Although some theorists and counseling practitioners have long emphasized the importance of the relationship (Taft, 1933; Allen, 1942; Axline, 1947; Rogers, 1951; Moustakas, 1959), recent writing and research activities have significantly increased this focus of attention.

It is important to remember that each counseling relationship is unique, for each child is unique and must be dealt with uniquely; hence, rigid counselor adherence to a set of principles and techniques applying across the board in the treatment of children is inappropriate. It should also be noted that the counseling relationship is not different in kind from other human relationships. It has many similarities to parent-child, teacher-student, and physician-patient relationships. Its uniqueness stems chiefly from the increased intensity and intimacy of the relationship and from the attitudes and behaviors evidenced by the counselor. We turn now to a discussion of these relationship variables.

FACILITATIVE COUNSELOR CONDITIONS

There is a growing body of research evidence to suggest that counseling effectiveness is much less dependent upon the counselor's theoretical orientation and technique than upon certain facilitative counselor conditions. Truax and Carkhuff (1967), after an extensive review of the literature related to counseling, concluded:

Despite the bewildering array of divergent theories and the difficulty in translating concepts from the language of one theory to that of another, several common threads weave their way through almost every major theory of psychotherapy and counseling, including the psychoanalytic, the client-centered, the behavioristic, and many of the more eclectic and derivative theories. In one way or another, all have emphasized the importance of the therapist's ability to be integrated, mature, genuine, authentic, or congruent in his relationship to the patient. They have all stressed also the importance of the therapist's ability to provide a nonthreatening, trusting, safe or secure atmosphere by his acceptance, nonpossessive warmth, unconditional positive regard, or love. Finally, virtually all theories of psychotherapy emphasize that for the therapist to be helpful he must be accurately empathic, be "with" the client, be understanding, or grasp the patient's meaning. (p. 25)

Although few of the studies conducted have related directly to the effect of the facilitative conditions in counseling with children, the evidence which is available seems to confirm the notion that children who experience high levels of empathy, genuineness, and respect also experience significantly greater constructive changes than those children who experience low levels of these conditions. In our experience, we have found that children are prone to more directly "read" the feelings of the counselor than are older clients. This is undoubtedly a result of their relative lack of dependence on verbal skills and cognitive approaches to life. Children are more affectively oriented and, consequently, directly feel the empathy, genuineness, and respect of the counselor. Moreover, these three human elements seem to be central to and cut across a wide variety of "helping" processes including the teacher-student and parent-child relationship (Wynne, et *al.,* 1958; Christensen, 1960; Baxter, Becker and Hooks, 1963; Ginott, 1965; Aspy, 1966). Simply stated, it would seem that the facilitative conditions are critical to all interpersonal processes which are designed to promote learning and relearning. Now that these conditions or characteristics have been labeled, let us proceed to develop a fuller understanding of their nature.

Genuineness

Among the three central therapeutic ingredients, genuineness seems to be the most basic. Truax and Carkhuff (1967) have suggested that to be a facilitative human being, one must be deeply sensitive and understanding of the moment-to-moment experience of the one being helped. Such sensitivity and understanding require that one must first have at least a degree of warmth and respect for the other person. However, the respect and understanding of the other person can only be "constructively meaningful" to him if it is without pretense.

Genuineness has been variously described as congruence, transparency, consistency, disclosure, authenticity, honesty, maturity, openness, and realness. It is antithetical to facade, masquerade, deceit, defensiveness, playing a role, artificiality, acting, pretense, and phoniness. To be genuine in the counseling relationship means to present oneself as a real person in a sincere and straightforward fashion—a fashion which minimizes discrepancy between what is verbalized and what is communicated nonverbally. Unlike much of our ordinary social conversation where the people involved tend to keep up a "front," counseling involves an openness and honest seriousness of purpose on the part of the counselor which allows the client to lay aside his deceits and facades in favor of a more genuine way of being. In other words, genuineness on the part of the counselor begets genuineness in the client. Can the counselor expect his client to be any more honest and straightforward than he, the counselor, is willing and able to be? We think not. Only inasmuch as the counselor can risk to be a real person in the counseling relationship can he facilitate realness in his client. Only to the degree that the counselor is aware of his own experience and is honest with himself can he enable another person to become aware of his experience and be honest with himself.

Does this mean that genuineness is categorically good in "helping" relationships? Is there no potentially harmful effect to be realized by the counselor's unqualified free expression of himself? Although it is extremely important for the counselor to avoid "playing the counselor role" in the counseling relationship, this does not give him license to do or say whatever he feels like doing or saying whenever he feels the urge. He must be facilitatively genuine (Carkhuff and Berenson, 1967). Jourard (1968) has discussed this issue in terms of what he calls "relevant authenticity." He suggests that before he, the counselor, can risk being authentic in the counseling relationship he must be sensitive to where his client is and with what his client can effectively deal. Being authentic for the sake of being authentic ignores the unique being of the client and renders the counselor authentically blind rather than authentically helpful. Being "relevantly authentic," however, takes into account the uniqueness of the client, who he is and where he is, and uses this information about him to be helpful to him. The extent of the counselor's authenticity or genuineness in the counseling relationship should therefore be determined by his own sensitivity to his client. His goal should be to continually work toward aiding his client in achieving increasingly authentic life experiences.

Another aspect of counselor genuineness which seems worthy of mention is what we choose to call counselor vulnerability. It is not unusual in helpful counseling relationships for the client to elevate the counselor to a position of near deification. Such elevation, although ego-inflating, may detract from a maximally productive relationship. We recognize that the counselor may contribute consciously or unconsciously to his own elevation by not allowing his fallibility to be known by his client. By frankly accepting his errors and shortcomings, the counselor will help the client realize a more equalitarian and mutually sharing relationship. When the counselor can openly own his vulnerability and admit to his error, the client can profit by realizing that it is possible for one to own one's mistakes without loss of self-respect or necessary denunciation of one's shortcomings.

Positive Regard

Positive regard is a difficult concept to discuss. So often it gets confused with sentimentality, sugar-coatedness, and role expectancy. However, sentimentality, sugar-coatedness, and role expectancy have little to do with honest expressions of positive regard between people.

All of us no doubt have had some experience with a person or persons who have made us feel comfortable, wanted, and important due to some sort of personal quality which they were able to convey to us. We like to be around such people simply because of the way they make us feel. Although positive regard can be communicated in a number of ways, what the person says does not seem to be as important as what he is as a human being. The central feeling communicated by such a person to the other in the relationship is one of deep caring and respect for the other person's worth and rights as a human. Such a feeling is expressed through verbal and nonverbal expressions.

Menninger (1958) emphasizes the importance of positive regard in the therapeutic relationship by stressing the need for the therapist to convey ". . . his poise, his patience, his fairness, his consistency, his rationality, his kindness, in short—his 'real' love for the patient." (p. 178) Moustakas (1959) out of his experience as a child therapist suggests that positive regard is conveyed to the child as

> . . . the therapist conveys his unqualified acceptance, respect, and faith in the child and the child's potentialities. He conveys these attitudes in many different ways. He encourages the child to make his own decisions, accepting and valuing everything the child does. He listens with complete attentiveness to every expression of the child. He urges the child to explore his thoughts and feelings further. He concentrates with his whole being on what the child is saying or doing. He insists that the child lead the way. He participates in the child's plans, sometimes playing with him, but more often by following his cues, listening with tenderness and concern, or by watching with a desire to understand. He attempts to see the child as he is and respects all that he sees. In effect he conveys to the child, by his words and feelings: 'These are your feelings. These are your ways. You have a right to cherish them because they belong to you. I hold your peculiarities, your loves and your hates, your mannerisms and your habits in esteem and honor as I do all aspects of your self. (p. 5)

As in the case of the concept of genuineness, it should be noted that there are many words that are nearly synonymous with positive regard. Such concepts as kindness, warmth, positive affect, altruistic love, respect, prizing, deep caring, genuine concern, and acceptance seem to be closely related to positive regard as they are discussed in the literature of counseling and psy-chotherapy. Although we do not feel that a comprehensive discussion of the nuances of meaning between and among these various concepts would sig-nificantly facilitate the reader's understanding of positive regard, we do believe that his understanding can be enhanced by a brief comment related to what it is not.

First of all, the communication of positive regard does not involve approval, condoning, or agreement. Rather, it means respecting and accepting the child as a human being who for his humanness alone is worthy of respect and dignity. The counselor neither approves or disapproves, condones or condemns, agrees or disagrees with what the child says or feels. He recognizes the unique life experiences of the child and realizes that these life experiences have in large part shaped the nature of the child's thoughts, feelings, and be-haviors. How then can the counselor presume to approve or disapprove? The child is what he is in the moment. His apparent behavior is a reflection of his best adjustment to that moment. The communication of positive regard is not without hazard, however, in the counseling relationship. The child may well misinterpret the counselor's regard in the direction of approval, especially in the early stages of the counseling process. It behooves the counselor to be aware of such a hazard and to be prepared to deal with it.

A second misconception regarding the nature of positive regard is that it implies the expression of sympathy for the child client. Sympathy involves sharing common feelings with another and may run the gamut from pity to sincere compassion for that person. While sympathy is intended to be sup-portive, it frequently has the net effect of minimizing the child's feelings. It conveys an attitude of "Poor little you. You are helpless. Let me help and encourage you." Implicit in this message is the notion, "I am better, or better off, than you." Such communication can have the result of fostering depen-dency in the child. In the counseling relationship, which is characterized by increasing equalitarianism and mutual sharing, the fostering of dependency would be contrary to desired outcomes. Sympathy, then, has the potential to be harmful and destructive to the development of a significant growth-pro-moting relationship.

A third misinterpretation of positive regard revolves around the notion that it involves tolerance of the child by the counselor. To be "put up with" is less than satisfactory to all of us. The counselor who dutifully acts tolerant because "counselors are supposed to act that way" denies both his own being and that of the child. Nothing positive and helpful can result from an inter-action between child and counselor which is built upon facade and decep-tion. The child cannot be expected to risk himself if the counselor is unwill-ing to cast aside role definitions and expectations in favor of his own unique self.

In summary, then, positive regard is that counselor-offered condition which communicates the counselor's appreciation of the client's person and life experience. Such a condition permits the client to feel safe and valued which in turn leads to client self-exploration.

Empathic Understanding

Empathic understanding has been defined as the ability of one person to understand another person from that other person's point of view. Stated differently, it is the ability to "climb into the other guy's skin," to see the world through his eyes and hear it through his ears, and to grasp what his life experiences mean to him. Such understanding is the antithesis of "objective" understanding which views people and happenings as they "objectively are" —not as the child experiences them to be. To move from "objective reality" to the internal "subjective reality" of the child requires the counselor to perceive the events and experiences of the child's life as if they were parts of the counselor's own life. The counselor's ability to "tune in" and "be with" the child as he explores his private thoughts and feelings provides an opportunity for the child to move toward overcoming his feelings of aloneness and alienation.

A short story told by Benjamin (1969) exemplifies the essence of empathic understanding. In one of Israel's kibbutz was a little donkey named Shlomo that all of the children dearly loved. One day, much to the dismay of the children, he disappeared. Searching for Shlomo proved futile, and the sadness of both children and adults became great. Finally, the kibbutz membership gathered together to try to decide what to do next.

In this kibbutz there also lived an old man—one for whom little respect was shown by either the children or the adults. While the membership had been meeting, he had been searching. When the gathering was almost to despair in finding Shlomo, in walked the old man with the donkey in tow. You can imagine the relief and excitement. While the children surrounded Shlomo, the adults in utter astonishment inquired of the old man how he had found the donkey when everyone else had failed.

His answer was simple. "I just asked myself where I would go if I were Shlomo. Then I went there and brought him back."

Not only does this folktale capture the essence of empathic understanding, it also suggests the infrequence of deep and meaningful empathic understanding in the life experiences of us all. It is critical to the effective counseling relationship that the counselor be able to set aside his own personal biases and beliefs and say, "I must try to understand this child and his concerns as he understands them so that he may be able to clarify his own thinking about possible courses of action."

INTERRELATEDNESS OF GENUINENESS, POSITIVE REGARD, AND EMPATHIC UNDERSTANDING

As has been stated earlier, effective learning is at least in part contingent upon the existence of high levels of core facilitative conditions in the learning environment. Even though these conditions have been discussed somewhat separately and discretely for the purpose of helping the reader grasp a fuller understanding of their natures, we hasten to emphasize that they are intertwined and interrelated. They are, as we see it, portions of a unified whole. They converge and blend as integrated dimensions of the essence or core being of the facilitative person. Ginott (1965) has emphasized the importance of these dimensions in the parent-child relationship.

The interrelatedness of these core conditions is stressed by Truax and Carkhuff (1967) when they state:

> The element of genuineness or authenticity is most basic to a relationship. Once this reality of the person of the therapist is established, the warmth and respect communicated to the patient becomes the second central ingredient in an effective relationship. Finally, given a relationship characterized by warmth and genuineness, the "work" of therapy or counseling proceeds through the therapist's moment-to-moment empathic grasp of the meaning and significance of the client's world. (p. 32)

This statement is not to suggest, however, a three-stage counseling process. It does not infer that the effective counselor says, "Okay, now that I've been genuine with this client I'll move on to being warm and respectful," or "Now that I've been genuine and warm I'll be empathic." Rather, it suggests a melting together of the three conditions so that they become pervasive in the counseling relationship.

One additional and important word with regard to the trinity of core dimensions is necessary. Namely, in the final analysis it is what is perceived by the client rather than what is offered by the counselor in the way of facilitative conditions that makes the difference. Even though the counselor may be maximally offering genuineness, respect, and empathy to the child, unless the child can see and feel it, it may be to no avail in terms of fostering growth and promoting positive gains.

HIGH AND LOW LEVELS OF FACILITATIVE CONDITIONS

To this point we have discussed the core facilitative conditions largely in dichotomous terms, that is, genuineness versus deception, respect versus pity, and the other's frame of reference versus one's own frame of reference. We have suggested, however, that such dichotomies only represent the poles of continua—that in fact facilitative conditions are offered at different levels from high to low by different persons regardless of their job titles.

Truax, Carkhuff, Berenson, their colleagues and students have boldly attempted to further our knowledge of human growth and potential through the development of rating scales designed to assess the quality or level of conditions offered. Although these scales are highly subjective, the findings which have evolved from their experimental use have contributed substantially to our understanding of growth-promoting relationships.

Operational definitions for the various levels have been established and presented by Truax and Carkhuff (1967) and Carkhuff and Berenson (1967). The reader is referred to these works for a comprehensive discussion of the levels.

TENTATIVE AND SPECULATIVE DIMENSIONS OF EFFECTIVE COUNSELING

Even though there is widespread agreement among counselors of varying theoretical orientations regarding the necessity for an understanding, respectful, and honest counseling relationship, it must be made clear that differences exist among counselors and across orientations. There are differences in the exact meanings and emphasis given to these concepts by different theorists and practitioners. Furthermore, although regarded as necessary, they are not considered to be sufficient in themselves to account for the totality of positive counseling outcomes. A number of additional dimensions have been proposed for consideration and experimental study.

Concreteness

There is a limited amount of evidence to indicate the importance of specificity of expression or concreteness in the production of positive counseling outcomes (Truax and Carkhuff, 1964). Concreteness involves ". . . the fluent, direct, and complete expression of specific feelings and experiences, regardless of their emotional content, by both therapist and client." (Carkhuff and Berenson, 1967, p. 29)

As in the case of the variables already discussed, this concept is presented by a continuum ranging from low to high levels of specificity. Low levels are characterized by vague generalities, abstraction, and discussion between the counselor and the client of a highly intellectual nature. In addition, the counselor makes no effort to direct and focus the client's attention on relevant specific situations and feelings. At high levels of concreteness, however, the counselor guides the client's expression to specific thoughts, feelings, situations, and events. He encourages and aids the client to involve himself in directly dealing with all personally relevant experiences and feelings in specific terms.

Carkhuff and Berenson (1967) identify the following three important functions which are served through concrete expressiveness.

First, the therapist's concreteness ensures that his response does not become too far removed emotionally from the client's feelings and experiences. Second, concreteness encourages the therapist to be more accurate in his understanding of the client, and thus misunderstandings can be clarified and corrections made when the feelings and experiences are stated in specific terms. Third, the client is directly influenced to attend specifically to problem areas and emotional conflicts. (p. 30)

In our work as counselors we have come to realize that both the quality of the counseling relationship and the positive movement of the client is at least in part dependent upon our ability to lead the client into expressing his feelings and experiences in specific terms. The counselor's willingness and ability to "zero in" on the conflict and painful life experiences of the client provide opportunity for the client to "zero in" on himself and to explore his feelings deeply.

Counselor Intensity

Some recent attention and discussion have been directed toward the potential relationship between counselor intensity and counseling outcome. Truax has pioneered efforts to experimentally determine the nature and extent of this relationship. He has speculated that the "Intensity and Intimacy of Interpersonal Contact" may be the "motor" which moves the counseling process forward.

In discussing the dimensions of this potentially important variable, Truax (1962) has suggested that at high levels it involves a counselor preoccupation and acute attentiveness to the feelings and life experiences of the client. It combines alertness, concentration, profound seriousness of purpose, deep sincerity, and intense absorption in the client by the counselor. The voice and manner of the counselor convey the deep concern which he has for the person of the client.

Although there is an absence of research evidence relating counselor intensity to counseling outcomes with children, our own subjective experience as counselors would seem to confirm this hypothesized therapeutic variable. A gentle touch, a genuine tear, a chosen closeness, a warm and compassionate tone of voice, a tender embrace given freely, spontaneously and unconditionally, have had significantly positive consequences on the quality and hence the outcome of relationships in which we have been privileged to participate as facilitators.

Dealing with the Existential Moment

Contrary to popular opinion, effective counseling is not a process which focuses primarily on the client's history. We recognize that the thoughts, feelings, and behaviors of the present are in large part a product of the client's background of experience. We also recognize that a recounting of the client's history may aid in the counselor's understanding of the client's present state of being. We submit, however, that little client benefit is derived from a comprehensive and chronological recapitulation of the events in his background. Only as specific antecedent experiences tie in directly to the client's current existence are they relevant and important dimensions of the productive counseling process. In other words, to dredge up background for the sake of dredging up background has little therapeutic value. The background which is relevant is that which intimately involves the on-going troublesome thoughts, feelings, and behaviors in the "right-now" experience of the client.

Similarly, we do not view the counseling process as future-oriented. Surely a by-product of counseling is a more fulfilling future. However, the thrust of the counseling experience involves much more than preparation for the tomorrows. It has been our experience that there is too much emphasis in our culture on "preparing today to live tomorrow" rather than on living today. This is not only true of adults but of children too. How often have we heard words similar to "When my dad gets a new job, then things are going to be okay," when in actuality, dad will not be getting a new job and things will not be changing. Certainly there is risk in involving oneself in the process of life on a "now," "today," "in this moment" basis. However, the alternative would seem to be toleration of existence rather than active participation in life in some meaningful way.

Effective counseling, then, is a vital, living relationship focusing on the here-and-now experiences of the client and the counselor as they interact together. When significant feelings are present in the existential moment, the counselor must not only be aware of them and understand them in that moment, but he must also be willing to work with them. The moment-to-moment happenings that occur in the relationship must be capitalized upon by the counselor's ability to be sensitive to them and to deal with them as they occur.

Trust

Perhaps it is perfunctory for us to devote a separate section to a discussion of trust. It should be obvious by this point that trust is a basic and integral component of genuineness, positive regard, empathic understanding, and significant communication. Yet, we would like to underscore its importance in the counseling relationship.

It is not profound to say that we learn to trust through healthy relationships with people who trust us and who in turn are trustworthy. Conversely, we learn to be suspicious, fearful, and lacking in trust through faulty relationships where trust cannot be experienced. Trust is a two-way street.

In our work with children, we have come to be keenly aware of how little trust is expressed in children by adults and of the resultant consequences—suspiciousness, constriction, tenseness, conformity, fearfulness, disability, dependence, and others. In the extreme, such attitudes and behaviors are very debilitating to the child. He cannot grow optimally when inhibited by a life style which denies trust in himself—thoughts, feelings, and actions.

A child's inability to trust is also learned through demonstration of untrustworthiness in significant persons in his environment. When on occasion the child's parent rewards a particular behavior and punishes it on another, the child learns to be suspicious of his own ability to judge what is right and wrong. As a concomitant, he also learns to be suspicious of his parent. Chronic inconsistency results in the destruction of the child's ability to trust in both himself and others.

With children who have learned not to trust through sad experiences with peers and adults, trust may be hard for the counselor to earn. He must realize that the child's behavior in the counseling relationship may be saying, "Okay, counselor, I'm going to put you through the mill to see if you are what you claim to be. I need to know if you can be trusted." To earn the child's trust, the counselor must demonstrate his trustworthiness by consistent word and deed.

Language Patterns and Usage

Although our emphasis throughout has been one of "actions speak louder than words," we recognize that the counselor's use of language has some impact on the counseling process. What that impact will be is determined by the unique combination of the child, the counselor, their interaction, and situational variables.

Quite obviously, the extent to which verbal counseling can take place is dependent upon the age and/or language skill and sophistication of the child. Generally, the older the child the more appropriate verbal counseling becomes. However, this rule of thumb needs at least one important qualification; namely, the child's level of cultural advantage-disadvantage must also be considered.

In our experiences, some six- and seven-year-old children are perfectly capable of effectively participating in verbal counseling. This is not to suggest that verbal counseling is necessarily the preferred approach, however, even when it is possible. There are also children who at the age of eleven, twelve, and beyond are incapable of such effective participation. Our speculation is that a major factor in such differences is the degree to which the child is talked to, read to, played with, and otherwise provided with the materials and encouragement to learn to communicate verbally. The child who is a product of an environment largely devoid of human interaction and impoverished in terms of stimulating materials available for browsing and reading will be less likely to participate effectively in verbal counseling than the child who represents the other extreme on the continuum. In such cases the counselor must be prepared to communicate with the child in alternative ways.

It is generally agreed that the counselor's verbal expressions to the child should be brief and simple but in the natural idiom of the counselor. Although some counselors suggest using the same words as the child to avoid talking over his head, we feel that such is not necessary provided the counselor is sensitive to the child's understanding of the counselor's communication. Children expect adults to act like adults rather than children. We believe the child has a right to expect the counselor to be a model of responsible and integrated adulthood. Moreover, the counselor has a responsibility to be such a model.

A final comment regarding the adult tendency to "talk down" to children is needed. We have tried to emphasize the idea that the counseling relationship is one of equality, of mutual sharing, and mutual respect. It is readily apparent that the eight-year-old child is not an equal of the middle-aged counselor in most respects; yet, in one very crucial and profoundly significant aspect they are equals—they are both human beings. Consequently, at that level the counselor must treat the child as an equal. Continued recognition of this mutual condition on the part of the counselor will aid him in coping with the common tendency to "talk down" to the child client.

Client Readiness

Readiness for learning is a long-established and well-known educational principle. Readiness for the counseling process is similar in that certain client needs must be felt before optimal use of the process can be made.

With older children, adolescents, and adults, recognition of the need for help in coping with life may begin with the prospective client. Although he may be reluctant and skeptical about seeking help, in the end he chooses to make or to avoid a commitment to the counseling process.

Young children may voluntarily seek the help of counselors too, although this choice is more often made by parents, guardians, or other significant persons in the world of the child. With the potential voluntary child client, readiness is strongly influenced by the child's perception of the counselor. This perception is a combination of rumors that the child has heard about the counselor from peers and adults, the child's observations of what the counselor does with children and how he treats them, and reactions to the noncounseling experiences that the child himself has had with the counselor. If this perception is favorable, the child may seek the help of the counselor in time of felt need.

The child who involuntarily approaches counseling presents a somewhat different readiness problem. There are children who do not see that they are in need of help. In some cases they are absolutely right, for the help is needed by the parent or by the teacher who refers the child for counseling. Such situations can be recognized by the counselor's use of data from the child and other sources. However, in those cases where there is need but seems to be no awareness of that need, the counselor can help the child to become aware and to ready himself for a counseling experience.

Group experiences where children can gain and give feedback about their respective impacts on each other provide a good medium for developing an awareness to problem areas. A variety of "orientation-to-counseling" procedures, including counselor talks, films, tapes, skits, and role-playing have been used to acquaint children with the work and the role of the counselor. Such procedures are potential readiness builders. (Specific suggested methodology for such techniques are discussed in chapter 11.)

COMMENT

In the preceding pages of this chapter, we have discussed those dimensions of the effective counseling process which seem to cut across or transcend parochial or theoretical allegiances. We have tried to include not only those dimensions for which there is empirical support but also dimensions which are tentative, speculative, and in need of experimental validation. In so doing we are hopeful that the reader may be able to use the discussion in any of three basic ways: (1) to increase his own understanding of the counseling process, (2) to examine his own personal life experience in the light of various dimensions presented, and (3) to stimulate the evolution of methods and procedures whereby these dimensions and others can be creatively researched.

We would also like to emphasize again that these dimensions are but parts of a complex whole—the counseling process. Although they can be separated for the sake of discussion, they cannot be separated in fact. They occur and exist together. They interrelate in unique configurations and amounts as the uniqueness of the child and the counselor meet and interact. In the final analysis it is the quality of that meeting and interaction that is critical to the outcome of the counseling process.

REFERENCES

ALLEN, F. H. *Psychotherapy With Children.* New York: W. W. Norton & Company, Inc., 1942.

ASPY, D. N. "The Relationship Between Teacher Functioning on Facilitative Dimensions and Student Performance on Intellective Indices." Unpublished doctoral dissertation, University of Kentucky, 1966.

AXLINE, VIRGINIA M. *Play Therapy.* Boston: Houghton Mifflin Company, 1947.

BAXTER, J. C.; BECKER, J.; AND HOOKS, W. "Defensive Style in the Families of Schizophrenics and Controls." *Journal of Abnormal and Social Psychology* 66 (1963): 512–518.

BENJAMIN, A. *The Helping Interview.* Boston: Houghton Mifflin Company, 1969.

BERGIN, A. E. "The Effects of Psychotherapy: Negative Results Revisited." *Journal of Counseling Psychology* 10 (1963):244–250.

BRAMMER, L. M., AND SHOSTROM, E. L. *Therapeutic Psychology.* 2nd ed. Englewood Cliffs, N.J.: Prentice-Hall, Inc., 1968.

CARKHUFF, R. R., AND BERENSON, B. *Beyond Counseling and Therapy.* New York: Holt, Rinehart & Winston, Inc., 1967.

CHRISTENSEN, C. M. "Relationships Between Pupil Achievement, Pupil Affect-Need, Teacher Warmth and Teacher Permissiveness." *Journal of Educational Psychology* 51 (1960):169–174.

EYSENCK, H. J. "The Effects of Psychotherapy: An Evaluation." *Journal of Consulting Psychology* 16 (1952):319–324.

———, ed. *Behavior Therapy and the Neurosis.* New York: Pergamon Press, Inc., 1960.

———. "The Effects of Psychotherapy." *International Journal of Psychiatry* 1 (1965):97–142.

GINOTT, H. G. *Between Parent and Child.* New York: The Macmillan Company, 1965.

JOURARD, S. M. *Disclosing Man to Himself.* Princeton, N.J.: D. Van Nostrand Co., Inc., 1968.

LEVITT, E. E. "The Results of Psychotherapy With Children: An Evaluation." *Journal of Consulting Psychology* 21 (1957):189–196.

———. "Psychotherapy With Children: A Further Evaluation." *Behavior Research and Therapy* 1 (1963):45–51.

MENNINGER, C. *Theories of Psychoanalytic Technique.* New York: Basic Books, Inc., Publishers, 1958.

MOUSTAKAS, C. E. *Psychotherapy With Children.* New York: Harper & Row, Publishers, 1959.

ROGERS, C. R. *Client-centered Therapy.* Boston: Houghton Mifflin Company, 1951.

TAFT, J. *The Dynamics of Therapy in a Controlled Relationship.* New York: The Macmillan Company, 1933.

TRUAX, C. B. Intensity and Intimacy of Interpersonal Contact: Effects of Therapists and Effects of Parents Upon the Level of Intensity and Intimacy of Interpersonal Contact Offered by the Therapist. *Brief Research Reports,* Wisconsin Psychiatric Institute, University of Wisconsin, 65, 1962.

———, AND CARKHUFF, R. R. "Concreteness: A Neglected Variable in the Psychotherapeutic Process." *Journal of Clinical Psychology* 20 (1964):264–267.

———. *Toward Effective Counseling and Psychotherapy: Training and Practice.* Chicago: Aldine Publishing Company, 1967.

WYNNE, L. C.; RYCKOFF, I. M.; DAY, J.; AND HIRSCH, S. I. "Pseudomutuality in the Family Relations of Schizophrenics." *Psychiatry* 21 (1958):205–220.

SELECTED ADDITIONAL READINGS

ARBUCKLE, D. S. *Counseling: Philosophy, Theory and Practice.* Boston: Allyn and Bacon, Inc., 1965.
BECK, CARLETON E., ed. *Guidelines for Guidance.* Dubuque, Ia.: Wm. C. Brown Company Publishers, 1966.
BERENSON, B., AND CARKHUFF, R. R., eds. *Sources of Gain in Counseling and Psychotherapy.* New York: Holt, Rinehart & Winston, Inc., 1967.
BLOCHER, D. H. *Developmental Counseling.* New York: The Ronald Press Company, 1966.
BORDIN, E. S. *Psychological Counseling.* New York: Appleton-Century-Crofts, 1968.
FRANK, J. D. *Persuasion and Healing.* New York: Schocken Books, Inc., 1963.
GEIS, H. J. "Toward a Comprehensive Framework Unifying All Systems of Counseling." *Educational Technology* 9 (1969):19–28.
GLASSER, W. *Reality Therapy.* New York: Harper & Row, Publishers, 1965.
LONDON, P. *Modes and Morals of Psychotherapy.* New York: Holt, Rinehart & Winston, Inc., 1964.
MAHRER, A. R., ed. *The Goals of Psychotherapy.* New York: Appleton-Century-Crofts, 1967.
McGOWAN, J. F., AND SCHMIDT, L. D. *Counseling: Readings in Theory and Practice.* New York: Holt, Rinehart & Winston, Inc., 1962.
ROGERS, C. R., ed. *The Therapeutic Relationship and Its Impact.* Madison, Wis.: University of Wisconsin Press, 1967.
————, and STEVENS, BARRY. *Person to Person.* Walnut Creek, Calif.: Real People Press, 1967.
SCHOFIELD, W. *Psychotherapy: The Purchase of Friendship.* Englewood Cliffs, N.J.: Prentice-Hall, Inc., 1964.
SHAPIRO, J. G. "Agreement Between Channels of Communication in Interviews." *Journal of Consulting Psychology* 30 (1966):535–538.
SNYDER, W. U. *The Psychotherapy Relationship.* New York: The Macmillan Company, 1961.
WOLBERG, L. R. *The Technique of Psychotherapy.* New York: Grune & Stratton, Inc., 1954.

6

The Counselor

Counseling outcome is dependent, to a significant degree, upon the personal characteristics and skills of the counselor; that is, counseling can be no more effective as a process of change than the counselor is effective as an agent of that process. But who is an effective counselor? What are the personal characteristics and skills that are requisite to positive counseling outcomes?

Many of the answers to these questions at this point in the evolution of counseling as a discipline are diverse, at times contradictory, and at best often tentative. The variety of "good counselor qualities" which is found in the literature of counseling has for the most part been arrived at through conjecture or subjective counselor experience. We are not suggesting that such procedures are inappropriate. Indeed, conjecture and personal experience are the beginnings of much innovation in all fields. There is a need in the area of counseling, however, for experimental evidence to indicate those qualities which are unquestionably positive factors, those which are neutral, and those which are negative in the counseling relationship. We do not propose to present the definitive evidence which is currently lacking. As has been the case in other discussions of counselor qualities, the following discussion largely represents our collective experiences as counselors. We most certainly do not intend to imply that our experience should be the reader's experience. Rather, it is our sincere hope that the reader will use our comments and experiences to reflect on and examine his own experience in working with children. From such examination we believe that those qualities having the most personal meaning for the reader will emerge. Furthermore, we are hopeful that there will be those who may be stimulated to do that needed experimental work in an attempt to further clarify our understanding of the qualities of the "good" counselor. If by our comments we stimulate or provoke the reader to turn inward in search of new meanings, we will have accomplished our intended purpose.

PERIPHERAL PERSONAL QUALITIES

In many listings of "good" counselor qualities and characteristics are such ambiguous inclusions as "demonstrate a keen sense of humor," "present a good personal appearance," "be well-founded in basic academics," and "present an above-average scholarship record," among others. The trouble with such statements is that there is no evidence that such qualities have anything whatsoever to do with the counselor's ability to help children. Nevertheless, prospective counselors continue to be selected for university training and for counseling positions largely on the basis of these criterion measures rather than on the qualities that facilitate children's growth. Some of these qualities were discussed in the preceding chapter. Judgments are often made by graduate school selection committees and employers with little or no regard for evidence that relates to the individual counselor's ability to benefit children in the counseling relationship.

Such a criterion as "a neat and orderly appearance" would certainly rule out a large number of today's nonconformist college students many of whom have deep personal commitments to helping others. There is absolutely no evidence to suggest that a male counselor with long hair, a beard, "unusual" or nonconventional clothes, will be any more or less successful in working with children than his "All-American boy" counterpart. It would, however, be an extremely rare school system or agency that would employ a teacher or counselor whose appearance and behavior did not conform to traditional standards.

If there is any relationship between high academic achievement as an undergraduate and success as a counselor, the evidence would seem to suggest the individuals with high grade-point averages as undergraduates tend to be less effective in counseling with children than are their peers with lower academic achievement records. Ability to jump hurdles in undergraduate school is a very good predictor of ability to jump hurdles in graduate school. Such abilities, however, have little relationship to creative, growth-promoting relationships. Yet, undergraduate grade-point averages continue to be used as a chief criterion for acceptance to counselor preparation programs. Rogers (1969) has suggested reasonable alternatives to such selection criteria. His alternatives, the degree of ability in problem-solving, the degree of spontaneous curiosity and originality, and the degree of empathic understanding of the prospective student, should be considered as more important criteria in current selection practices.

Such characteristics and attributes are not, however, the usual choices of training programs and employees. In a survey of elementary school administrators and counselor educators who were asked to rank a variety of counselor characteristics (Dimick, 1966), such qualities as "being well respected in the community," "demonstrating courteousness," and "demonstrating a neat and orderly appearance" were items to which both groups gave high importance. An amusing side note to the study, although not evident as a direct comparison in the questioning, was that both groups thought it more important that elementary school counselors be parents than that they be married. It is doubtful that either counselor educators or administrators would look upon being an unwed parent as a particularly desirable characteristic for being a counselor of children, yet from a purely statistical point of view, such was indicated.

Our point in singling out those characteristics which have been mentioned above is not to suggest that such characteristics are inconsequential. It may very well be that Counselor A, an effective counselor, does present "a neat and orderly appearance," "an allegiance to community standards," and so on. Such attributes are not "put on" to meet a role expectation but are expressions of him as a person. To do or be otherwise would render him less effective as a person. We do, however, categorically reject the idea that all effective counselors should conform to such standards. We submit, furthermore, that such considerations are of a peripheral nature; that is, they are of less consequence in the counseling relationship than other, more central counselor qualities.

THE COUNSELOR AS A PERSON

The key variables that exist between the facilitative and the nonfacilitative counselor is the person of the counselor. In the helping interview the counselor brings his knowledge, his experience, his professional skill, the information process, but most important he brings himself. Therefore, it is the evolving person of the counselor which is the vital dynamic for therapeutic change or significant learning to take place.

For the counselor to be most effective in working with others, in a "helpful" capacity, it is essential that he know what and who his "person" is. If he is to have the kind of potent influence that he desires, he must know his biases, his commitments, his vulnerable spots, his weaknesses, his strengths, his fears, his defenses, his total impact on others. Only inasmuch as he is aware of the dimensions of his "self" will he be able to use his "self" to benefit others. Specific considerations relative to the development of "self" knowledge and other facilitative counselor qualities are discussed in chapter 12.

In addition to being aware of "self," the facilitative counselor must also communicate his facilitative qualities to the other person in the relationship.

It is not enough that they are internally felt by the counselor. They must be perceived and experienced by the child client. To the degree that the real self of the counselor communicates the counselor's facilitative qualities to others, to that degree he will be able to benefit those others whether they be children, teachers, parents, or administrators.

As an introduction to the consideration of counselor qualities in some of our graduate classes, we have asked students to write down some personal secret that they have never shared with anyone. We have then asked these students to describe what a person would have to be in order for each of them to feel free enough to share that secret with him. Rather than such characteristics as three years of teaching experience, an *A* in a Counseling Techniques course, or a high percentile ranking on the Miller's Analogy Test, they have usually arrived at lists of qualities embodied by terms such as warmth, openness, trust, deep caring, honesty, and others. Some of these qualities have been discussed in the preceding chapter. The discussion which follows attempts to clarify additional counselor characteristics which from our experience contribute to positive counseling outcomes. The order of presentation is not intended to reflect their relative importance.

Spontaneity

The counselor's willingness and ability to change and venture into the counseling relationship is possibly one of the counselor's greatest assets. The successful "lesson plan" for counseling with children does not exist, nor can it exist. The counselor must be able to respond in the moment to the situation as he sees it. Instead of reacting in a preplanned or rehearsed and, hence, sterile way, the effective counselor responds spontaneously in a way that seems to fit the needs of the moment. Thus the helping relationship becomes a creatively dynamic and vital "right now" human growth experience for the child and for the counselor. Such willingness to venture on the part of the counselor aids the child in risking to be creative in moving toward the resolution of conflicts and concerns in uniquely personal ways. In other words, the child is encouraged through behavior of the counselor to search for solutions which evolve from his own inner resources rather than from the prescriptions of others. Conversely, the counselor who is unable to be spontaneous in the child-counselor relationship provides a model for the child which precludes to large extent the child's opportunity to go beyond prescribed solutions to creative ones.

Going into the counseling interview can be likened to going into an athletic contest. Like the athlete, the counselor does not plan to do *A, B,* and *C,* but rather gets himself "ready" to interact. This readiness can best be defined as an attitude which conveys the counselor's deep desire to be with his client and to devote his total organism to being as helpful as possible in spite of the inherent risks. Experience and intimate self-knowledge help the counselor to anticipate his responses with some degree of precision, but meeting the living moment at hand with ingenuity and courage plays a major role.

Flexibility

Flexibility is a quality that seems to come from a high degree of personal security and the awareness that there is no "right" or "fixed" way for *all* counselors to counsel. It also suggests that there is no "right" way for a particular counselor to work with all children, nor a "fixed" way for a counselor to work with a particular client. Flexibility implies an ability and willingness to change, to modify, to amend, when such movement becomes necessary. Flexibility involves spontaneity and creativity and indeed cannot be separated from them. Creativity, spontaneity, and flexibility as ends in the helping relationship, however, serve no purpose. Only inasmuch as these qualities become means to the ends of meeting the child's needs and in helping the child become better able to realize his potentials are they vital in the counseling relationship.

Concentration

The helping relationship is demanding of both the child and the counselor. Of the counselor, it demands that he attend to and concentrate as completely as possible on what is going on right in the "here and now" of the relationship. That is to say that the counselor must "tune out" all external interference that would hinder his concentration. Moreover, he must be internally free from interruptions so that the child can be the total focus of his attention. This latter condition suggests that the counselor's "own house" should be in order so that he does not have to attend unduly to his own needs in the relationship.

Concentration on the child client involves two dimensions of client behavior—verbal and nonverbal. Listening with the eyes, the ears, and the heart is an essential skill by which concentration is accomplished. Verbally, the child expresses himself by describing incidents, by talking about ideas, and by stating feelings. The counselor listens to see *what* the content of the child's verbalizations is, the *way* that this content is presented, and the personal *meanings* for the child which may be behind the words and ideas. Nonverbally, he "tunes in" on gestures, facial expressions, mannerisms, intonations, body movements, and other behaviors which may add to his understanding of the total child.

We have found that concentration on nonverbal child behaviors is more crucial than such concentration with adolescents and adults. This is probably due to the child's relative lack of language sophistication as compared to adolescents and adults. No matter what client-age, however, counselor attunement to nonverbal communication is essential. Such attunement can be accomplished only through intense concentration.

Openness

Each person has countless beliefs from which he functions as a person. Rokeach (1960) has discussed man's use of these beliefs in terms of open and closed mindedness. We suggest that a person's belief system is open or closed to the extent to which that person can "receive, evaluate, and act on relevant information received from the outside on its own intrinsic merits unencumbered by irrelevant factors in the situation arising from the person or from the outside." (p. 57) Simply stated, openness is the counselor's ability to hear and accept the values of the other person without needing to distort them to meet his own needs. This is not to suggest, however, that the counselor is without values, for such a notion is unrealistic and absurd. Neither is it a suggestion that the counselor does not make value judgments. That is also absurd. To be human involves "valuing."

No real quarrel can be had with the fact that counselors make value judgments. Problems arise, however, when the counselor's need to impose his values on the client becomes dominant over the client's human right to self-determination. The child counselor must be particularly aware of this tendency, since it is relatively easy to view the child as being inferior in many ways to the adult counselor. The effective counseling relationship requires that the counselor be open enough to allow the child to make his own value judgments even though they may not correspond with those of the counselor.

The quality of openness is also quite different from simply refraining from making value judgments. People, including children, will think and feel whatever they think and feel whether the counselor thinks they should or not. Because a counselor may not want a child to think or do something and tells the child, "You shouldn't think or do that," there is no guarantee that the counselor's admonition will in any way affect what the child thinks or does. It may, however, have much to do with what the child will tell the counselor. On the other hand, the admonition of the counselor may indeed affect the child. That is, the child may develop feelings of guilt for having these thoughts about which the counselor has admonished him; or he may develop resentment for the counselor who has tried to impose his own personal values on the child. In either case, little has been accomplished toward aiding the child in the realization of his potentials.

Openness, then, does not mean that the counselor approves or disapproves of what the client thinks, feels, or says. It does connote a counselor's willingness to work hard to accept from the child's point of view what he is experiencing and/or communicating. Openness also implies a willingness on the part of the counselor to continually reexamine and reassess his own values in light of his growth and development through new experience.

Emotional Stability

Emotional stability is often discussed in terms of freedom from pathology. Although we strongly affirm that the counselor should be relatively free of pathological qualities, we are more interested in focusing on the personal characteristics which are presented at the healthy end of the continuum.

A common misconception regarding the stable person is that he is continually the same; that is to say, the individual who seems to be externally consistent by appearing "even-tempered," "happy," "congenial," and "adjusted" all of the time may not necessarily be genuinely stable. It is impossible for us to conceive of a well-adjusted, well-integrated person as not experiencing the heights of joy and the depths of depression upon occasion. To be otherwise would suggest an "out-of-touchness" with the vicissitudes of life.

To be emotionally stable, as we see it, involves an ability on the part of the individual to "flow with" the experiences of life—to be sad when life's experiences produce sadness and to be openly joyful when joy is the individual's response to his life experience. To be so suggests a confidence in self on the part of the individual that his own personal resources will "see him through." The events do not take control of him. He is their master. He experiences life appropriately for him.

Experiences of emotional instability in the counselor's life are, however, not without merit. It appears to be less possible to deeply understand and empathize when some of the feelings that are paired with emotional instability have never been experienced by the counselor. This is not to suggest that those who have experienced life deeply and broadly may bring better opportunity for profound understanding to the counseling relationship. This individual must, however, be able to accept, understand, and cope with his own feelings so that they do not negatively affect the counseling relationship.

Belief in People's Ability to Change

It seems only logical that a belief in people's ability to change should be taken for granted in the fields of psychology, education, and counseling. For what are these fields if they are not processes for changing the behaviors, attitudes, beliefs, and feelings of individuals?

If children do not have the ability to change, we most assuredly have wasted vast amounts of time, effort, and money sending them to school. But children can change. They do change. These changes, however, are often influenced by the beliefs and expectations held by significant persons in their worlds.

It should be emphasized that an intellectual belief in people's ability to change is not enough. It is one thing for the counselor to say "people can change," but an entirely different thing to have that assurance integrated into his behavior. He must behave as though change can and will occur if he is to be maximally helpful. This belief communicated to the child will ultimately give the child courage to face change and effectively cope with it.

Commitment to People

Counseling as we view it involves a deep commitment to humanness and the fulfillment of human potentials. Again we would like to emphasize that this commitment goes well beyond the oft-recited euphemisms about the inherent worth and innate goodness of man. It requires the counselor to "put his money where his mouth is," to act out his convictions in his life style, to be what he professes to be.

In the counseling relationship, the fully-functioning counselor communicates his desire to "stick by" the child client, to see him through his time of need, and to continue to care outside the confines of his professional role. In other words, the counselor's attitudes about the ultimate importance of people is demonstrated in word and deed regardless of the setting. It is this kind of deep counselor commitment that helps instill trust, hope, respect, and the willingness to try in the child client.

The Responsible Anarchist

Jourard (1968) has defined effective counselors as "reponsible anarchists," as "the 'loyal opposition' committed to an endless search for ways of life that foster growth, well-being, idiosyncrasy, freedom, and authenticity." (p. 42) We contend, with Jourard, that many practicing counselors have tended to function only as agents of socialization, conformity, and "averageness." They have tended to make or help the child "fit" his environment rather than to help him transcend and change it. They have tended to support the establishment which stifles and constricts man's inherent potentials rather than challenging and working to effect societal changes which can aid in man's liberation.

Most certainly, children are not as free as adults to unilaterally choose those ways of living which could be most enhancing to them. They do live in a more controlling environment where adult expectations for children are well defined; hence, the role of the counselor is to help the child live more fully through direct and indirect means. Directly, he can aid children in the evolution of attitudes and behaviors which promote growth toward their optimal functioning levels. Indirectly, he can help those adults who control the child's world to modify their attitudes and behaviors so that the environment of the child allows for the realization of his potentials.

In the event that the child's environment is resistant to change and modification, then the responsible counselor is obligated to aid the child in the development of compensating methods for coping with that environment. In our experience, we have found that children are highly adaptable and can cope with seemingly intolerable environmental conditions provided there is someone who deeply cares for them and in whom they can trust and find significance for themselves. In such a circumstance, the counselor, as responsible anarchist, may be able to do nothing more than be a point of stability and reference for children.

Swimming upstream takes much courage, deep commitment and strength. This is, however, the lot of the counselor who is concerned about man's destiny and the realization of man's "self." We are encouraged by what appears to be a growing trend among concerned persons to search for new ways of liberating man.

Counselor Knowledge

If wholeness begets wholeness, and if the primary goal of counseling is to promote wholeness in clients, then the counselor himself must be a whole person (Carkhuff and Berenson, 1967). Many of the specifics which are involved in wholeness have been or will be discussed at other places in this volume; hence, they will not be reiterated here. It is perhaps sufficient to say that all knowledge is valuable, particularly when it promotes wholeness in the individual. For some, this may mean intense concentration on the "behavioral sciences"; for others it may mean a primary focusing on philosophical questions; and for others it may require involvements of other sorts. In the final analysis, however, the counselor must be a "wise" person—wise in his own personal understandings of self; wise in his understandings of others; wise in his understandings of conditions and experiences which promote self-actualizing whole people.

Gestalt of Factors

We have talked of personal qualities of the counselor as if each were somewhat distinct and different. It should be apparent from the overlapping and interweaving of these qualities that they are, in reality, not distinct from one another. What really makes the difference is the combination or blending of these factors in the individual. Qualities such as the ones we have discussed do not seem to be learned or maintained separate from each other. They are only parts of a whole—a gestalt.

The Gestalt principle that the whole is truly greater than the sum of its parts has relevance in viewing the personal characteristics of the effective counselor.

Self-actualization is a term applied by Maslow and others to the gestalt of human qualities and characteristics of people at the positive end of the mental health continuum. Many counseling theorists as well as counseling practitioners list as the desired result of counseling the movement by the client toward self-actualization.

It seems more than coincidental that the characteristics of effective counselors and characteristics of self-actualizing people so closely parallel each other. Perhaps our discussion of the counselor as a person could have been greatly abbreviated had we stated that it seems necessary that the counselor demonstrate the qualities of the self-actualizing person if the client is going to be positively affected by the counselor. In the final analysis, it may very well be that the characteristics ascribed to the self-actualized person are identical to the qualities of the effective counselor.

For a comprehensive discussion of the concept of self-actualization and its identified characteristics, the reader is referred to Maslow (1954, 1962).

A word of caution is necessary. The counselor qualities which we have discussed and the characteristics of self-actualized people developed by Maslow are descriptions which fall along a continuum. They are descriptions relating to a process, a process which shows movement in a positive human direction. Consequently, it is inappropriate for the reader to say, "I do this, but I don't do that. So I had better start." We believe that all people possess these qualities in varying degrees. Furthermore, it is particularly necessary for the counselor to evolve his potentials by beginning with his unique degree of each quality and developing each in the desired direction.

THE COUNSELOR AS A PROFESSIONAL

Professionalism

Just like teaching, counseling is not a profession because its practitioners wish it to be so or choose to label it that. "Wishing and labeling" seem to have little to do with the real questions of professionalism.

All too often professionalism has come to be viewed as synonymous with membership in professional organizations. This too is a hollow kind of professionalism. Arbuckle (1961) comments on such attempts at professionalism by saying:

> It is true of course that there are counselors who wish to join everything in sight so that they can add up the number of organizations to which they belong. But the responsible counselor, while he will carefully budget his time and money, will feel that part of his professional responsibility is to be an active member of his professional organizations at a local, state, and a national level. (pp. 77–78)

Moreover, Sweeny (1966), after surveying a group of counselors and their administrators, reported finding no significant differences between counselors that were members of local and national guidance associations and counselors without professional affiliation.

Another view of professionalism suggests that reading and contributing to professional journals constitute professionalism. We submit that much of what is written in such journals is a product of school "publish or perish" policies rather than investigations and discussions of searching questions and burning issues. It is our experience that few journal articles have significant personal meaning and relevance for the individual counselor. Although vast quantities of literature are being produced, the quality of these productions leaves these readers questioning the *raison d'être*. It seems unfortunate that some feel they must produce articles to insure professional survival and enhancement even when they feel little commitment to that task.

Still another way of assessing professionalism is through the counselor's participation in formal counseling activities such as conventions, area conferences, in-service meetings. In the main, however, we have personally found formalized activities to be less beneficial, less stimulating, less meaningful, and less relevant than informal get-togethers. To assemble with other people for some formal program or activity often precludes the spontaneous encounters between people which promote growth. Whether it be midnight in a hotel room with colleagues at a national convention or breakfast with the counselor from the nearby elementary school, these have been the professional activities which have meant the most to us.

To this point we have stated and implied that professionalism is more than labels, affiliations, obligations, and formal meetings. What then is the "more than" dimension? It is giving and receiving. Professionalism, as we see it, involves two basic questions: (1) What of myself can I offer to other counselors? and (2) What can I gain from other counselors and their experiences? The manner in which a counselor can best answer these questions is the manner in which that counselor can best obtain professionalism for himself. The "how" of meeting his obligations to colleagues and of obtaining and utilizing help from them is a matter which must be worked out personally by the child counselor himself.

Ethical Issues

Perhaps the most important professional consideration for the counselor pertains to his ethical and moral behavior. Again, the counselor must examine himself in terms of his beliefs and commitments to determine his personal stance with regard to matters of client confidentiality, referral, treatment, and so on, and also the behavior of his professional colleagues. In matters of client confidentiality, for instance, the counselor must determine the point beyond which he can no longer maintain the child's confidence. This may be viewed in two dimensions: (1) What kinds of behavior is the counselor unwilling to maintain confidence about; and (2) Under what amount of pressure is he unwilling to maintain confidence. To illustrate, let us suppose that eight-year-old Tom has told the counselor about his theft of some small items from a department store. What does the counselor do? Let us suppose next that these small items were a pistol and some ammunition. What does the counselor do? Now suppose that the counselor is aware of Tom's hatred for his younger brother and that Tom is carrying the pistol on his person. What does the counselor do? Now suppose that Tom has talked about his wish to kill his brother. What does the counselor do? Suppose Tom does shoot his brother and later confesses his crime to the counselor. What does the counselor do? Suppose the counselor is subpoenaed into court to testify regarding his knowledge of Tom's behavior. What does the counselor do? Finally, the counselor is informed that he will be charged with contempt unless he testifies. What does the counselor do?

Our point in developing this illustration is to demonstrate that there are numerous considerations which must go into judgments regarding confidentiality and other ethical issues. These judgments must be made independently by each counselor and with consideration for each unique situation. However, it is important that the counselor has considered questions of ethics as they relate to him as a person and that he have some ideas formulated to assist him in making ethical decisions.

THE COUNSELOR AS A TEAM MEMBER

It is easy and sometimes tempting for the counselor to sit back smugly and act as though he is the only person dealing with children who really knows about children and their behavior. Certainly such a position is narrow, if not to some degree irresponsible, for there are many disciplines that can be legitimately called upon to provide insights into child behavior. What is needed is a comprehensive and interdisciplinary team approach to the questions of child behavior. Only by bringing together what is known from the various sources of knowledge can we best service children.

The team approach has been a popular method, especially in child guidance clinic programs and in education. Almost all functions in the public schools have been talked about as team functions and almost all functionaries have been described as team members. From our experience, it seems important to emphasize, however, that a key member of any team designed to be of service to a child is that child himself. Often team efforts have proved less than efficient by failing to recognize and pay heed to this basic consideration.

In the discussion which follows, we have chosen to focus on the counselor as a team member, a coordinator, and a consultant in the public school setting. With limited modifications this discussion would seem applicable to counselors in other settings.

We have tried to look at the counselor as functioning as a team member in three different ways: (1) intraschool teams, (2) interschool teams, and (3) extraschool teams. In each instance, the team will not maximize its effect toward the betterment of the child unless the child is included as an integral part of the functioning team.

Intraschool Teams

The idea of a team without a purpose doesn't make much sense. Purposes for teams can vary just as roles for the counselor on the team can vary. However, purposes in terms of benefit to the child should be the number one consideration for the team's existence and specific structure.

In some cases the counselor may assume the leadership of the team. In other cases he may be a team member under the leadership of someone else. In any case, his role and responsibilities should be defined at the onset and in terms of the team goals.

Just what the counselor role will or should be or just who should make up the team is a function of the particular school and/or the particular child for whom the team has been designed. The school employs a number of workers whose primary concern is the welfare of the child. To work together toward this end as a unit with each member benefiting each other member is much more profitable than the competitive and duplicated efforts that so often take place in the name of benefiting children.

Particularly within the school the team does not need to function on a formal basis. This is not to suggest that the counselor pass on to other team members all the information he has from or about the child. In fact much of such information was obtained by the counselor in a confidential relationship and cannot be ethically discussed with teachers, principles, and others unless the client so agrees. Similarly, information is given the counselor by the teacher in a framework that assumes confidentiality and must be treated by the counselor in such a manner.

The counselor, the child, the teachers, the administrators, the school nurse, the reading and speech therapist, together with the parent and other individuals whose primary concern is the betterment of the child within the school, can work cooperatively toward their common goal.

Interschool Teams

The elementary school classroom has often been referred to as an island unto itself. If this is true, it is equally as valid a description of an elementary school. Elementary schools communicate between and among each other very infrequently. As with intraschool teams, it does not seem as important just what methodology is employed to facilitate communication or just who the team members are as it does that the counselor considers himself as a potential team member of any team constituted with the purpose of benefiting a child.

Certainly, when schools work together, effective means for accomplishing desired results can be shared so that children on a broader scale can benefit.

Interschool teams can be formulated in both formal and informal ways. The most important function of the interschool team seems to be one of establishing and solidifying lines of communication. Much of what could be discussed in terms of interschool teams has already been covered in this chapter under the heading of the counselor as a professional. The reader is referred to that section for additional thoughts regarding interschool teams.

Extraschool Teams

The child spends much more time outside of school than in school. There are a great many people outside of the school setting who are vitally concerned with the development of the child. Again, it seems crucial to coordinate the inter-, intra-, and extraschool efforts in order that the child receive the maximum benefit.

Traditionally, the school counselor has waited until an outside agency such as a child guidance clinic or an individual such as the child's physician invites the counselor to participate. In this way the counselor often feels like a second-class citizen rather than a fully enfranchised team member. We contend that this has come about by the counselor's not usually taking the initiative in formulating the extraschool team.

This is not meant to be taken as an indictment against the counselor. In the main, training programs have not encouraged or provided experiences in working with professionals outside the field of education. For this reason, counselors often do not feel competent to work with, let alone initiate contacts with, such extraschool professionals.

THE COUNSELOR AS A COORDINATOR

The ASCA-ACES joint statement cited in chapter 1 regarding the elementary school counselor lists coordination as one of his three major functions(We would like to reemphasize our position that such functions as coordination are legitimate functions of the elementary school counselor but are secondary to the counselor's major function of counseling.)

We have just discussed three ways that the elementary school counselor might function as a team coordinator. Counselors are often the coordinators of the pupil personnel services of the school. The trouble with such a function is that coordination so often gets confused with administration and the counselor bogs himself down or gets bogged down in work that could more efficiently and less expensively be done by a qualified secretary. It becomes so easy for the counselor to take charge of the testing program, the cumulative records system, and so forth, that there is not time left to counsel.

The guidance services in the school do, however, require coordination. We suggest that the counselor be aware of the role that he can play in his own unique situation as a coordinator in developing teams to serve the student without losing sight of his major counseling function.

THE COUNSELOR AS A CONSULTANT

Some literature in counseling suggests that the elementary school counselor of the future will become more and more of a consultant. This would seem to be taking place in that the teacher will be performing many counseling functions heretofore considered the province of the counselor. As an expert in child behavior and in the forming of relationships with children, the counselor may spend a great deal of time helping to teach others the skills that are associated with counseling (Faust, 1968).

Consulting can encompass both the role of working with teachers and other school personnel and the role of working with groups and individuals outside the school setting. Just what the counselor does as a consultant will depend on his own unique expertise. We would hope, however, that the counselor in the elementary school would not limit his professional experiences to the confines of the school which employs him.

Work with service clubs, churches, groups of parents and others can be considered consulting. On the other hand, formal and informal meetings with teachers and administrators and eventually the child can likewise be considered consulting and are within the legitimate province of the counselor.

Most often consulting on the part of the elementary school counselor has taken the form of "suggestion giving" and "question answering" with teachers. In that the counselor does assume the role of an expert in child behavior and communication, he most likely does have some suggestions and some answers to questions. However, confining his consultative role to answering and advising teachers is restrictive.

We would also like to comment on the similarities between counseling and consulting. From our point of view both are human relationships requiring that the counselor demonstrate the personal qualities which have been discussed in the preceding pages of this chapter. Whether the counselor is providing information about the child development, advising the parent of the importance of "limits," or listening to the teacher vent her feelings about Tommy's disruptive classroom behavior, he must perform the various tasks within a facilitative human relationship. The setting and the role of the individual being served by the counselor seem to be the most important differences between counseling and consulting.

COMMENT

The counselor as a person is the major variable in the counseling process that makes a difference in whether positive change is facilitated in the child. We have tried to describe some of the personal qualities that counselors might demonstrate to children in order to be effective. We have emphasized that these qualities can be learned and in many ways parallel the qualities of the self-actualized person. Team participation and leadership on the part of the counselor is one of the effective ways the counselor can work with others toward the ultimate benefit of the child.

The elementary school counselor can assume a number of roles in addition to counseling. The important aspect of these roles is that they be assumed in light of the benefit to the child. It is important that these roles be internally consistent and that they not replace the counselor's major function —counseling.

REFERENCES

ARBUCKLE, D. S. *Counseling: An Introduction.* Boston: Allyn & Bacon, Inc., 1961.

CARKHUFF, R.R., AND BERENSON, B. *Beyond Counseling and Therapy.* New York: Holt, Rinehart & Winston, Inc., 1967.

DIMICK, K. M. "The Elementary School Counselor as Perceived by Counselor Educators and Elementary School Administrators." Unpublished doctoral dissertation, University of Arizona, 1966.

FAUST, V. *The Counselor-consultant in the Elementary School.* Boston: Houghton Mifflin Company, 1968.

JOURARD, S. M. *Disclosing Man to Himself.* Princeton, N.J.: D. Van Nostrand Co., Inc., 1968.

MASLOW, A. *Motivation and Personality*. New York: Harper & Row, Publishers, 1954.

————. *Toward a Psychology of Being*. Princeton, N.J.: D. Van Nostrand Co., Inc., 1962.

ROGERS, C. R. *Freedom To Learn*. Columbus, Ohio: Charles E. Merrill Publishing Co., 1969.

ROKEACH, M. *The Open and Closed Mind*. New York: Basic Books, Inc., Publishers, 1960.

SWEENY, T. J. "The School Counselor as Perceived by School Counselors and Their Principals." *Personnel and Guidance Journal* 44 (1966):844–849.

SELECTED ADDITIONAL READINGS

ALLEN, T. W., AND WHITELEY, J. M. *Dimensions of Effective Counseling*. Columbus, Ohio: Charles E. Merrill Publishing Co., 1968.

BECK, C. E., ed. *Guidelines for Guidance*. Dubuque, Ia.: Wm. C. Brown Company Publishers, 1967.

BENTLEY, J. C., ed. *The Counselor's Role*. Boston: Houghton Mifflin Company, 1968.

BOY, A. V., AND PINE, G. J. *The Counselor in the Schools*. Boston: Houghton Mifflin Company, 1968.

BRAMMER, L. M., AND SHOSTROM, E. L. *Therapeutic Psychology*. 2nd ed. Englewood Cliffs, N.J.: Prentice-Hall, Inc., 1968.

BUGENTAL, J. F. T. *The Search for Authenticity*. New York: Holt, Rinehart & Winston, Inc., 1965.

DINKMEYER, D. C., ed. *Guidance and Counseling in the Elementary School*. New York: Holt, Rinehart & Winston, Inc., 1968.

FITTS, W. *The Experience of Psychotherapy*. New York: D. Van Nostrand Co., Inc., 1965.

FRANK, J. D. *Persuasion and Healing*. New York: Schocken Books, Inc., 1963.

JOURARD, S. M. *The Transparent Self*. New York: D. Van Nostrand Co., Inc., 1964.

KOPLITZ, E. D., ed. *Guidance in the Elementary School: Theory, Research and Practice*. Dubuque, Ia.: Wm. C. Brown Company Publishers, 1968.

MULLAN, H., AND SANGIULIANO, IRIS. *The Therapists' Contribution to the Treatment Process*. Springfield, Ill.: Charles C Thomas, Publisher, 1964.

ROGERS, C. R. *On Becoming A Person*. Boston: Houghton Mifflin Company, 1961.

SCHOFIELD, W. *Psychotherapy: The Purchase of Friendship*. Englewood Cliffs, N.J.: Prentice-Hall, Inc., 1964.

SHERTZER, B., AND STONE, S. C. *Fundamentals of Counseling*. Boston: Houghton Mifflin Company, 1968.

SNYDER, R. *On Becoming Human*. New York: Abingdon Press, 1967.

TRUAX, C. B., AND CARKHUFF, R. R. *Toward Effective Counseling and Psychotherapy*. Chicago: Aldine Publishing Company, 1967.

TYLER, LEONA E. *The Work of the Counselor*. New York: Appleton-Century-Crofts, 1969.

7

Individual Interview

The majority of formal counseling, including counseling with children, is accomplished through the use of the individual interview. So universal is this concept that most definitions of counseling and therapy specify the one-to-one relationship as a basic essential.

In trying to discuss the *hows* and *whys* of the individual interview, it is easy to compare individual and group counseling. A certain amount of comparison cannot and should not be avoided. In this chapter, we have tried to present the individual interview as an entity with its own distinct advantages and disadvantages.

RATIONALE FOR INDIVIDUAL COUNSELING

There are a number of reasons why individual counseling has been and will continue to be the preferred "helping" approach of many who work with children. Some of these reasons are discussed below.

Tradition

Although tradition is hardly a sufficient rationale for the continuance of an established practice, it is nevertheless a significant determiner of what will be done in child counseling in the future. Part of the responsibility for this tradition's being carried forward is that of counselor preparation programs. That is, most training programs focus on the development of skills related to one-to-one relationships. Moreover, most facilities designed and constructed to house the counseling service are ones which lend themselves most effectively to individual interviews. Perhaps if training programs had different emphases and if facilities had more flexible designs, the individual interview would not be the preferred "helping" approach.

Confidentiality

The issue of confidentiality is a very important consideration in individual counseling. The counselor cannot ask the child to be free and open in his self-disclosures if there is no assurance that the counselor will not use these disclosures against the child or to effect a change in the child's life that he does not want. Certainly the child can expect a greater degree of confidentiality from the counselor in the individual interview than he can from peers in a group-counseling experience; hence, the individual interview provides greater safety, at least initially, for the child client who may be inhibited from self-disclosure.

Preparation for Group

There is a process of learning how to be a client which is accomplished in the individual interview. Experientially, the client learns how to let others help him, how to express his feelings, and how to become the focus of attention. Such learnings are crucial to effective participation for group counseling and may be acquired through individual counseling experiences, the primary purpose of which is to prepare the child for group counseling.

We have done some work with young adults using various methods of preparing them for a group experience. It is our conclusion that those individuals who function most effectively in groups (personally benefiting from the experience as well as being of benefit to others) are those who have first participated in individual counseling. Much of the initial exploratory behavior ("What am I supposed to do?" "What am I supposed to say?" "What does the counselor do?" etc.) is eliminated since the "experienced" client is aware of basic counseling ground rules.

Although we recognize that our experience along these lines has not been with young children, we believe that the idea is applicable to work with children. We hypothesize that the process may go something like this. The child is having difficulty coping with or developing adequately in his environment. He enters individual counseling, learns to talk about and understand some of the dynamics of his behaviors. He experiences the development of a relationship. He then moves to a group experience where he is afforded the opportunity to "field test" and practice new behaviors. From this "more real" environment, he can then move more easily back into the original environment with his new coping behaviors.

Counselor Attention

Since there is but one relationship in the individual interview, the counselor is able to devote his full attention to the child and to his interaction with the child. In a society where many children tend to be detached and alienated from adults and where children are often to be seen and not heard, the single fact that the adult counselor devotes his full attention to the child and treats him as worthwhile may be of great consequence to the child. Attention in this context involves the counselor's attitude toward the child; his willingness to let the child speak and act for himself; his interest in understanding how the child's world appears to him; his sensitivity to the child's needs, fears, wishes; his willingness to listen and "hear" the child's communications both verbal and nonverbal.

Learning Appropriate Defenses

As suggested earlier in this work, all people need and use defense mechanisms to protect their egos from attack and devaluation. Moreover, the appropriateness of these protective mechanisms has to do with their degree of flexibility and their availability for use by the individual when they are needed. That is to say, the individual who is able to function well in society is the one who is able to control the flexible use of his defenses rather than being controlled by them.

Some children and adults, however, have never learned to use their defenses flexibly in ways which help them function well. Such persons are set and rigid in their behavior patterns and tend to use the same defensive strategies to the same degree regardless of the threat posed. Other children and adults have such poorly structured defenses that in each human interaction or relationship they put themselves at the mercy of those around them. Both extremes seem to be deficient ways of dealing with life.

Certainly we all have need to "cover up" from time to time and from situation to situation. We all feel threat. We all become intimidated. These reactions to life are all perfectly healthy and appropriate. It is also healthy and appropriate for the individual to learn effective and flexible ways of protecting his "self"—ways which prevent him from being overly vulnerable to the vicissitudes of life, but ways which also can be set aside when the risk to "self" is not too great.

With the child who has rigid and stereotyped defense patterns for himself, the counselor can aid in the examination of their appropriateness. To accomplish this, the threat to the child must be minimized so that the defense strategies can be safely dropped. With the child who is exceptionally vulnerable, the counselor can help in the building of appropriate defenses that can serve the child in the protection of his "self."

A final comment about the development of functional and appropriate defenses is necessary. If an individual can learn to have confidence in his own defense mechanisms, that is, if he can feel his defenses are adequate to serve him in time of need, he will be more open to experience. The child, for instance, often avoids situations because of the negative potentials that exist. If, however, the child felt he could protect himself from such negative outcomes, he would be more willing to involve himself in experiences.

Needs of the Child

Perhaps the entire rationale for the individual interview process can be summed up in the statement that the needs of some children can be met more adequately through the use of the one-to-one relationship. In the final analysis, we believe that this criterion ought to supersede considerations of counselor theoretical orientation, personal bias, and counselor comfort. Only inasmuch as the counselor can operationally transcend such considerations will he be able to most effectively help children meet the needs which they have.

Recently we conducted a psychodrama (see chapter 8 for a discussion of psychodrama) using as protagonist (the central character) a counselor of fine skill and extensive experience. She was told about her selection as protagonist approximately a week in advance. Following the psychodramatic experience she said, "You know, the most significant part of the experience was my worrying all week about the session. I am so used to being a counselor that I hadn't thought of the fear that a child must have in anticipating that first counseling session. This experience has brought that home to me."

Just the thought of sitting down and expressing oneself totally in a society which teaches that what children think and feel is relatively unimportant is at best a very threatening experience for most children. The threat is minimized, however, in the one-to-one relationship where an amosphere of respect and safety can be experienced by the child—where his needs can be accepted and ultimately met.

School Needs

Throughout this text we have emphasized that a major responsibility of the child counselor is one of helping children meet their unique needs. It should be pointed out, however, that the school child exists in a highly structured and complex organization. Moreover, counseling is not the major function of the school; hence, it is usually easier and much more practical to remove one child at a time from a classroom for counseling without undue disruption than to remove several.

In situations where counseling can only be done during the times when children are free from their "academic pursuits," the logistical problems of trying to establish and maintain working counseling groups is discouraging to most counselors. Therefore, even though a group experience might be the preferred "helping" approach, the counselor may often resort to individual counseling in order to avoid the practical problems of getting groups of children together.

POSITIVE POTENTIALS OF THE INDIVIDUAL INTERVIEW

It is difficult to separate the positive potentials of counseling with children on a one-to-one basis from the rationale for such a process. Although we will focus on the following paragraphs on the "what can happen" aspect of the individual interview, it should be noted that the *why* aspect will be an integral part of these potentials.

Optimal Learning Laboratory

Earlier in this volume we discussed learning and conditions which promote the most effective learning experiences. The individual interview in many senses epitomizes an optimal learning laboratory especially with matters having to do with decision-making processes, self-awareness and understanding, and interpersonal relationships. As we have defined the productive counseling relationship, we have noted the necessity of certain counselor-offered facilitative conditions in order for behavioral change to occur. We also emphasized the significance of these conditions in learning experiences outside the counseling relationship.

What better learning environment and opportunity can be conceived than that of the one-to-one relationship? The counselor, an expert in human relations, learning, and behavior, focuses his entire attention on providing the most facilitative learning experiences for the child client. There are minimal child resistances and impediments to the learning process since the need for defensive behaviors is minimized. Even physical setting contributes to optimal learning since client comfort, confidentiality, and freedom from intrusion are assured. The child is provided a laboratory where he can learn about himself, about others, and about relationships. Moreover, he is free to "try out" alternative behaviors without fear of ridicule or censure. The productive individual counseling session is an optimal learning laboratory for children.

Forming Positive Adult Relationships

Children are obviously smaller, in some ways less skilled, and in many ways less experienced than adults. Because of such factors, it becomes easy for adults to consciously and unconsciously treat children as inferior beings. By being so treated, children can learn to see themselves as inferior and can tend to regard adults as punitive, controlling, superior, domineering, and so forth. Such child attitudes are restrictive in that they prevent the child from experiencing adults as human beings subject to all the aspects of being human, both positive and negative.

This kind of child "set" regarding adults can be reassessed by the child if he has adult experiences with adults—experiences of a kind which demonstrate to him that he is respected, worthwhile, capable, and trusted as a human being. The counselor is in a position to be able to help the child make such a reassessment as a function of the one-to-one relationship between counselor and child. Moreover, this experience can be generalized to other adult-child relationships by the child as he learns to accept and trust himself and the counselor.

Modeling

The expected outcomes of counseling are increased self-understanding, behavioral change, and a fuller realization of potentials. Counselor modeling, whether incidental or planned, gives the child an alternative way of behaving. It is almost inevitable that the child who is cared about by the counselor will reciprocate by caring about the counselor. He may manifest this caring in a number of ways including a kind of "copying" of the admired counselor behaviors.

If the characteristics evidenced by the counselor convey to the child respect, understanding, equality, worth, and acceptance, then the child is in a position to discover his "self" and more fully realize his growth potentials. The counselor as a model of positive attitudes toward people can positively influence the child's attitudes toward himself and toward others.

Stability and Sanctuary

Perhaps the greatest single service that the counselor, and hence the individual interview, provides is that of a safe and stable sanctuary from the client's everyday world. A client once remarked that her whole world was spinning and unpredictable outside of the counselor's office. But once in that office she had the assurance that the situation was predictable, stable, and secure. "I always knew that I whould have my feet on the floor in the counseling session even though my other world was mixed up and spinning."

The individual counseling session can become a haven, a place where the client does not have to defend against being hurt, worry about being accepted, or concern himself about being respected as a person. It can be a place where the child has no fear of being what he is. Only in such an atmosphere can the child optimally discover his "self" and learn alternative ways of meeting his needs and actualizing his potentials.

NEGATIVE POTENTIALS OF THE INDIVIDUAL INTERVIEW

The individual interview is not without potential liability. Just as every coin and every issue has two sides, so it is with the one-to-one counseling relationship.

Counselor Responsibility

Like it or not, the day you start calling yourself a "helping person"— counselor, psychologist, therapist—you give up some of the rights afforded human beings in other walks of life.

If you are a truck driver and your next door neighbor comes to you telling of his marital difficulties, that neighbor has a set of expectations for you. If, however, you are a "helping person" of whatever label and this same neighbor comes to you, a whole different set of expectations are held. In or out of your office, you are "expected" to be helpful in time of need.

We know of a young girl who before her self-inflicted death told us of her unrealized expectations for counseling. Before having sought counseling, she had always believed that when things got too bad she could seek a counselor and he would "cure" her. That was her "ace in the hole." When that "too bad" day came, however, she discovered that her expectations were unwarranted. She had "played her ace" and it had been "trumped." From that experience she lost hope and finally concluded that she was "incurable."

We fully realize that no counselor can be all things to all people. We do, however, suggest that the counselor has the responsibility of either helping the person in need who seeks his help or of getting that person to someone else who is able and willing to assume that responsibility.

Fostering Dependency

In most discussions of potential liabilities for the individual interview the question of dependency is raised. This is an especially critical issue in counseling with children for in many ways children must be dependent.

At birth they are totally dependent upon adults for the meeting of all their needs. As they grow, develop, and mature, they become increasingly able to assume responsibilities if they are permitted to do so by the adults in their environments. Often, however, the child seen in counseling has not had such an opportunity. He is excessively dependent for his years and tends to be a real challenge to the counselor.

The development of dependency is an insidious process. As we have implied, it results from the responsibility for decision-making being usurped from the child by adults and older children. When mother decides what clothes to buy eight-year-old Tony, when he should wear what, who his play-mates should be, what games he should avoid, what foods he should eat, how he should cut and comb his hair, and so forth, Tony is set up with the poten-tial for becoming an overly dependent child. It is with such children that the counselor can have a positive or negative influence. The difference will result from how the dependency is dealt with.

Let us suppose that seven-year-old Alice has been referred to the coun-selor because of excessive expressions of dependency. Her life experiences before and since her introduction to school have left her with little confidence in her abilities to do things for herself. Consequently, she has developed clever habits patterned to get others (peers and adults) to do things for her. It is these same clever habit patterns that she brings to the counseling relationship. Since Alice has had extensive experience and is skilled in using these behavior patterns to get others to do for her, she is going to use them to deal with the counselor. It therefore behooves the counselor to be "on top of" the dynamics of the relationship so that he does not fall prey to Alice's dependency and does not wind up reinforcing rather than eliminating such behaviors.

It is not profound to state the dependency is at best in part related to the age of the child. That is, individual children naturally experience decreasing degrees of dependency as they mature and develop. It is only when this "natural" process is stifled that children develop excessive reliance on others for the gratification of their needs.

In our experience we have found it very difficult to not "jump in" and "do for" the overly dependent and frightened child. To wait for such a child to come to grips with the decisions which are a part of his world and to watch him struggle and wrestle with the process of choosing is agonizing for us. We realize, however, that only inasmuch as the child learns to make choices for himself will he be able to become a free and responsible human being. To "jump in" and needlessly "do for" denies the child his basic human rights and potentials.

Counselor Status

It is not uncommon for the child client to put the effective counselor up on a pedestal. This is especially true if the counselor has weathered through some rough times with the child or if the child has had no positive adult relationships apart from his relationship with the counselor. This is not in itself a liability, although it has that potential.

Due to the quality of the counselor-child relationship (a novel experience for many children), it is sometimes possible for the child to view the counselor as a paragon of all that is good, virtuous, and proper. A hazard growing out of such an elevated perception is that the counselor can become a "one-of-a-kind" in the world. No other person could possibly fill his shoes, and furthermore, no lowly child could ever aspire to be like him. So why even try?

We suspect that in many cases where the counselor has been regarded with such awe and reverence, he has contributed to that perception by permitting himself to be only partially "known" (the positive part). If the counselor will allow himself to be "known" in his negative aspects as well as his positive ones, if he can allow children to see and feel his vulnerability, he can diminish to a great extent, if not eliminate, the "perfect" image.

But what of the liabilities of the counselor expressing negative feelings in the counseling interview? Shouldn't he have more self-control than that? Won't he frighten or confuse the child? Won't that damage the relationship? These certainly are potentials which can result from the counselor's expression of negative feelings. From our experience, however, such negative consequences need not result. The counselor can nondestructively express his anger at a child by focusing on the counselor's feelings and the child's behavior rather than on the person of the child. For example, "I really get mad when you hit smaller children," rather than, "You make me mad when you are so bad." Moreover, the child may learn an important lesson about how to handle his own negative feelings safely through the open expression of negative feeling by the counselor.

Child-Client Labeling

We have tried to emphasize the perils and hazards in the common practice of labeling children by the use of psychological jargon. Such labeling denies to a large extent the uniqueness of the individual child so labeled and has little, if anything, to do with treatment methods; hence, we tend to avoid such labeling procedures.

There is another kind of child-client labeling which occurs, however, that is less easily controlled but equally as harmful. It stems from attitudes and perceptions of parents, teachers, and other children which are held about the counselor and his responsibilities. It is not unusual for the counselor who really makes a difference in the lives of children to be sought out and used by the "extreme" child; hence, the counselor can get the reputation of working with only "seriously disturbed," "crazy," "weird," and "far-out" children.

Such a reputation can certainly limit the impact of the counselor inasmuch as the more "normal" youngster with "normal" problems may tend to shy away from being identified as "crazy," "weird," and "far-out" as a function of seeking the help of the counselor. These children need the help of the counselor too. It is important, therefore, that the counselor clarify his function and responsibility through word and deed so that his service to children can be seen by all who have needs.

THE COUNSELING PROCESS

The word *process* has many connotations. Factories process foods. Banks process checks. Colleges process applications. In all cases, however, the central idea of processing is that a procedure characterized by a variety of steps is used to produce a product. This is also largely true of the counseling process, although the steps in the procedure are not highly differentiated and discrete. Simply stated, the counseling process is an alive, dynamic human growth interaction which can be loosely characterized as consisting of initiation, relationship development, search for self, integration of self, self in action, and termination.

Initiating Counseling

Much has been written about "what ought to be done" to get the first counselor-client contact off on a positive note. From our perspective, this initial contact is critical to the establishment of a productive counseling relationship. Therefore, the counselor must demonstrate his respect, concern, and understanding for the child and his experiences from the inception of the counselor-child contact. In that initial meeting, the child will most likely be "sizing up" the counselor. The counselor must understand the feelings and behaviors of the child in these moments. If, for whatever reasons, the counselor assumes responsibility for asking questions about home, siblings, peer relations, and a variety of other things, the child may get the "set" that the counseling relationship will be a "question-and-answer game" with the counselor asking all the questions. If this is the intent of the counselor, that is, to gain an abundance of information, then such a "set" is appropriate for the child to develop. If such questions are only intended as "ice-breakers," then the "question-and-answer game" set has the potential for getting the relationship off on the wrong foot.

It has been our experience that the beginning child counselor in the initial interview is particularly prone to question, question, question. When asked to explain the "why" of the questioning, they are usually at a loss.

"What else could I do?" "He wouldn't talk when I didn't ask questions" are common responses. Certainly the counselor is doing what he at the moment thinks to be best. However, this "best" may be providing a "set" to the child regarding counseling that will be difficult to overcome.

Another issue that is critical to the establishment of a positive counseling "set" is that of counselor consistency. So many times we have seen the initial counselor-child interview begin with the counselor's saying something like, "Okay, John, this is your time to do what you'd like to do, to talk about things that are important to you." John, somewhat taken aback by seemingly being given responsibility for what will happen between him and the counselor, and having a long history of experiences with adults who say one thing and mean something else, silently sits assessing the meaning of the counselor's statement. Two minutes pass in silence and the counselor's anxiety builds, for he is supposed to be "doing" something. Finally, as a desperate move to get the interview going and because his anxiety can no longer be quelled, the counselor "jumps in" by asking, "By the way, John, how are your grades?" The question may relieve the counselor's anxiety, he may even feel accomplishment in getting the interview going, but what is John's reaction? Could it be that his suspicions about adults who "talk out of both sides of their mouths" has been affirmed? Might it be that he could evaluate the situation as being one more where he was told something but it was obviously not true? Could it be that John has "set the counselor up" to fail? We feel that such a potential is real.

By this illustration we are not suggesting that the counselor ought or ought not to begin a counseling relationship with a statement giving the child major responsibility for what transpires. Rather, we are pointing out the importance of the counselor's being consistent. The counselor must be willing and able to match his words with his behaviors if the child is going to learn to trust in the relationship.

Developing a Relationship

From the tentative commitment of the child that he can trust the counselor comes the development of a significant counseling relationship. Early in this stage the counselor and child mutually determine goals and purposes for their continuing relationship. This relationship characterized by counselor honesty, warmth, understanding, acceptance, and mutual respect allows the child to see the counselor as an ally in his struggle with himself and his phenomenal world. The counseling relationship is one for the child to rely upon and gain strength from until his own inner growth forces are able to function adequately apart from the support, encouragement, and caring of the counselor. In the safety of the relationship the child can examine his feelings, thoughts, and behaviors without having to defend or justify them. In the relative absence of external threat, the child can discover who and what he is.

Searching for the "Self"

As the relationship becomes more "solid" between counselor and child, the search for "self" intensifies. Generally, this search involves self-disclosure which is characterized by release and awareness of feelings mainly through play and language media. It may also come through direct forms like crying, however.

Often the counseling relationship is the first opportunity where the "locked up" feelings have had opportunity for open and free expression. A "ventilation" of these feelings, then, has the potential benefits of (1) releasing physiological and emotional tension, (2) developing a sense of satisfaction and courage, (3) freedom from having to defend against these feelings, and (4) the release of new creative energy to be constructively used in the resolution of the child's concerns. But "ventilation" is not enough. Once the pent-up feelings have been released, the counselor and client work together to explore underlying attitudes and values of the child's self system as well as distortions in his perceptions.

This "searching" and exploration of underlying attitudes and values is typically the stage which involves the longest duration. Uncovering and assessing attitudes and values, and reexamining perceptions in order to correct distortions, however, are basic to the child's developing understanding of the inner and outer worlds of his existence.

Integrating the Self

The search and exploration stage of counseling helps the child see himself, his perceptions, and his phenomenal world in a more "real" and undistorted fashion. With his new awarenesses and understandings, the child must then work toward putting them all together into some personally meaningful gestalt—an integrated "self."

As the integration process evolves, feelings and thoughts become aligned, previously perceived contradictions are understood, conflicts are resolved, and the child develops a feeling of personal wholeness. Defensiveness is minimized and positive feelings are experienced. The attitudinal self, the physical self, the intellectual self, the psychosexual self, the social self, and the emotional self become united in the uniquely personal SELF.

Self in Action

The final test of the meaningful integration of "awareness" and "understanding" is the child client's increased ability to act responsibly and effectively outside the counseling relationship. Only inasmuch as the child's extracounseling behavior is more effective in helping him with his needs is counseling successful. Changes in the child's thoughts, feelings, perceptions, and/or behaviors are the real measures of counseling efficacy.

Termination

Termination of the counseling relationship is often an awkward event. Both counselor and child in the "integrating" and "acting out of self" stages become increasingly aware of the time when their professional relationship must end. Often the counselor is fearful that the child will experience feelings of rejection if he, the counselor, suggests that "the time has come." Similarly the child may be very reluctant to leave the sanctuary epitomized by the counselor and hence will be hesitant to conclude the relationship, and yet, the issue of termination must be confronted.

It has been our experience that counselor openness and honesty in this event is critical to a fulfilling termination of the counseling relationship. To sensitively deal with the child's feelings and to unreservedly express his own will profit both the counselor and the child. Assurances of a continuing relationship on an informal basis or of the counselor's availability in times of future need can make the parting a happy rather than somber event in the total counseling process.

Follow-up

Although follow-up is generally not considered to be an integral part of the counseling process, it can be an important adjustment for both counselor and child. It seems inconceivable to us that an "all caring" relationship can become a "no caring" one as a result of the child's termination of counseling; hence, we suggest that the counselor consider the possibility of formally or informally getting together with ex-clients for the purpose of keeping abreast of the child's progress and of displaying his continuing interest in and concern for the child's welfare.

CRITICAL POINTS IN THE COUNSELING PROCESS

As was implied earlier in our discussion, the initial contact between counselor and client is a critical point in the process. As the child "sizes up" the counselor and decides whether or not the counselor can be trusted, he also decides whether or not he will commit himself to the process.

Another critical point occurs subsequent to the "ventilation" of pent-up feelings. The tension release resulting from this experience may be great enough so that the child will feel able to cope with his situation without further counseling. In other cases, if the child is permitted to "ventilate" to excess, revealing too much of himself too fast, he may feel guilty about these revelations and be ashamed to return to counseling. Still in other cases the client may feel afraid to "face" exploration of underlying attitudes and feelings and will choose to terminate counseling prematurely.

More generally, it should be pointed out that early or premature termination of counseling may occur at many other points in the total process when the child has experienced considerable success in meeting his life situation, or when he is confronted with particularly difficult or threatening "self" material and/or choices. In the former case, he may feel as though he no longer has a need for help. In the latter, he may shy away from the challenge of the difficult or threatening task before him. Although we do not believe in keeping children in counseling against their wills, the greatest gains are often missed through premature termination of the counseling process.

OTHER CONSIDERATIONS

There are a number of considerations and aspects which impinge in one way or another on the counseling process. Although they could have been interwoven into the preceding discussion of the process, we have chosen to discuss them in this separate "catch all" section. We would emphasize, however, that the reader consider the ways that these other considerations and aspects relate to the total counseling process.

The Involuntary Client

The child who comes to the counselor of his own free will obviously has some reason for being there. It is not, however, necessarily the reason which may be initially stated.

The involuntary client also has a reason for being in the counselor's office, but it is not his reason. He is there because someone else thinks he needs to be. Beier (1952) gives three alternative ways of working with such clients: (1) The counselor can refuse to work with the involuntary child client. (2) The counselor can ignore the fact that the child doesn't want to be there and can proceed to "shape up" his behavior. (3) The counselor can deal with the child's feelings in an empathic way.

The first alternative is an approach subscribed to by those counselors who believe that no one can be helped who doesn't voluntarily seek that help. Even though such an approach would seem to be an ideal way of working with children, it does seem somewhat irresponsible of the counselor to work only with voluntary clients.

The second alternative is one practiced by those counselors who feel that the job of the counselor is largely one of modifying behavior through the use of influences external to the child. The child is viewed as having to meet standards and having to learn to fit in with societal expectations; hence, the counselor acts as a teacher of the status quo and agent of society. How the child feels is of little consequence. It is his behavior which must be "shaped up" so that he is not a "thorn in the side" of others. This approach is especially useful when the child feels no need for change or does not understand how to proceed.

The third approach is most compatible to us. The counselor who can be sensitive to the feelings of the involuntary child client (confusion, resentment, puzzlement, etc.) and who can communicate empathic understanding of the child's feelings and respect for his person can "get through" to him. Once this has happened, the child may choose to continue his contact with the counselor.

Although we have talked about the involuntary child client using the assumption that he is in need of help, this is not always true. Children may come involuntarily to counselors as the result of referrals from adults (teachers, parents, etc.) who themselves are the "needy" individuals. In such instances, the counselor may assume responsibility for offering his services to these "needy" adults. Again the key to success in this type of situation is the counselor's sensitivity to that adult, his genuineness in desiring to be of help, his deep respect for the person of the individual, and his ability to communicate his understanding of that individual's phenomenal world to him.

Counselor-Child Expectations

The expectations of the child and the counselor need to be essentially congruent in order for the counseling process to be maximally effective. In other words, child and counselor must be cooperative and unified in the goals and purposes that they define for the process. Mutual concurrence can be achieved and maintained if the possibility of open dialogue between counselor and child exists. In an atmosphere where incompatibilities and conflicting expectations can be explored and resolved, the counseling process can be maximally productive.

Ground Rules

Related to the clarification of goals, purposes, and expectations is the consideration of establishing counselor ground rules. Each counselor has his own personal set of ground rules from which he can function most adequately. Moreover, these ground rules may shift from client to client as well as from situation to situation. For instance, the counselor in a residential treatment center for children may allow himself more latitude in working with children and may be afforded more opportunity to work effectively by his employment setting than the counselor who works in an elementary school where greater personal limits and environmental restrictions are experienced.

We are not proposing to discuss what ground rules ought or ought not to exist, for such decisions most legitimately grow out of a combination of the child, the counselor, and the setting. We do suggest, however, that the counselor give serious thought to those behaviors which he is able and willing to accept in the counseling relationship. The child has a right to know where he stands.

The Counseling Contract

We have found it helpful to work out a flexible, tentative, and informal "contract" between ourselves and child clients. Such a "contract" grows logically out of the clarification of goals, purposes, and expectations and gives specific emphasis to key considerations. Essentially the counselor and child commit themselves to each other by agreeing to do and to be certain things in the relationship. This process is also referred to by some authors as structuring the relationship.

Case Notes

A number of different points of view are reflected by counselor answers to the question, "Case notes for what?" These answers vary from "Case notes are of no value to me or the child" to "Case notes are a very critical part of the total counseling process."

It seems obvious that case notes ought to have as their major *raison d'être* the ultimate benefit to the child client. This can be directly accomplished by the counselor's making his notes available to the child who could benefit from such a procedure (Tyler, 1961). In so doing, the child may be able to gain a better understanding of the counselor's perceptions and impressions. More frequently, however, the benefit to the child is indirect through the counselor's use of his own notes to help him be of aid to the child. In our experience we have found that notes help us recapture impressions and observations which may be crucial to the ongoing counseling relationship. Moreover, they can provide an index of change or movement in the client, movement which otherwise may be difficult to assess owing to the usual gradual and imperceptible nature of such change.

The form and content of notes also vary widely. They may consist of counselor feelings expressed in sketchy, idiosyncratic terms, client expressions of movement and change, comprehensive descriptions of the total counseling process, and a host of other focuses. Again, the criterion for inclusion should relate to the ultimate benefit of the child. Case notes have little reason for being, apart from their service to the child.

Recording

Electrical recording of counseling interviews has a long history of use (Kogan, 1950). First employed as an alternative to note-taking, it later came into use as a method for studying client behavior, counselor behavior, and their combined interactions in the counseling relationship. Today, there are few, if any, programs designed to train counselors where audio- and/or video-taping is not used as a basic technique for studying the counseling relationship.

In that the counselor is continually in the process of learning beyond his formal training, it would seem advisable to use interview recording as a learning experience. By relistening to oneself, or better still, by having some other counselor listen to and critique one's counseling sessions, the counselor on the job can continue to professionalize himself and enhance his ability in becoming an "agent of change."

Another use of tape-recorded interviews is also possible. Several studies have pointed out the significance of interview replay in enhancing client growth (Schmeding, 1962; Kagan, Krathwahl and Miller 1963; Holmes 1964; Huff, 1966). Basically, the client listens to and/or watches a replay of his last counseling session and is able to gain increased self-understanding and self-awareness from his experience. It should be noted that none of these studies has been accomplished using children as clients. It is our contention that such a practice would, however, have merit in working with child clients.

In all instances of interview tape-recording, the permission of the client should be elicited before recording is begun. Such is a common courtesy which demonstrates to the child respect for him. When resistance to being recorded is encountered, the counselor can choose to deal with the feelings of the child which underlie his resistance; he can choose to respect the wishes of the child and not record; or he can choose some combination of the two approaches. Occasionally, resistance can result from the anxiety of the counselor which is picked up by the child. Long-involved counselor explanations about the taping process may generate concerns about the process which would never have occurred if the counselor's own concern about taping had not been so manifest. Resistance to recording tends to be minimized when the counselor gives an honest but concise explanation of its intended purposes.

Evaluation

How does one go about evaluating one's effectiveness as a counselor? This question is one which has stirred up considerable debate and a wide variety of evaluation procedures. Much of this controversy and variety results from diversity in counseling goals from counselor to counselor. Moreover, there is dispute and variation relative to what constitutes the effective counseling process. In addition, the criterion for assessing counseling outcomes is also of a controversial nature. How then has evaluation taken place?

Some investigations have chosen to use criterion such as changes in psychological test scores, differences in self-report inventories, and modifications in interview content. Others have measured physiological differences accompanying the counseling process. Still others have looked at measures of change in achievement and in ability to perform certain tasks. And others have considered factors such as behavior reports from peers, teachers, parents, and the child himself as being legitimate sources of data regarding the effects of the counseling process.

It is apparent that at this point in time there is no "the way" of evaluating counseling outcomes. It would seem most defensible to use multifactor approaches similar to that of Daldrup, Hubbert and Hamilton (1968), Truax (study in progress), and others. Such an approach to the evaluation of counseling can provide a more comprehensive and theoretically bias-free picture of changes which result from effective counseling.

COUNSELOR RESPONSE CONTINUUM

Much attention has been directed to what counselors say and do in the counseling interview. Moreover, a list of constructs have been devised to describe the many different counselor response techniques which occur in counseling. Benjamin (1969) and Brammer and Shostrom (1968) have comprehensively discussed these varied response techniques; hence, they will not be presented here. We would, however, like to stress that all counselor responses are for the purpose of facilitating client self-exploration and understanding. This is accomplished only when the counselor is able to do the "right" thing at the "right" moment in the "right" tone of voice.

The Right Thing at the Right Time

Counselor responses should be interpretations of client verbal and/or nonverbal behaviors. These interpretations are intended to present the client with tentative "hunches" about the potential meanings of events in the client's life. They attempt to bring a ". . . fresh look at the behavior in the forms of different language, new frame of reference, or revised theoretical outlook." (Brammer and Shostrom, 1968, p. 268) Interpretations range, however, from being very conservative and mild where the counselor goes no further than the client has explicitly gone, to depth interpretations where the counselor assumes responsibility for introducing new concepts, relationships, and meanings which relate to unconscious and implicit client attitudes, feelings, and behaviors.

Knowledge of what to respond to is partly determined by the stage in the counseling process. In earlier interviews it may be most appropriate for the counselor to respond to attitudes toward counseling and toward the counselor. These responses early in the process will tend to be general and tentative since they are focused on developing a favorable climate for an effective working relationship. As counseling progresses, effective counselor responses will tend to become more specific and concrete, although a certain tentativeness which allows the client to reject a response is always advisable.

Perhaps the most important consideration in a discussion of counselor response is the matter of timing. In general, the type of response and the timing of it are matters of counselor judgment and are contingent upon the counselor's assessment of the client's readiness to accept them. A responsible assessment, in turn, can only be made out of the counselor's understanding of the psychodynamics of the individual client. In other words, the counselor's sensitivity to the child and to the situation will help him determine "the right thing at the right time"—that timely response which will aid the child in his development of self-awareness and understanding.

MULTIPLE COUNSELING

Multiple counseling (two counselors working with one child) is technically not an individual counseling process. However, it is more like individual counseling than like group counseling; hence, we have decided to include a brief discussion of multiple counseling in this chapter.

Although the practice and research evidence regarding the merits of this approach is limited, the precedent for such an approach dates back to Adler's work with children in the early twentieth century (1930). There seem to be two fundamental potential advantages to the multiple counseling approach. The first relates to the resolution of impasses and the second to the provision of a symbolic healthy marriage model.

All counseling relationships experience impasses when little or no client movement and growth seem to be occurring. In such instances when the impasse is prolonged and crippling to the facilitative relationship, the introduction of a second counselor into the relationship may prove helpful. This second counselor, unencumbered by the dynamics of the existing relationship, may be able to point out to the other counselor and the child the reason why the impasse has occurred and why and how it is being maintained. In so doing, the impasse can be understood, broken, and new growth potentials realized in the relationship.

A second productive use of a multiple counseling approach requires a male-female counselor team. Troubled children often have poor male and female adult models in their everyday lives. Moreover, the relationships between fathers and mothers are also frequently inadequate; hence, a multiple counseling situation where the child can learn to relate to an adult male and an adult female, and where he can observe a healthy interaction between that male and the female, can be a productive experience for the child. Such an approach, however, assumes that the adult male-female relationship has been "worked out" prior to the introduction of the child in the multiple counseling process.

COMMENT

The majority of counseling with children is conducted on a one-to-one basis. This individual approach has certain rationales and assets in facilitating child growth, and it also has certain liabilities.

The counseling process is a complex human interaction. A number of stages can be identified, although these stages are not discrete and exist for varying amounts of times with different child clients and work situations. Special consideration must be given to certain ground rule issues such as confidentiality, record-keeping, and so on, by the counselor prior to the counselor-client contact.

A variety of counselor response techniques are used in order to promote client self-awareness and understanding. The "what" and the "when" of counselor responses are largely governed by counselor judgment resulting from counselor understanding of the child.

Multiple counseling can be helpful in "breaking" impasses and in providing healthy adult male-female modeling opportunity. In general, we have tried to stress the point that child benefit should be the primary criterion for deciding "what" approach is used, "when" it is used, and "how" it is used. The individual interview may be the most beneficial approach for some children and some counselors, while group approaches or play may be the most productive for other children and other counselors. The decision is a function of the child's needs, the counselor's needs, and the requirements of the situation.

References

ADLER, A. *Guiding the Child*. New York: Greenberg, Publisher, 1930.

BEIER, E. G. "Client-centered Therapy and the Involuntary Client." *Journal of Consulting Psychology* 16 (1952):332–337.

BENJAMIN, A. *The Helping Interview*. Boston: Houghton Mifflin Company, 1969.

BRAMMER, L. M., AND SHOSTROM, E. L. *Therapeutic Psychology*. 2nd ed. Englewood Cliffs, N.J.: Prentice-Hall, Inc., 1968.

DALDRUP, R. J.; HUBBERT, ARDELLE; AND HAMILTON, J. "Evaluation of an Initial Elementary School Counseling Program." *Elementary School Guidance and Counseling* 3 (1968):118–125.

HOLMES, JUNE E. "Counselee Listening: Another Dimension of the Counseling Process." *Counselor Education and Supervision* 3 (1964):153–157.

HUFF, V. E. "The Effect of Interview Replay on Client Movement Toward Psychological Health." Unpublished doctoral dissertation, University of Arizona, 1966.

KAGAN, N.; KRATHWAHL, D. R.; AND MILLER, R. "Stimulated Recall in Therapy Using Video-tapes: A Case Study." *Journal of Counseling Psychology* 10 (1963):237–243.

KOGAN, L. S. "The Electrical Recordings of Social Casework Interviews." *Social Casework* 31 (1950):371–378.

SCHMEDING, R. W. "The Use of Playback in the Counseling Session." *Vocational Guidance Quarterly* 11 (1962):64–67.

TYLER, LEONA E. *The Work of the Counselor*. New York: Appleton-Century-Crofts, 1961.

Selected Additional Readings

ARBUCKLE, D. S. *Counseling: Philosophy, Theory and Practice*. Boston: Allyn & Bacon, Inc., 1965.

BORDIN, E. S. *Psychological Counseling*. New York: Appleton-Century-Crofts, 1968.

BOY, A. V., AND PINE, G. J. *The Counselor in the Schools*. Boston: Houghton Mifflin Company, 1968.

PARKER, BEULAH. *My Language Is Me*. New York: Basic Books, Inc., Publishers, 1962.

REIK, T. *Listening With the Third Ear*. New York: Farrar, Straus, and Company, 1949.

ROGERS, C. R. *Counseling and Psychotherapy*. Boston: Houghton Mifflin Company, 1942.

————, AND STEVENS, BARRY. *Person to Person*. Walnut Creek, Calif.: Real People Press, 1967.

WOLBERG, L. R. *The Technique of Psychotherapy*. New York: Grune & Stratton, Inc., 1954.

8

Group Counseling
with Children

Group membership and group participation are indigenous to all people of all cultures. Family groups, friendship groups, religious groups, work groups, play groups—all suggest some commonality which is a condition for membership. Although historically groups have been responsible for our social and technological advances, it is only in recent times that systematic attempts have been made to study and develop an understanding of the dynamics of the group process. One application of this study has been the evolution of group counseling.

Group counseling has been rapidly increasing in popularity as an approach to dealing with individuals who face stresses and conflicts in life with which they are unable to effectively cope. Although initially thought of as an expedient, economical, and superficial method, group counseling has been found to be more than a time-saver. Many counselors and clients now regard group counseling as a powerful therapeutic technique—one which has some unique advantages over individual counseling and one which also complements individual counseling.

Basically, group counseling is a social and psychological process in which learning about oneself and others can occur. Although group counseling can be tied to theoretical orientation, there are certain features which transcend theoretical orientation. Moreover, there are perhaps as many variations in group counseling as there are in individual counseling. Common to most, however, are such discussions of group counseling considerations as group type, the potential of the group experience, the logistics of group counseling, the group process and product, and the complexity of group interrelationships.

TYPES OF GROUPS

Groups have been variously defined and discussed along a number of dimensions. For our development, we have chosen to discuss group type from the perspective of the kind of leadership that is evidenced by the group leader. The leadership models which are presented are not found in pure types. However, for the sake of description and discussion, the following five models have been isolated.

Laissez-faire Leadership

The laissez-faire group is characterized by complete leader permissiveness. There is no guidance or control by the leader who remains uninvolved and passive. The assumption underlying such leadership is that the group members are capable of planning, initiating, and bringing any endeavor to a successful conclusion or resolution (Kemp, 1964).

Authoritarian Leadership

Under authoritarian group leadership the leader exercises control over the group members. He plans in advance the content, method, and outcomes and presents them to the group members for their consideration and acceptance. The assumptions are that the leader has greater knowledge and capability which in turn justifies the imposition of his ideas on the group membership. The rewards which he offers to the members in terms of new behaviors ensure the motivation to action of the group members (Kemp, 1964).

Democratic Leadership

In a democratic group, the leader and the group members work together cooperatively throughout the total group process. The assumptions underlying this type of leadership are that the members of the groups are capable and motivated and that they can perform more efficiently with better outcomes with the leader's assistance than without it (Kemp, 1964).

Group-Centered Leadership

The group-centered process is one in which members select the subject for discussion and carry it through to its resolution. The leader refrains from questioning and evaluation. Instead, his role is to facilitate communication and understanding among group members and to maintain a psychological climate characterized by acceptance, warmth, and with an emphasis on feelings. The assumption here is that the leader can aid the group members in making maximum use of their individual potentials. They will be able to gain insights which can be applied to their personal lives (Kemp, 1964).

Leaderless

Most recently some experimentation has begun with leaderless or self-directed groups (Berzon and Solomon, 1966; Gibb and Gibb, 1968). The self-directed group is one that meets without a professionally-trained leader present to guide and/or participate in the group interaction. However, a professional leader is readily available to join the group should the need for his services arise. The assumption underlying this approach is that untrained group members are capable of defining the purposes of the group and working toward the realization of these purposes without the benefit of a professional leader. Moreover, Berzon, Solomon, and Davis (1966) contend that the effectiveness of the self-directed group can be enhanced through the use of selected planned experiences. As a consequence, they have developed an audio-tape program which can be used with self-directed groups.

Authors' Statement

At this point the reader may be saying to himself, "Okay, all of these categories are fine, but what does it all have to do with me and with group counseling with children?" Firm answers to this question are impossible for several reasons: (1) The question is a personal one and must have a personal answer to be meaningful to the individual; and (2) Research related to group counseling with children is meager and is unable to give us much direction at this time. What limited evidence we do have, however, suggests that children as young as four years of age do respond to group counseling (Bessell, 1968); and that the group experience is most profitable when specific topics and tasks are introduced by the adult leader. After being introduced, however, the children are free to discuss and express themselves freely with the leader functioning as a facilitator of communication and understanding among and between group members.

It has been our experience that the need for leader-structured topics and tasks gradually decreases as the group members gain a fuller understanding of the intent of their group meetings, that is, to talk openly about one's feelings, ideas, and concerns. Perhaps the key to effective group leadership is best summed up by saying that the group leader must be sensitive to the needs of the group at any given point in time. If the leader's sensitivity to the needs of the group and to the individual children suggests that additional leader-structure will facilitate the group process, then it would seem only reasonable to provide such structure. The type of group leadership must be fluid and reflect the need of the moment, not some preconceived theoretical formulation. A leader may function from any one of the aforementioned models of leadership at given points in time; hence, one should not feel the need to categorize himself as a "this" or a "that." In the final analysis, it is what the group leader is and does rather than how he labels himself which makes the difference.

POTENTIALS OF THE GROUP EXPERIENCE

One of the most important products of the group experience is for individual group members to find out that their peers have problems too. The child who has felt very different and alone and somehow inferior becomes less concerned about his differences and thus better able to feel a sense of belonging when he discovers that other children have concerns which are similar to his. Often the single event of realizing that his feelings are not that unique gives the child incentive to increase his personal involvement with other children.

As a corollary to the child's reduction in feelings of being different, the group experience produces an opportunity for the child to learn and improve his social skills through modeling and experimentation. Unlike individual counseling where the interaction takes place between a counselor who is warm and acceptant and is "paid to be so" and the child client, group counseling provides a more nearly real-life situation with the child interacting with his peers. The opportunity in such a situation is to work out and learn more effective ways of relating to people through trial-and-error explorations. Although the child still has to apply his new learning when he returns to his own everyday environment from the group, the jump is not so great as having to apply new learning gained from individual counseling where much less opportunity is afforded for reality testing. The child who is having difficulty with peer relations and who can try out new ways of relating to peers in a peer group has the opportunity of getting immediate reactions regarding his new behaviors—a type of feedback which is essential to the development and maintenance of more effective behavior.

Still another dimension of the group experience which seems to benefit group members is the opportunity for vicarious learning. Children who are reticent to openly participate in the group and who have difficulty talking about their concerns can gain insights and personal understandings. From listening to and observing other members' behaviors and expressions, they can experience feelings and interactions of other children without becoming openly involved in discussion which focuses on them, their feelings, and their concerns. Evidence of the involvement of a child in the group process, even though he is silent, is often communicated nonverbally through gestures, fidgeting, or facial expressions.

The importance of being able to help someone else with problems is another potential of group counseling. It is therapeutic for one person with problems to learn to get outside of himself and to become "other-centered" rather than self-centered. This requires the group members to learn how to trust each other. It requires that each invest something of himself in other group members if sharing and mutual benefit are to occur. It requires that the group members learn how to "care" and show that they care. Moreover, the opportunity for intimate emotional identification is greater in a group experience than in individual counseling. By that we mean that the group leader and others in the group may be able to understand in an empathic way the experiences of a group member but are unable to identify with that member as if they were deeply sharing those experiences. As Haigh (1968) has said, "One outstanding value of a group experience is that there is often at least one member of the group who is personally stirred by the expression of deep feeling and who closely identifies with the person expressing the feeling." (p. 99)

Many children seem to be convinced that their worth is pretty much dependent on what they *do,* not on what they *are;* hence, they become "doing-to-please-others" oriented and tend to "tune out" or disown their own private feelings if those feelings are not compatible with what is expected. Feelings such as anger come to be regarded as unacceptable by the child because his adult models regard them so. But the child *does* feel angry—a feeling that results in depreciated self-worth because of its unacceptable nature. Group counseling provides an experience where all feelings can be expressed and where the child can learn that negative as well as positive feelings are natural and acceptable human feelings.

The group experience also provides an opportunity for children to explore their ideas and beliefs. Through a cooperative and mutual give-and-take the child is able to gain additional information and perspective on his ideas and eventually will be better able to crystallize and integrate beliefs and ideas which have personalized meaning for him.

At the same time that group counseling provides the opportunity for a child to discover that his feelings and attitudes are not unique, it provides him with the chance to develop his uniqueness. This statement may sound contradictory, and yet our experience seems to point to its validity. Perhaps an example will clarify the apparent paradox. Billy enters the group believing that his feelings of resentment for his new baby brother are bad and unique; hence, he is hesitant to discuss them. As the individual children explore their feelings about siblings, Billy realizes that other children can feel resentful of a younger brother. This reduces his feeling of uniqueness and helps him to accept those "bad" feelings he has had. As the group interaction progresses, Billy continues to explore his ideas and feelings about various things and gradually evolves his own personalized and unique way of believing and feeling. In other words, he is able to actualize his own unique self. While false differences between children are eliminated, real individual differences are encouraged and rewarded.

The foregoing discussion of potentials for the group experience has focused on positive potentials. This is not to suggest, however, that the group experience is without liability. Even though there is much professional support for group counseling, the topic still remains controversial. Such weaknesses as (1) the difficulty in using group counseling with people who know each other; (2) the potential for the rapid stripping of defenses; (3) the slowness of the group process; (4) the superficiality of the process; (5) the inability of the counselor to deal with all of the feelings and interactions among group members; and (6) the potential dependency of the group member upon the group have been cited by various critics of group counseling. It should be noted, however, that the majority of the objections stem from personal bias and not from empirical evidence. The question of the relative merits and limitations of group counseling remains yet to be subjected to rigorous objective evaluation.

LOGISTICS OF GROUP COUNSELING

A number of factors must be considered prior to the formulation of a group. Such considerations as purposes, group composition, group size, group duration, and physical setting are basic to the establishment of a productive group.

Group Purposes

Generally speaking, counseling groups exist in order to benefit the group members in some way. Such a loose statement, however, obviously applies to a host of other experiences also; hence, more specific purposes for the group counseling experience must be defined.

Dreikurs and Sonstegard (Dinkmeyer, 1968) have defined the purposes of group counseling as consisting of "(1) the establishment and maintenance of proper relationships; (2) an examination of the purpose of each group member's action or behavior; (3) revealing to each student the goals he is pursuing, called psychological disclosure; and (4) a re-orientation and direction." (pp. 284–285) They suggest that the counselor must establish himself as the leader of the group. However, the group atmosphere must be democratic, and an attitude of mutual respect must prevail between and among the members of an effective group. They emphasize the importance of firm but kind leadership.

They also stress the need for the counselor to be able to identify the "private logic" of each child's behavior in the group as he or she interacts in the group. By so doing, the "private logic" can become public and the group can aid the individual youngster in gaining insight into his behavior and in reexamining his behavioral goals. From such reassessment the child can redirect his behavior in ways that are more satisfying.

Seeman (1963) from a somewhat different framework sees the purpose of the group experience as one of setting up optimal conditions for learning. He sees the productive group as providing a safe environment, an understanding environment, a caring environment, a participating environment, and an approving environment for the child.

The purposes defined for more behaviorally-oriented group counseling tend to be quite specific. For example, shy children who have a difficult time talking to their teachers might comprise a group. The purpose and focus of the counselor would be to increase each child's ability to talk to his teacher. This might be accomplished in a variety of ways such as role-playing and systematic desensitization. However, the major emphasis would constantly be directed toward that specific goal.

What we have attempted to point out in this brief discussion of purposes is that the assumptions about human behavior that the counselor holds dictate in part the purposes which the group will have. For that matter, counselor beliefs and biases tend in part to account for differences of opinion with respect to group size, composition, duration, and ground rules. This is not to suggest that the current diversity is unwarranted. It often underscores the variety and the uniqueness of each author's human experience and points out the need for additional research.

Group Composition

The question of group composition in counseling with children seems also to reflect more counselor speculation than empirical validation. Ohlsen's experience (Dinkmeyer, 1968) suggests, "children who seem to profit most from group counseling include shy children, children who have difficulty participating in class discussion, children who want to make friends, and children who have better ability than their performance indicates." (p. 289) He is quick to point out, however, the inadvisability of creating groups comprised of a single client type. He feels that balanced groups are more to be desired. Frank and Zilback (1968) also emphasize the need for group balance in comprising counseling groups for children.

Bessell (1968) in his discussion of his group experiences with preschool and early-elementary-school-aged children implies the use of heterogeneous grouping. He seems to assume that a high degree of homogeneity exists in any group of children regardless of the uniqueness of their life styles and experiences. "Every child wants to succeed; every child has the same questions when he starts to school: 'Am I safe? Can I cope with this? Will I be accepted?' " (p. 34) Ginott (1961) from his experiences as a child therapist, however, cautions against group formation on the basis of an accidental conglomeration. He contends that the composition of a group ". . . must be carefully planned and balanced for the impact of members upon each other." (p. 35)

Our experience with groups of elementary-school-aged children tends to place a somewhat different focus on the question of homogeneity and heterogeneity. Similar to Bessell, we have found that so-called heterogeneous groups do in fact have a great deal in common—commonalities which engender communication and cohesiveness. Homogeneous groups on the other hand are characterized by a great deal of diversity apart from the common symptoms or complaints of the group participants. Perhaps an important distinction to be made between homogeneous and heterogeneous group preferences is closely associated with counselor comfort.

Our experience again suggests that groups which have a balance of client types tend to be easier, especially in the initial stages of counseling, for us to work with. Children with similar problems, such as nonassertiveness or aggressiveness, require more counselor energy and investment in the initial stages of the counseling process. Once cohesion and mutuality have developed in a group, however, the importance of the initial composition of that group seems to be considerably diminished.

In summary, we would like to emphasize the importance of the counselor's doing what he believes he does best to benefit children. He must have the opportunity to work with those children whom he feels reasonably certain he can help. If this involves homogeneous grouping, then his potential impact on children will be diminished with other than a homogeneous group of children.

Group Size

Technically, a group can be of any size from three on up. Bessell (1968) in working with children ranging in age from four years to six years has found that an ideal group is made up of ten children. "Smaller groups offer the children less opportunity to discover the large range of individual differences in human reactions while larger groups demand too much patience from the children while they wait to hold the center of attention." (p. 35)

On the basis of their experiences at the Ventura School for Girls, Glasser and Iverson (1966) have advocated the use of Large Group Counseling (L.G.C.) in working with delinquent girls. Basically, the school is designed for girls ranging in age from eight to twenty-one who have long histories of "irresponsible" behavior. Glasser and Iverson contend that such behavior can best be modified through the use of a therapeutic living community with L.G.C. sessions held five days per week for all the residents and the staff of that community. This amounts to a total of sixty or more people in each session.

Ohlsen and Gazda (1965) and Combs, Cohn, Gibrian, and Sniffen (1963) have suggested that group size should depend upon the age and maturity of the children involved. Since younger children are neither as verbal nor as group-oriented as older children, the younger children seem to be afforded a greater opportunity to interact with their peers when the group consists of four to six children. Older children are better able to profit from a somewhat larger group of six to eight members.

It should be pointed out that the preceding comments on the size of a productive child counseling group reflect different theoretical orientations, different clientele, and, at least to some degree, different methods. However, each of these approaches has the common purpose of promoting more acceptable child behaviors through the use of the group process. The diversity in opinion relative to group size once again underscores the need for research in the area. At this stage in the evolution of group counseling with children, few definite statements can be made. However, it seems appropriate to suggest that group size should be determined in part by (1) the opportunity that is afforded each member to talk, to listen, and to be inactive if he wishes; (2) the ability of the counselor to be aware of and deal effectively with the number of interactions which occur in the group; and (3) the composition of the group (the more antisocial the child, the smaller the group).

Group Duration

Diversity also exists with regard to the number of sessions per week, the length of each session, and the desirability of setting a definite termination date in working with child counseling groups.

Ohlsen (1968) has recommended that younger children be treated in groups which meet for forty to forty-five minutes three times per week. Combs, Cohn, Gibrian and Sniffen, however, suggest that group counseling with children is most effective "on a one-period-per-week basis running approximately fifteen to twenty weeks." (Dinkmeyer, 1968, p. 301) They also emphasize the need to avoid interruptions of the group meetings caused by vacations and holidays, pointing out that consistency especially in the early stages of the group process is important in developing a cohesive "working" group.

Other authors have suggested daily group meetings, twice-weekly meetings, group meetings lasting approximately thirty minutes, group meetings lasting up to seventy minutes. Once again this diversity of opinion suggests the need for empirical data from which we can gain some directions for effectively working with child counseling groups. Until definitive data is available, the experience of others at least provides a starting point for the beginning counselor—a starting point from which he can experiment and discover what works for him.

Physical Setting

Group counseling can be carried on in most facilities large enough to comfortably accommodate six to ten children; that is, children should be close enough together so they can readily communicate with all the other group members but not so close that they are tempted to diversionary activity (Combs, Cohn, Gibrian and Sniffen, 1963).

It is most advantageous to have group members sitting in a circle so that each member is able to have direct visual contact with the other members. Frequently, group counseling is conducted around a table. It is our experience that such a procedure has advantages and disadvantages. Among the advantages is the security which sitting around a table provides to the group members. However, the opportunity is limited for the group leader and other group members to be aware of nonverbal behaviors which may be very important but which are cut off from view by the table.

A most important setting consideration, however, is the need for privacy —both from being seen and heard by others and from seeing and hearing others. Although the question of confidentiality becomes a function of group trust in group counseling, each group member should have the assurance that his thoughts and feelings are not for the ears of the whole world. A soundproof and private meeting room can in part provide such assurance.

Ground Rules

A wide variety of ground rules have been proposed for group counseling experiences with children. Combs, Cohn, Gibrian, and Sniffen (1963) have suggested eight principles which promote an effective group counseling experience. They suggest that the children should know that group counseling is (1) an experience in which everyone must cooperate to help each other; (2) an opportunity for children to look at their problems honestly; (3) an opportunity to really listen to and try to understand other children; (4) an experience in which members should stick to the topic and not get sidetracked; (5) a chance to say whatever one wants to say; (6) an opportunity to let other children know that their feelings are not unique; (7) a place to develop your own solutions to problems with the help of others; and (8) an experience in which members must trust each other in order to benefit from the experience.

An additional ground rule which has been useful to us is the establishment of a "contract" with group members. In our work with children, we have requested each child participating in a group experience to make a commitment to attend regularly for four times. At the end of this period of time, he then reassesses his desire to continue with the group. We have used this technique in order to reduce the number of dropouts which might occur before the group really gets "off the ground." A comprehensive discussion of the initial stages of the group counseling process follows and will provide the reader with a better understanding of the usefulness of the "contract" idea.

INTRODUCING THE GROUP EXPERIENCE

Frank (1967) has discussed the use of "role-induction" as a device for preparing individuals for a counseling experience. The purpose of this technique is to give clients appropriate expectations about counseling which facilitate the counseling process and its outcome. We propose the use of a similar procedure in introducing the individual child to group counseling. Through the use of an audio or video tape recording of a group counseling session where group members are interacting openly and freely, the child can gain an understanding of what to expect and how he might act in a group experience; hence, he can enter the group expecting to build trust and honesty with other group members.

A second but somewhat similar approach to introducing the child to the group experience has been used by the authors. A tape recording was made in which a role-played client and a counselor discussed a wide variety of questions which a client might have regarding group counseling. Such questions as "What does the group do?" "What do people talk about?" "What is the leader's role?" "How confidential is this situation?" are discussed. By listening to this tape recording, the child who is about to enter a group is provided the opportunity of gaining understanding of group purposes. In addition, the child is made aware that the counselor expects him to have reservations, questions, and some confusion about the group experience, and thus the child's anxiety is reduced.

BEGINNING THE GROUP

"Well begun is half done" is a proverb which has meaning for the initiation of a counseling group. From the very beginning, the counselor sets the pattern and tone for the group. Most clients are suspicious and uncertain at first and are inclined to listen and watch rather than participate. They look to the counselor for direction and structure. If he is uncertain, members may lose confidence in him. If he is overbearing, they may become dependent or hostile. The counselor, however, at the same time realizes that only through participation will group members benefit. Consequently, he assumes the task of leading members into voluntary interaction as quickly and sensitively as possible.

Typically, the counselor begins by greeting the group members and by asking them to give their names and expectations for the group experience. He may also suggest icebreaker-type experiences through which group members can more quickly get to know one another (Schutz, 1968). He may then follow with a statement of his own intentions and expectations, leading into a discussion of ground rules. During this introductory phase and following it and frequently during the early sessions, periods of silence will occur. How the counselor handles these silent periods will have considerable bearing on the development of an effective group process.

PHASES IN GROUP COUNSELING

Any particular session may vary according to the demands of the group members or it may follow a pattern. In any event, certain natural phases through which most groups go are identifiable:

1. There is a phase of hesitant participation with individuals operating as separate units. Members are self-centered and are testing out the situation and the group leader. Johnson (1963) suggests that group members compete for the favor and acceptance of the counselor in this initial phase. The members express attitudes of fear and suspicion and tend to keep the focus of discussion on "safe" topics; hence, operations in the group are at a surface level with members being polite and attempting to favorably impress each other. Evolving from this superficial initial stage are the beginnings of mutual cooperation and increased closeness among group members. The closeness, however, increases the anxiety of group members since increased closeness means the exposure of real feelings.
2. The second phase emerges imperceptibly from the first and is characterized by an increase in the exposure of real feelings and other-centeredness. Individual members begin to discuss sensitive matters, including their own feelings and behaviors, their relationships with others, and their own group behaviors. During this phase, individual members begin to feel that other members are like themselves and that there is greater similarity in feelings and thoughts among group members than had been expected. This reduces feelings of "aloneness" and helps to overcome the need for defensive behavior on the part of the various group members. Members are also provided the opportunity of extending themselves to help other group members which adds to their feelings of adequacy and usefulness. A cooperative, cohesive "working" group gradually develops.

3. In the third phase of the group process, solutions and reorientation develop. Feelings of freedom and interdependence evolve and strengthen, and group members begin to take action—action which receives support and encouragement from the group. Reports of behavior changes are made by group members, and the results of these changes discussed. When changes have not resulted in the outcomes desired, alternative behaviors are evolved in the group. These alternatives are then "field tested" and subsequently reported on to the group. During this phase, individual members often come to an "aha" moment when they are able to relate the experiences of other group members to their own lives. This moment of insight can lead to changed behavior. The feelings between and among group members deepen as members share varying degrees of responsibility for each other's growth and development.

4. Termination of the group counseling experience is in part dependent upon the ground rules established for the group. Generally, when the counselor becomes aware of desire for closure on the part of the group, he should begin to taper off the group experience. During this tapering-off period, the counselor should assist group members in summarizing and clarifying the problems discussed and solutions explored (Dinkmeyer, 1968). He should also emphasize that the group can resume its activity if members so desire.

In summary, the group process from its inception to its termination is characterized by movement—from individual self-centeredness to group centeredness; from defensiveness to openness among members; from feelings of uniqueness to feelings of commonality; from intellectual "safe" topics to deep personal communication; from competition to cooperation and mutual help. Above all, respect for group members and group decisions must be upheld.

GROUP INTERRELATIONSHIPS

Counselor Role

As was suggested earlier, the counselor is largely responsible for getting the group "off the ground." In addition, he is responsible for facilitating communication between and among group members throughout the course of the group experience. In order to accomplish the latter responsibility, it becomes necessary for the counselor to be aware of the verbal and nonverbal communications. Quite obviously this is a large task. In a group of eight (including the counselor) there is the potential for more than 200 different relationships between and among group members; hence, the need for the counselor to be a highly sensitized and perceptive individual is emphasized. Due to the complexity of these relationships, co-counselors are often found to be advantageous in working effectively with groups.

In the early phase of the group experience the counselor also has the responsibility of being a model of the products of the group experience which were discussed earlier, that is, other-centeredness, openness, cooperativeness, genuineness, and so forth. In other words, through the counselor's actions, verbal and nonverbal, group members can gain an understanding of how to listen to others, what to listen to, and how to express themselves more adequately.

Group Member's Role

In small groups it is possible to identify characteristic patterns of behavior for individual members and to relate these roles to the functioning of the group. This is not to suggest that an individual group member assumes a role and continues to function in that role throughout the group experience. Roles continually change in group counseling and shift from individual to individual. For example, a particular member may at one time assume the "giving information" role, at another time the "tension release" role, and at a third time the role of antagonist in a group (Bales, 1950). (For a comprehensive discussion of specific roles assumed by members in group counseling the reader is referred to Kemp [1964].)

More generally, group members are participants in a communication process. This process pertains to both articulated words and thoughts and to unvocalized feelings and attitudes which are manifest in behaviors. Communication is also concerned with the intentions of the communicator and the impressions received by the one to whom the communication is directed. Difficulties in communication often result from poor quality listening.

Listening to others is of great importance in the group process. Although it is regarded as a simple task, listening takes time, effort, and skill if one is to seriously attend to and attempt to understand the speaker. Many of our everyday listening experiences, when examined more carefully, are really tolerant periods of silence when the "listener" is waiting for the speaker to stop speaking so he, the "listener," can say what he wants to say. Little attempt is made to understand the speaker's communication.

At another level, "listening" involves attending to the words of the speaker and attempting to understand the *content* of what is being communicated. This type of "listening" involves more effort and attention on the listener's part than the "waiting-for-the-speaker-to-stop-speaking" type. This is also the type of communication which characterizes our better relationships with others. However, a third level of "listening" involves the most meaning-ful communication between people.

This third level of "listening" involves attending to and understanding the *meaning* of the speaker's communications. In other words, the listener tunes in on the feelings and attitudes which are implicit in the communicator's communication as well as the content of the words expressed. It is toward this level of listening and communication among group members that group counseling experiences move as cohesion and mutual cooperation evolve. Fitts (1965) has stated that group counseling is conducted by the group for the group. This becomes increasingly true as the group members develop their abilities to listen and understand each other and to communicate this understanding.

SPECIALIZED GROUP EXPERIENCES

Considerable attention has been directed in recent years to specialized uses of the group process. Such procedures as family group counseling, role-playing, sociometric ratings, sociodrama, group play, and sensitivity groups have been advanced as effective direct child treatment procedures. Indirect effects on children can be accomplished through the use of parent and teacher groups.

Family Group Counseling

Dreikurs (1967) is credited with introducing family group counseling to America. Recognizing the impact of the family group on the child's be-havior and vice versa, Dreikurs and others have suggested treatment of the entire family constellation. By so doing, faulty communication and disrup-tive behaviors can be observed and dealt with in the actual situation in which they occur. Furthermore, analysis of the various roles played by family mem-bers can be made, and awareness of the needs, rights, and responsibilities of each family member developed. In addition, the individual family members in the freedom of the group counseling situation can become consciously aware of the impact that each member has on each other member and can work toward the resolution of differences and evolution of family cooperation.

Groups of family groups in counseling have also been effectively used in promoting a healthier family environment. The assumption underlying this method is that members of one family will be able to gain insights into their behaviors by observing and discussing with other families.

It is our belief and experience that family counseling, when feasible, can often be the preferred approach to helping children develop more adaptive behaviors. Moreover, we predict that in the future the child counselor will be called upon with increasing frequency to work with families.

Role-Playing

Moreno is the recognized author of role-playing approaches in working with groups (Corsini, 1957). Basically, the technique involves acting out one's problems with group members assuming the roles of significant others in the life of the main person in a simulated situation. Such an approach is particularly "effective when the child has difficulty describing a situation or conveying to others how he feels about it; or when he wants to obtain others' reactions to his way of meeting a situation; or when he feels he needs practice in meeting a situation." (Ohlsen, 1964, p. 174) Often when a child is afforded the opportunity of describing a troublesome situation and the people involved in that situation, he gains understanding of himself and of the situation even before the role-playing experience itself.

Sociometric Ratings

Sociometric ratings are techniques used to assess the relative standing or distance between people on a given dimension. Group members are typically asked to indicate the names of other group members with whom they would prefer to work closely on some activity. By tallying the number of times each person is chosen, an assessment of the relationships which exist in the group can be made. By so doing, individuals who are most in need of help can be identified, and provisions for helping initiated.

Sociometric devices can also be used to give the person being rated an objective picture of how other group members see him. If the feedback from other members is fairly consistent with the child's own self-image, the child will not need to feel threatened. When, however, differences between the child's self-concept and the opinion of others occur, the child may feel considerable threat. For this reason, it is desirable for the group to be available to help the individual child reconcile the disparity between his own perceptions and those of the group after the sociometric ratings are made.

Sociodrama

Similar to role-playing, sociodrama simulates a real-life drama. However, unlike role-playing where the clients are participants in the role-played situation, the clients who are to benefit from sociodrama do so as spectators. The real-life situation is enacted in front of an audience and can be effectively accomplished through the use of puppetry when working with children. The assumption underlying this approach is that "spectators" can gain personal meaning and insight from viewing situations which enact personal conflicts or difficulties of individual children.

Group Play

Group play is especially useful in working with groups of younger children who have minimal verbal skills. Although our experience suggests that children of primary school age are capable of putting their feelings in words, the use of play media can be useful in facilitating the child's communication. Materials such as doll families, hand puppets, finger paints, clay, and others can be used effectively by children to act out their feelings. The reader is referred to chapter 9 for a more comprehensive discussion of play and the use of media.

Sensitivity Groups

Much attention has been given in recent years to the use of a variety of sensory awakening and sensitivity experiences in promoting more fulfilling and effective living for the so-called "normal" individual (Bradford, Gibb & Benne, 1964; Otto and Mann, 1968; Schutz, 1968). Although the majority of this attention has been directed toward adolescent and adult populations, increasing emphasis is being turned to the elementary-school-aged child (Gibb, 1964). Meeks (1965) in the address to the American Personnel and Guidance Association's National Convention implied the need for such a direction when she stated:

If the youngster is going to learn about himself, he's got to start early. I like to think of him using the counseling, especially in groups, to learn to listen to other people as a counselor does. I believe that we can actually teach youngsters to listen with the counselor's ear, and mind, and heart. I think we could change the face of human relations in this great country of ours with two generations of helping youngsters through counseling to become the kind of person who tries to understand what the other fellow is saying. (p. 6)

It should be noted that this direction suggests the need for those children who are making a "normal" adjustment to life to have the opportunity to learn to be more sensitive to others. The hope for our future rests in the hands of our children. If we can make the "well" ones "weller" by the use of experiences designed to increase communication and understanding between and among people, our future can be a brighter, more optimistic one indeed.

Bessell (1968) has made application of group process in aiding "normally functioning" children to maximize their human potentials.

Through the use of a specially guided group encounter experience, children as young as prekindergarten age learn to express their feelings and increase their sensitivity to one another and hence to people in their larger everyday environments.

Less formal and public sensitivity experiences are being provided in selected elementary school settings. Experiences which range from children providing honest feedback to each other about their respective perceptions to heterogeneous groups of children, teachers, and parents openly interacting together for the purposes of increased mutual communication and understanding are being experimented with (Rogers, 1969).

Much of the alienation that is being experienced in our society is in part a result of a general cultural fear of emotion and interpersonal intimacy. We believe that this trend can be arrested and reversed. The sensitivity group experience with children in which they can learn to trust and share feelings seems to be one very legitimate point at which to attempt to reverse the current trend.

APPLYING GROUP TECHNIQUES IN THE CLASSROOM

Much of what has been discussed in this chapter has application to working with the group process in the classroom. The differences between the group counseling situation and the classroom are more a matter of degree than of basic essentials. Important to the group counseling experience is the sensitivity of the counselor to the needs of the children at any given moment. Similarly, the classroom teacher should "tune-in" as much as possible to the feelings and attitudes of the children in the classroom from moment to moment. It hardly seems necessary to point out that the arithmetic lesson for the day may mean little to Mary if she is upset upon her arrival at school by the argument which occurred between her parents at the breakfast table. Interest in the individual child can be expressed by the teacher's being sensitive to the child's immediate need. Techniques such as role-playing, group discussion, or sociodrama can be used to effectively help the child cope with the troublesome feelings of the moment.

Basically, the teacher's responsibility in the area of guidance is to listen to and try to understand individual children. Communication of respect and concern for the child can be accomplished by doing so. Special times can be set aside by the interested teacher for children to air topics of particular concern to them, affording them an opportunity to check out ideas and share feelings with peers. Knowledge of and attunement to the feelings of the child are basic to understanding the child and in aiding him toward the attainment of his unique potentials.

COMMENT

In this chapter the authors have attempted to focus the reader's attention on a number of issues. Among these issues are the following which seem to be of major consequence: (1) group counseling is as yet a controversial treatment process although its use is rapidly increasing; (2) a wide variety of approaches, techniques, and considerations germane to the group composition, size, and function exist; (3) the group experience has unique potentials in comparison to individual counseling; (4) many of the rationales for group counseling with children reflect more personal bias than empirical validation; and (5) due to the lack of definitive evidence at this time, the counselor must use his own unique experience as well as that of others in arriving at meaningful answers to the many questions which relate to group counseling with elementary-school-aged children.

REFERENCES

BALES, R. F. *Interaction Process Analysis.* Reading, Mass.: Addison-Wesley Publishing Co., Inc., 1950.

BERZON, BETTY, AND SOLOMON, L. "The Self-Directed Therapeutic Group: Three Studies." *Journal Counseling Psychology* 13 (1966):491–497.

————, AND DAVIS, D. P. "A Personal Growth Program for Self-Directed Groups," Paper read at American Psychological Association, New York, 1966.

BESSELL, H. "The Content is the Medium: The Confidence the Message." *Psychology Today* 1 (1968):32–35.

BRADFORD, L. P.; GIBB, J. R.; AND BENNE, K. D. *T-Group Theory and Laboratory Method.* New York: John Wiley & Sons, Inc., 1964.

COMBS, C. F.; COHN, B.; GIBRIAN, E. J.; AND SNIFFEN, A. M. "Group Counseling: Applying the Technique." *The School Counselor* 11 (1963):12–18.

CORSINI, R. *Methods of Group Psychotherapy.* Chicago: William James Press, 1957.

DINKMEYER, D. C., ed. *Guidance and Counseling in the Elementary School.* New York: Holt, Rinehart & Winston, Inc., 1968.

DREIKURS, R. "Counseling for Family Adjustment." *Psychodynamics, Psychotherapy and Counseling.* Chicago: Alfred Adler Institute, 1967, pp. 248–262.

FARNSWORTH, D. *Psychiatry, Education, and the Young Adult.* Springfield, Ill.: Charles C Thomas, Publisher, 1966.

FITTS, W. H. *The Experience of Psychotherapy.* New York: D. Van Nostrand Co., Inc., 1965.

FRANK, J. D. "How Do Emotionally Sick People Get Better?" *Mental Health Program Reports.* Bethesda, Md.: National Institute of Mental Health, 1967, pp. 205–216.

FRANK, MARGARET G., AND ZILBACK, JOAN. "Current Trends in Group Therapy with Children." *International Journal of Group Psychotherapy* 18 (1968):447–460.

GIBB, J. R. "Climate for Trust Formation." In *T-Group Theory and Laboratory Method,* edited by L. P. Bradford, J. R. Gibb, and K. D. Benne. New York: John Wiley & Sons, Inc., 1964.

————, AND GIBB, LORRAINE M. "Leaderless Groups: Growth-centered Values and Potentialities." In *Ways of Growth,* edited by H. A. Otto and J. Mann. New York: Grossman Publishers, Inc., 1968, pp. 101–114.

GINOTT, H. G. *Group Psychotherapy With Children.* New York: McGraw-Hill, Inc., 1961.

GLASSER, W., AND IVERSON, N. *Reality Therapy in Large Group Counseling.* Los Angeles: Reality Press, 1966.

HAIGH, G. "The Residential Basic Encounter Groups." In *Ways of Growth,* edited by H. A. Otto and J. Mann. New York: Grossman Publishers, Inc., 1968, pp. 86–100.

JOHNSON, J. A. *Group Therapy: A Practical Approach.* New York: McGraw-Hill, Inc., 1963.

KEMP, C. G., ed. *Prespectives on the Group Process.* Boston: Houghton Mifflin Company, 1964.

MEEKS, ANNA R. "Consensus of Thinking in Elementary School Guidance." Paper read at American Personnel and Guidance Association, Minneapolis, 1965.

OHLSEN, M. M. *Guidance Services in the Modern School.* New York: Harcourt, Brace & World, Inc., 1964.

————. "Counseling Children in Groups." *The School Counselor* 15 (1968):343–349.

————, AND GAZDA, G. M. "Counseling Underachieving Bright Pupils." *Education* 86 (1965):78–81.

OTTO, H. A., AND MANN, J., eds. *Ways of Growth.* New York: Grossman Publishers, Inc., 1968.

ROGERS, C. R. *Freedom to Learn.* Columbus, Ohio: Charles E. Merrill Publishing Co., 1969.

SEEMAN, J. *Motivations to High Achievement.* Guidance Summer Lecture at University of Colorado, 1963.

SCHUTZ, W. C. *Joy: Expanding Human Awareness.* New York: Grove Press, Inc., 1968.

SELECTED ADDITIONAL READINGS

BERNE, E. *Principles of Group Treatment.* New York: Oxford University Press, Inc., 1966.

BERGIN, A. E., AND GARFIELD, S. L. eds. *Handbook of Psychotherapy and Behavior Change.* New York: John Wiley & Sons, Inc., 1969.

BION, W. R. *Experience in Groups.* New York: Basic Books, Inc., Publishers, 1961.

BUGENTAL, J. F. T., ed. *Challenges of Humanistic Psychology.* New York: McGraw-Hill, Inc., 1967.

DREIKURS, R.; CORSINI, R.; LOWE, R.; AND SONSTEGARD, M. *Alderian Family Counseling.* Eugene, Oregon: University of Oregon Press, 1959.

FARSON, R. E., ed. *Science and Human Affairs.* Palo Alto: Science and Behavior Books, 1965.

GAZDA, G. M., ed. *Basic Approaches to Group Psychotherapy and Group Counseling.* Springfield, Ill.: Charles C Thomas, Publisher, 1968.

————, ed. *Innovations to Group Psychotherapy.* Springfield, Ill.: Charles C Thomas, Publisher, 1968.

GIBB, J. R., AND GIBB, LORRAINE M. "Role Freedom in a TORI Group." In *Encounter: A Primer on Sensitivity Training and Encounter Groups,* edited by A. Burton. San Francisco: Jossey-Bass, Inc., Publishers, 1969.

GREENBERG, I. A. *Psychodrama and Audience Attitude Change.* Beverly Hills: Behavioral Studies Press, 1968.

HANSEN, J. C.; NILAND, T. M.; AND ZANI, L. P. "Model Reinforcement in Group Counseling With Elementary School Children." *Personnel and Guidance Journal* 47 (1969):741–744.

MACLENNAN, BERYCE W., AND FELSENFELD, NAOMI. *Group Counseling and Psychotherapy With Adolescents.* New York: Columbia University Press, 1968.

MAHLER, C. A. *Group Counseling in the Schools.* Boston: Houghton Mifflin Company, 1969.

MAYER, G. R.; ROHEN, T. M.; AND WHITLEY, A. D. "Group Counseling With Children: A Cognitive-Behavioral Approach." *Journal of Counseling Psychology* 16 (1969):142–149.

MOWRER, O. H. *The New Group Therapy.* New York: D. Van Nostrand Co., Inc. 1964.

MURO, J. J., AND FREEMAN, S. L. eds. *Readings in Group Counseling.* Scranton, Pa.: International Textbook Company, 1968.

SATIR, VIRGINIA, *Conjoint Family Therapy.* Palo Alto: Science and Behavior Books, 1966.

SHEPHERD, C. R. *Small Groups: Some Sociological Perspectives.* San Francisco: Chandler Publishing Company, 1964.

YABLONSKY, L. *Synanon: The Tunnel Back.* Baltimore: Penguin Books, Inc., 1967.

9

Play and the Use of Media

It may seem unusual at first glance to find a chapter entitled "Play and the Use of Media" in a book dealing with counseling of elementary-school-aged children. The authors, however, feel that the medium of play can be successfully used in working with children in many settings, including elementary schools, head-start programs, and others. In fact, such a medium may indeed be mandatory if significant communication is to take place between the child and the counselor.

Play is a child's natural method of self-expression and communication. A vast majority of the young child's free time is spent in play through which he explores roles, refines skills, develops social relationships, and acts out his feelings. In other words, play is the child's language and his play materials and objects become the words by which he communicates himself to others. As a child enters school, progresses through the grades, and becomes increasingly skilled in the use of formal language, his need to use play as a means of communication and self-expression is diminished. However, until the child reaches a level of facility and sophistication with verbal communication that will allow him to express himself fully and effectively to others, it would seem only appropriate to supplement talking with play so that the opportunity for maximal self-expression and communication can be realized. As has been suggested by Nelson (Dinkmeyer, 1968), to limit the young child strictly to verbal modes of communication is to make an unrealistic demand upon him. Having to rely on talking through his feelings and attitudes may indeed handicap him from being able to communicate in the most effective and meaningful way available to him. Moreover, effective communication necessitates that both parties involved in the process participate on essentially the same level; hence, it would seem that the counselor would have the responsibility for participating at the child's level, rather than expecting the child to move out of his own natural mode of communication and into the more foreign communication system of the counselor. Since counseling is a process which at least in part emphasizes the need for significant communication between the child and the counselor, it would seem appropriate for the counselor to employ those procedures which have the potential for enabling the child to engage in significant communication and self-expression. We believe that play media can be used with children to facilitate such communication.

Play, then, is another tool which can be used to enhance the counseling relationship. The carpenter who attempts to construct a building with only a hammer and saw is obviously handicapped when compared to a similarly skilled craftsman with a wide variety of tools. By the same token, we most certainly do not advocate the exclusive use of one therapeutic tool by the counselor as he seeks to effect changes in the behavior of children. We do suggest that the counselor will be most likely to make a significant difference in the lives of children when he is able to use a variety of tools. Moreover, no one can dictate when and where a particular tool will prove to be most effective for a given counselor. Such decisions must emerge from the experience of the individual counselor. Only through his creative use of various therapeutic tools can he realize his fullest potential as a helping person.

We recognize that to advocate the availability of a specially equipped playroom staffed by a highly trained therapist in elementary schools is unrealistic in many settings. Although such a facility might be ideal, it by no means is necessary. A child's communication may be facilitated by as little as a hastily constructed hand puppet, a stick used as a gun, finger paints, or a chunk of malleable clay. The vehicle of play then becomes an adjunct to other methods of communication and a means through which the child can share his world with other people.

THE DEVELOPMENT OF PLAY

Play as a technique for understanding and aiding children can be traced to Rousseau and the eighteenth century. In advocating that the teacher enter into the play of the child at the child's level in order to "reach" the child, he formulated a principle which was later to be the foundation of some modern approaches to child therapy. Rosseau's references to play, however, were directed toward education and training purposes rather than toward current investigative and therapeutic uses of play (Rousseau, 1957).

The first use of play in a therapeutic context is attributed to Freud (1955). His treatment of little Hans, a five-year-old boy with a violent fear of horses, was based in large part upon observations collected and submitted to Freud by the boy's parents. Using these observations and other data, Freud concluded that Hans' play with toy horses and his fantasies about being a horse were symptomatic of his anxieties about himself and his fears about his father, mother, and the new baby. From this formulation, Freud was able to offer therapeutic advice to the parents. Freud's treatment had the objective of aiding Hans in the development of more mature and adult thought and behavior patterns. Such an approach was somewhat different from meeting the child on his own ground as had been advocated by Rousseau (Freud, 1955).

Prior to the early 1920s, child therapy had been largely unsuccessful. The application of adult techniques of free association, dream analysis, verbalization of anxiety, exploration of the past, and analysis of developmental stages were at best difficult, if not impossible, with most children. As a result, little therapeutic assistance was available for children until Melanie Klein in the early 1920s evolved her psychological principles of child analysis (1955). During the same decade, Anna Freud, daughter of Sigmund, published her formulation of the classical Freudian theory as applied to child therapy (Freud, 1946). Klein developed the so-called play technique of child analysis as a method which would give direct access to the child's unconscious. The spontaneous play activity of the child during the therapy hour was substituted for free association and was considered to be the symbolic expression of the child's fears, conflicts, wishes, pleasures, and preoccupations. Moreover, this play activity was given symbolic interpretation by the therapist. The technique was later borrowed and adapted for use by therapists with other than the analytic orientation of Klein. The technique came to be known as play therapy.

EXPLANATIONS OF PLAY

A variety of explanations have been advanced for the meaning of play. By some it is considered to be a creative act; and by others it is thought to be regressive behavior. Some view play as attempts at age enhancement, while others interpret it as a desire to escape reality. Some believe that play represents the child's experimentation with various roles; and yet others see play as an expression of unconscious conflicts, desires, and/or wishes. Regardless of the explanation, however, play is regarded as a means of tapping more fully and directly the child's communication and his unique world. Moreover, all therapists seem to work with some concentration directed toward the meaning, the form, or the process of play.

Meaning in Play

Anna Freud, Melanie Klein, and their disciples have focused on the meaning of the child's play. From this focus, the role of the therapist is to analyze the child's play using the Freudian model and then to interpret the meaning of his play to the child. Ostensibly, the child's unconscious desires, conflicts, and feelings are tapped in his spontaneous play activities, and the therapist explains what the behavior means and why it is being engaged in. By explaining the behavior dynamics of the child to the child it is assumed that the child increases in his understanding of himself and is able to behave differently as a result of his new knowledge about himself. The play therapy experience is one containing the following elements:

1. Careful observation of the child's play behavior by the therapist.
2. Investment of "meaning," often of a symbolic nature, into the child's play behavior by the therapist—"meaning" arrived at through inferences drawn from the observed behavior.
3. Interpretation of the "meaning" of the child's play behavior to the child.
4. Increased understanding (insight) of his behavior on the child's part.
5. Use of this new understanding in developing more adaptive ways of meeting the world.

The following paragraphs describe Mary's behavior. A symbolic interpretation is given to the child's play behavior by the therapist.

Seven-year-old Mary had been playing with the dolls in the playroom and was observed to grow increasingly aggressive in her play. Her play activity finally culminated in attempts to destroy the female adult doll figure by violently beating it on a nearby shelf. This outburst was immediately followed by an outburst of tears and deep sobs from the child. At this point the therapist provided the following interpretation of the meaning of Mary's play behavior.

"You are very angry, Mary, with your mother because you have to share your father with her. You would like to have him all for yourself. You are so angry that you would like to kill your mother. Then you could do all the things that mamma and daddy do together. But now you feel very afraid and bad for having such bad thoughts."

Although it is obvious that this excerpt has lost some of its potential for interpretation by being considered out of its total context, the interpretation given seems to illustrate some important points. On the basis of the therapist's observations of Mary's behavior, some inferences about her feelings and unspoken attitudes about real world situations were made. What other potential interpretations could have been given to the same behavior? Note that the variation in interpretations relates to some "theory" of human behavior which is held by the observer. By giving the above interpretation to Mary's play behavior, the therapist provided Mary with new insights into why she felt and acted as she did. The assumption implied in so doing is that Mary will be able to take these insights and apply them to her real world situations, that is, Mary will be able to become a happier and more productive child. Note that this assumption also is tied into a theoretical position with respect to human behavior. Other belief systems would have dictated a different approach on the part of the therapist.

Form in Play

Lowenfeld (1935) introduced the idea of being concerned about the form of play, that is, the way the child plays as well as its unconscious and symbolic meanings. In emphasizing play as practice for life she stated, "Play in children is the expression of the child's relation to the whole of life. And no theory of play is possible which is not also a theory which will cover the whole of the child's relation to life." (Lowenfeld, 1935, p. 6) Play in this sense, therefore, refers to all behaviors of children that are spontaneous and self-generated. Furthermore, these behaviors can be considered ends in themselves and do not of necessity have to be interpreted in terms of unconscious motives and drives. Contemporary behavioral therapists seem to have emphasized the idea of focusing on the form of the child's play. The role of the therapist who functions from such a position is to aid the child in becoming "a more skillful player"; that is, play is an experience in which the child can be taught more skillful or adaptive behaviors by application of appropriate principles of learning. It is the child's overt behavior that is the primary focus of the form-oriented counselor. Specific maladaptive behaviors are determined by the counselor and then specific remedial procedures are employed in the play situation.

Behavioral therapists may employ a variety of techniques to bring about behavioral change in play therapy. These techniques include desensitization, shaping, role-playing, modeling, and others which are derived directly from scientific learning principles. The particular technique or treatment approach that is used is largely determined by a diagnosis of those specific child behaviors which are maladaptive. Suppose, for example, that seven-year-old Johnny is suffering from school phobia. The play therapist sets up a series of situations in the playroom which are associated with school attendance and activities and which represent an hierarchy of threatening situations to Johnny. In his play, Johnny is presented with the various school-related situations by the therapist until each fails to elicit anxious responses from him and he is able to return to school. Johnny has been desensitized to the threat which was producing his school phobia behavior. The reader is referred to Wolpe and Lazarus (1966) for further clarification of these principles.

Jimmy, age nine, has been observed by his teacher to be quite withdrawn in the classroom and on the playground. The therapist who is working with Jimmy has observed him in the classroom and on the playground and has concluded that Jimmy is lacking in social skills—hence, his withdrawn behavior. As a consequence, Jimmy and the therapist have met in the playroom with the specific purpose of helping Jimmy develop social skills. With Jimmy, the toys in the playroom are used to role-play various social skills and to practice more effective ways of relating in social contexts. The therapist actively reinforces this behavior through praise or by the use of some tangible reward such as candy. The therapist also consciously presents his own social skills as a model for Jimmy who carefully observes the therapist and learns to imitate the therapist's behavior. As new and more efficient skills are learned and reinforced, they replace the older maladaptive behaviors which have not been reinforced; hence Jimmy is better able to participate in the classroom and on the playground. Moreover, since counseling has a basic goal of changing behavior in the "real world" and not just the office of the therapist, play can be used to more closely approximate real-life situations. Unlike the symbolic meaning-oriented therapists, the form-oriented therapist is concerned most with overt behavior and makes few inferences since he does not concern himself with unconscious motives and processes. Similarly, he is uninterested in promoting insight but rather is focusing on the promotion of more effective behaviors. In one sense the form-oriented therapist becomes a "social reinforcement machine" in his relationship with the child (Ullmann and Krasner, 1965).

Process in Play

The works of Jesse Taft (1933), Carl Rogers (1939), Frederick Allen (1942), and Virginia Axline (1947) have stimulated the process orientation to play which tends to focus on the growth of the child. Play is seen as an opportunity for the child to "become" when provided with a psychological climate which is conducive to self-realization. It is neither the meaning of play nor its form but the quality of the experience itself which is of central importance. As Moustakas (1959) has emphasized, "the ongoing, dynamic, right-now, living relationship between the child and the therapist is the primary focus. The only thing the therapist can do for the child is help him gradually to be himself and to make creative, responsible use of his capacities and abilities." (p. 3). The play activity of the child becomes a vehicle by which a significant relationship between the child and the therapist is developed and through which the child's potentials are realized. A quality relationship between the child and the therapist frees the child to grow and to "become." This relationship, characterized by deep respect for the child and honesty in relating to him, allows the child to become increasingly able to rely on his inner capacities for self-fulfillment. The following segment from a play therapy session illustrates the process orientation to play. Note that the therapist is focusing on what is happening between the child and himself. How might a meaning- or form-oriented therapist have dealt with this play experience?

Eight-year-old Diane has been playing with paints in the corner of the playroom and all of a sudden begins spilling the paints on the rug. She says somewhat gleefully, "There, I've spilled them all over the floor, all over the rug. It's all ruined."

Therapist: You've really messed it up.

Diane: Yeah, Goodie!

Therapist: You're happy now.

Diane: Yeah, but you aren't.

Therapist: You want to make me angry with you.

Diane: You are kind of angry.

Therapist: You think I am?

Diane: Yeah, I'll cut this crayon. (*defiantly*)

Therapist: You want to keep on messing things up—to make me more angry.

Diane: I think you're angry. (*pause*) I want to go home. (*fearfully*)

Therapist: Now, you've made me angry and want to go home.

Diane: I don't want you to be angry at me.

Therapist: You wish I wouldn't.

Diane: But you really are.

Therapist: You wanted to make me angry at you and now you're sorry and afraid.

At this point Diane runs toward the therapist, throws her arms around his neck and clings to him desperately. The therapist holds her gently and after some time begins to talk with her about her fear of not being loved.

Even though it is possible to discretely separate the meaning, form, and process orientations to play, it must be remembered that such divisions really do not occur in practice. It is only for the sake of discussion that divisions such as these can be made. It is seldom that a therapist will fit neatly into one of these three orientations. Only the emphasis given to one of these orientations by the therapist allows us to talk about one therapist operating from a form orientation while another operates from a process orientation. It should also be stressed that any given therapist may emphasize one approach to play with one child and yet another with a second child. The criterion by which the therapist makes these choices would seem to be how he can use himself most effectively to work with the child needing his help. Although an attempt has been made in the illustrations to separate the three orientations so that they appear to be rather distinct and discrete, it is also obvious that such a task is impossible, for there is considerable overlap in the orientations. Moreover, the degree of overlap becomes more a function of the individual therapist than his adherence to a particular orientation.

STRUCTURE OF PLAY

Play has two loci from which its structure can emerge—the locus of the child and the locus of the therapist. When the child is totally responsible for structuring play, he is given complete freedom in his choice of toys, in setting the stage, and in carrying out his play activities. Moreover, the therapist becomes whatever the child wants him to become. He may actively engage in the child's activities or not, just as the child desires. At the opposite end of the continuum is therapist-structured play. From this point of view the therapist is responsible for the selection of specific toys which he feels will be most helpful in aiding the child in communicating himself. He sets the stage for play and requests the child to act out what would happen in a situation presented. The choice of toys and situations to be played out are arrived at by a diagnosis of the child's problem. Proponents of therapist-structured play point out the advantages of getting to the root of the child's problem more quickly than with child-structured play. They emphasize that therapist-structured play minimizes the diffuse and irrelevant play activity of the child. However, other child therapists caution that therapist-structured play should be used selectively with different patients and at different times during the treatment of one patient. With some it should not be used at all.

Advocates of child-structured play challenge the assumption that behavior not stimulated by the therapist is diffuse and irrelevant to the child. Moreover, they propose that the opportunity for the child to become better able to make decisions and to assume responsibility for his decisions is diminished when a therapist imposes structure on a child's play. Although these polar positions exist at least in theory, most practitioners fall somewhere between the extremes of totally child-determined or totally therapist-determined play structure. Moreover, individual therapists may also provide various degrees of structure for their clients based on what they perceive the client's needs to be at any one point in time. This position is in part a function of the therapist's theoretical orientation and his own personally determined limits for the play therapy situation.

RELATIONSHIP IN PLAY

The importance of the relationship between the therapist and the child is fundamental with nearly all therapists regardless of orientation. The central, or core, position of the relationship, particularly in adult therapy, has recently been emphasized by Carkhuff and Berenson (1967). It is of even greater importance in working with children because of their relative lack of verbal facility and sophistication, and because children "feel" adults directly. Our view of the significance of the relationship has been discussed in chapter 5. At this point it seems sufficient to say that play can be a vehicle by which the relationship between the child and therapist is afforded the opportunity of becoming more significant. It gives the child an opportunity to express himself in his most natural mode, and also it gives the therapist an understanding of the child's unique world.

Although, as stated earlier, little disagreement exists with respect to the importance of the child-therapist relationship, concurrence among practitioners with respect to the exact nature of the ideal relationship is more difficult to achieve. Whitmer (1946) in her discussion of the elements which are important in this relationship describes therapists as being

... friendly and kind and keenly sensitive to the child's moods, actions, and words. They may anticipate his fears and doubts and explicitly or more likely by implication let him know that his ideas will receive serious attention. They are very careful to be non-judgmental, neither condemning nor praising, but receiving all information in an accepting manner and permitting free expression of feeling and opinion even if the accompanying behavior is forbidden. (p. 40)

Axline (1947) emphasizes "complete acceptance of the client as he is and permissiveness to use the counseling hour in any way he sees fit." (p. 27) She further states that the atmosphere of mutual respect which characterizes the child-therapist relationship allows the child to set "a positive course of action that correlates with his inner drive toward maturity." (p. 28)

Moustakas (1959) views the therapist in a therapeutic relationship as conveying to the child "a deep belief in him as a person and in his potentialities for growth. He respects the child's values, his ways, peculiarities and symbolisms and lets the child know that these are worthy because they are part of him." (p. 27)

Common to these descriptions seem to be respect for the experience of the child, sensitivity to the child's meaning, and acceptance of the child even though his behavior may be limited.

LIMITS

Although most therapists would agree that the opportunity for the child's free expression is essential in play therapy, basic differences in professional opinion do exist with regard to the extent of permissiveness which should prevail in the relationship with regard to the application of limits in play therapy. Some practitioners consider completely unrestrained acting out as essential to effective child therapy (Slavson, 1952). They contend that the imposition of limits by the therapist may be antithetical to understanding and meeting the needs of the child. Others, however, view limits as an integral and essential part of the therapeutic process.

Without limits there could be no therapy. Limits define the boundaries of the relationship and tie it to reality. They remind the child of his responsibility to himself, the therapist and the playroom. They offer security and at the same time permit the child to move freely and safely in his play. They help to make the playroom experience a living reality. (Moustakas, 1959, p. 10)

Even though therapists differ with respect to the question of limits and their use, they agree that there are two essential differences between limits in the playroom and those in the outside world. First, the playroom limits are far fewer. Second, there is acceptance of the child's need to break them. In an attempt to assess the importance of the therapist's theoretical orientation on the use of limits in play therapy, Ginott and Lebo (1961) found no differences in the number of limits employed by different workers. However, different kinds of limits were used by therapists representing different orientations. Even though there are differences in the kinds of limits employed by various therapists, there are some limits which are widely accepted. These include (1) limits preventing the child from endangering his own health and safety, (2) limits preventing the child from doing injury to the therapist, and (3) limits preventing unrestrained destruction of the playroom materials and equipment. Other limits such as those placed on the span of time during which the child is involved in play activities, the action to be taken if the child voluntarily leaves the playroom, the prohibition placed on various socially unaccepted behaviors, and others are more controversial and appear to reflect a greater degree of therapist bias than empirical confirmation of the procedures used.

EMPLOYING LIMITS

Regardless of the number or kinds of limits established, they only have meaning to the relationship inasmuch as they are justly and consistently used. If the playroom experience is tied to reality through the limits which are set, then it is essential that these limits be delineated in a manner which leaves no doubt in the child's mind as to what constitutes acceptable and unacceptable behavior. Ginott (1961) has emphasized, "Little child security can be gained from limits which are arbitrary and capricious." (p. 102) Allen (1942) has stressed the need for valid limits to grow out of the situation and belong to it. Moreover, he suggests that limits should be unique to the particular child and should not represent a demonstration of personal power by the therapist. It is generally held that limits should be stated in a friendly but firm manner which tends to minimize the arousal of resentment in the child. However, when resentment occurs as a result of various restrictions being enforced, the therapist then focuses on helping the child accept the imposed restrictions.

Although much emphasis has been placed on the therapeutic value of limits, little attention has been devoted to the enforcement of them. Some therapists recommend expelling the child from the playroom as a result of a broken limit, while others reject such a course of action. Moustakas (1959) suggests placing areas or toys out of bounds and holding the child when a particular limit is broken. This is only recommended, however, after the therapist is certain that the limit is fully understood by the child. He quickly points out that the enforcement of limits should not become a punitive act against the child. "Whatever the therapist does, he must continue to help the child feel accepted even though he cannot be permitted to do certain things." (Moustakas, 1959, pp. 10–11)

Differing opinions are also held with respect to when limits ought to be introduced to the child. The authors are of the opinion that limits should not be mentioned or presented before a need for them arises; that is, it may be an important part of the therapy process to allow the child to discover the limits for himself. Furthermore, if the limits are presented to the child on his initial contact with the therapist, the potential for the child to view the therapy situation as one which is restrictive and punitive is quite possible. Such an initial set on the part of the child could be quite inhibiting to the establishment of a sound relationship and consequently to the process of therapy. For a more comprehensive discussion of the theory and practice of limits in play therapy, the reader is referred to Ginott's book, *Group Psychotherapy With Children.*

SELECTION OF TOYS AND OTHER MEDIA

Considerable variation exists among therapists with respect to the kinds of toys selected for use in play therapy. Most of the selection rationales devised are more a reflection of the therapist's preference than the result of empirical investigation. It is generally conceded that the toys available for the child's use should be within his realm of play; that is, toys which are too advanced or too simple for the individual child's level of development may not elicit the expression from the child which is essential for maximum therapeutic gains to occur. Ginott (1961) has presented five major criteria for selecting materials for play therapy. He maintains that a treatment toy should (1) facilitate the establishment of contact with the child, (2) evoke and encourage catharsis, (3) aid in developing insights, (4) furnish opportunities for reality testing, and (5) provide a media for sublimation (p. 53).

Specific toys and supplies which meet these criteria tend to vary with individual children. For some the unstructured media of clay, drawing, finger paints, sand, water, pipe cleaners, and so forth, tend to elicit the most therapeutic play behavior. It is held by those who advocate unstructured materials that such materials allow the child to more fully invest his unique self into the media used. For other children the more structured media such as doll families, hand puppets, blocks, animal toys, comeback figures, and various aggressive toys tend to maximize the child's expression of himself. Highly structured play materials are advised by some therapists as most useful with children diagnosed to be suffering a particular maladaptive behavior pattern. For example, the child who is severely repressed and unable to express anger might most effectively be treated by exclusive exposure to toys through which he could act out his anger without fear of censure or reprisal.

It has also been observed that the most appropriate media for expression may change during the course of therapy; that is, at one point in the therapeutic process highly structured materials might be most appropriate, while unstructured materials would be most useful at another stage. Again, it would seem that the therapist who is sensitive to the child's needs and his individual modes of expression would provide toys which could be used most effectively by that individual child. With some children this might involve a wide spectrum of toys which could be used by the child, and for other children a more narrow selection of toys would be effective. Perhaps an ideal situation would be one in which a wide variety of toys are available from which the child could choose that with which he seems to be able to communicate himself most effectively.

AGE AND PLAY

The effective use of play with children of varying ages has not been extensively investigated. It has been suggested that play therapy is facilitative with children as young as four years of age. By this age, they can perform two simultaneous motor acts, play and talk, although play activity at this age tends to far exceed the incidence and importance of talk. Lebo's findings (1956) seem to support such a position and further suggest that play as a medium of expression sharply loses its effectiveness at the twelve-year-old level. In discussing the suitability of play therapy with young adolescents, Dorfman (1951) concludes, "a young adolescent may be humiliated at finding himself compelled to occupy a room where everything seems to be in miniature." (Rogers, 1951, p. 265) In order to avoid such potential humiliation, she suggests that the child of approximately eleven years of age and older be permitted to choose between the playroom and an office; that is, between play therapy and the more traditional interview therapy. Ginott (1961) has suggested the use of ". . . a variety of penny arcade machines such as rifle galleries, table bowling and boxing machines," as therapeutic media for older children (p. 75). Such equipment represents a challenge to children who might feel resentful of being asked to play with toys. Activity therapy has also been suggested as a more appropriate means of expression for older children (Slavson, 1950). In such a situation, children are provided with raw materials and tools which can be used to construct things. Recommended for boys are work benches, hammers, saws, clamps, leather craft tools, and so forth; and weaving, sewing, beadwork, and similar activities have been recommended for girls. Even though Slavson's recommendations pertain directly to working with children in groups, it would seem that activity therapy would also have application to working with individual children.

THE PLAYROOM

Although few settings may have the economic resources or the inclination to consider the development of a playroom in the setting, it does seem appropriate to briefly mention some of the considerations which go into the development of such a facility. One such consideration is size. From his experiences as a play therapist, Ginott has found that a room of 150 to 200 square feet for individual play therapy and a room of 300 to 400 square feet for group play therapy are most desirable. He explains his choice on the basis that a playroom which is too small tends to make children hostile and frustrated owing to the close proximity with the therapist and with other children in a group setting. At the other extreme, a playroom which is too large invites "wild running and rough play in aggressive children and permits withdrawn children to avoid contact with the therapist and the group members." (Ginott, 1961, p. 64)

Care should be taken in the selection of basic furniture such as chairs and tables. The furnishings should be functional and of appropriate size. They also must be able to withstand rough usage. In addition, all facilities and fixtures should be selected so that the potential for physical injury to the child is minimized. Shelving which houses toys and play equipment should be of a height so that easy access is afforded to the child. In addition to the toys provided, a sandbox and a source of water are also recommended for the well-equipped playroom. Ginott (1961) has found these substances to be particularly effective in allowing the child to express himself since they require no special skills of the child; hence, he is better able to experience a sense of accomplishment in his play activity.

Care of the playroom and equipment is also a factor to be considered. When possible, it seems most advisable to have someone other than the therapist or the child be responsible for cleaning the playroom. If prior to leaving the playroom the child is held responsible for replacing all toys and materials in the places where they were initially found and for cleaning up his mess, the child may not feel as free to use the toys and materials, thus the usefulness of the playroom and its equipment in aiding children is diminished.

It is also undesirable to have the therapist responsible for the care of the playroom. Realizing this responsibility may cause the therapist to inhibit the child's spontaneous expression rather than facilitate it, since the therapist also has no desire to clean up the child's mess. Moreover, attitudes of acceptance and respect for the child are apt to be lessened if the therapist has the responsibility for clean-up. It is difficult for a person to fully accept a child who causes him to engage in some onerous task.

BEGINNING PLAY

Regardless of the orientation of the therapist, whether he accepts or rejects the child's right to reject therapy, each therapist should formulate his own policies prior to his first contact with the child. The therapeutic process begins with the initial contact, and the success of that process may be largely determined by the initial encounter between the child and the therapist. Once in the playroom or therapist's office, it is important to convey to the child the nature of the therapeutic situation. It should be made clear to him that he should express himself freely in his own way and at his own rate. Due to the uniqueness of the situation, the child may spend time testing and exploring the authenticity of the therapist's explanation. Once assured of the genuineness of the explanation, he can indulge in expressing himself through the use of the provided toys and other media. Theoretical orientation to some degree determines the behavior of the therapist in working with a child. There is, however, general agreement on the necessity of the therapist to be highly sensitive to the verbal and nonverbal communication of the child. No matter whether the therapist interprets the child's behavior to him or reflects his feelings and demonstrated attitudes, the focus of the therapist's response is directed toward communicating his understanding of the child to the child.

The degree of involvement of the therapist in the play activity of the child is also a matter which to some extent is dictated by the personal needs of the therapist and his theoretical orientation. According to Ginott (1961), those workers who believe in participating with the child in his play do so for two reasons: (1) "They are impressed with the role of parental cruelty in the etiology of childhood neurosis and they aim to neutralize the ill effect of early unkindness with a second edition of motherly love"; and (2) "They attempt to win the child's confidence by eliminating the traditional distance between adult and child." (p. 92) In speaking against the therapist's active participation in the child's play, he states his belief that therapy is retarded when the therapist participates with the child in play activities since the child may then more easily exploit the adult. Since the therapist-child relationship must be built on mutual respect and the therapist must maintain his adult therapeutic role, Ginott suggests that the therapist assume the role of sensitive listener and observer to the child's play. By implication, the therapist cannot be as deeply sensitive to the child's meaning if he is at the same time engaged as a participant in the child's play activities.

COMMENT

The view taken in this chapter suggests the use of play as a tool which can be used to enhance the counseling relationship. Although the literature pertaining to the appropriateness and the usefulness of play as a therapeutic approach is sparse and although most stated positions with respect to play reflect more conjecture than evidence, it seems clear that play is the child's most natural mode of communication. Moreover, to ask the young child to give up his most natural mode of communication for the counselor's highly verbal method is to make an unreasonable request of the child. Hence, it would appear appropriate and even necessary in some cases to employ play as a method of facilitating the child's communication, self-exploration, and understanding.

It should be stressed that the authors do not advocate the exclusive use of play or, for that matter, the exclusive use of any other specific approach to working with young children. Their intent has been to suggest *another* tool that the creative counselor might call upon when the need arises. The emphasis which we have attempted to convey might be summed up in the suggestion that play is most validly used when it benefits the child and the child-counselor relationship.

REFERENCES

ALLEN, F. H. *Psychotherapy With Children.* New York: W. W. Norton Press, 1942.
AXLINE, VIRGINIA M. *Play Therapy.* Boston: Houghton Mifflin Company, 1947.
CARKHUFF, R. R., AND BERENSON, B. *Beyond Counseling and Therapy.* New York: Holt, Rinehart & Winston, Inc., 1967.
DORFMAN, ELAINE. "Play Therapy." In *Client-centered Therapy* by C. R. Rogers. Boston: Houghton Mifflin Company, 1951, pp. 235–277.
FREUD, ANNA. *The Psychoanalytic Treatment of Children.* New York: International Universities Press, 1946.
FREUD, S. "The Cases of 'Little Hans' and the 'Rat Man.' " *Complete Works, Vol. 10,* London: Hogarth Press, 1955.
GINOTT, H. G. *Group Psychotherapy With Children.* New York: McGraw-Hill, Inc., 1961.
————, AND LEBO, D. "Play Therapy—Limits and Theoretical Orientation." *Journal of Consulting Psychology* 25 (1961):337–340.
KLEIN, MELANIE. "The Psychoanalytic Play-Technique." *American Journal of Orthopsychiatry* 25 (1955):223–227.
LEBO, D. "Age and Suitability for Non-directive Play Therapy." *Journal of Genetic Psychology* 89 (1956):231–238.

LOWENFELD, MARGARET. *Play in Childhood*. London: Victor Gollancz, 1935.

MOUSTAKAS, C. E. *Psychotherapy With Children*. New York: Harper & Row, Publishers, 1959.

NELSON, R. C. "Play Media and the Elementary School Counselor." In *Guidance and Counseling in the Elementary School,* edited by D. C. Dinkmeyer. New York: Holt, Rinehart & Winston, Inc., 1968, pp. 267–270.

ROGERS, C. R. *Clinical Treatment of the Problem Child*. New York: Houghton Mifflin Company, 1939.

ROUSSEAU, J. J. *Emile*. New York: E. P. Dutton & Co., Inc., 1957.

SLAVSON, S. R. *Analytic Group Psychotherapy With Children, Adolescents, and Adults*. New York: Columbia University Press, 1950.

———. *Child Psychotherapy*. New York: Columbia University Press, 1952.

TAFT, JESSIE. *The Dynamics of Therapy in a Controlled Relationship*. New York: The Macmillan Company, 1933.

ULLMANN, L. P., AND KRASNER, L., eds. *Case Studies in Behavior Modification*. New York: Holt, Rinehart & Winston, Inc., 1965.

WHITMER, HELEN L. *Psychiatric Interviews With Children*. New York: Commonwealth Fund, 1946.

WOLPE, J., AND LAZARUS, A. A. *Behavior Therapy Techniques*. London: Pergamon Press, Inc., 1966.

SELECTED ADDITIONAL READINGS

ALEXANDER, E. D. "School-centered Play Therapy Program." *Personnel and Guidance Journal* 43 (1964):256–261.

AXLINE, VIRGINIA M. *Dibs: In Search of Self*. Boston: Houghton Mifflin Company, 1964.

BARUCH, DOROTHY. *One Little Boy*. New York: Julian Press, Inc., 1952.

DESPERT, J. LOUISE. "Play Analysis." In *Modern Trends in Child Psychiatry,* edited by N. D. C. Nolan and B. L. Pacella. New York: International Universities Press, 1945, pp. 219–256.

GONDOR, E. I. *Art and Play Therapy*. New York: Random House, Inc., 1954.

MILLAR, SUSANNA. *The Psychology of Play*. Baltimore: Penguin Books, Inc., 1968.

MOUSTAKAS, C. E. *Children in Play Therapy*. New York: McGraw-Hill, Inc., 1953.

MURO, J. J. "Play Media in Counseling." *Elementary School Guidance and Counseling* 3 (1968): 104–110.

MURPHY, L. B. *Methods for the Study of Personality in Young Children*. New York: Basic Books, Inc., Publishers, 1957.

PIAGET, J. *Play, Dreams and Imitation in Childhood*. New York: James H. Heinemann, Inc., 1951.

"Symposium, Therapeutic Play Techniques." *American Journal of Orthopsychiatry* 25 (1955):574–626.

10

Information and Counseling

Living is a process of making choices, of choosing from alternatives. Basic to decisions and choices of wisdom is the use of information which informs the chooser of the possible implications and consequences of various courses of action. Wise choices are at least limited when all these bits of relevant data are not available for use in the decision-making process.

Counseling is a process which involves the weighing of alternatives and the making of choices. Since information is critical to wise choice, information is critical to the counseling process. What, then, should be considered in choosing and using information with children.

ESSENTIALS OF INFORMATION

Central to our discussion is the notion that when information is provided it must have the potential for affecting the child's present or future behavior. If such potential does not exist, the information will be of little benefit or consequence to the child. A number of considerations would seem to be required in order for this to become a reality. Some of these considerations are presented below.

The Need to Know

Fundamental to the useful application of information in counseling is an unmet need on the part of the child. In other words, when a demonstrated need to know, a searching, a desire, a readiness for information is evidenced by the child, that is the point at which the introduction of relevant information is maximally useful to the child.

This is contrasted to the idea that "all fourth graders need to know" about such things as changes in boy-girl relationships during puberty, high school and college curricula, or social service occupations. This is not to imply that such information is unimportant in itself, for information of all

182

kinds is important. It is just not important to all people at the same time. Consequently, the presentation of information for use by the child must be dependent upon the child's individual needs at the moment.

Generally speaking, when in our everyday lives we hear a question asked, we assume that the question is a request for information. For example, "How long does it take to become a doctor?" asks for information. But what does the question "Am I the only kid in this school who thinks that teacher is unfair?" mean? Our point is that all questions are not requests for information input. Questions are often disguises for more penetrating and deep concerns. It is a job of the counselor to assess the nature of the question—to "hear" what is meant by the child. When a legitimate request for information is "heard," then the counselor responds with whatever data resources he may have. When some other request is "heard," he responds to that need.

Personal Meaning

It is not only important to have a need for information before it can be effectively used, it is also crucial that the information presented have personal meaning for the needing child. In other words, the information must relate to the phenomenological world of the child. It must have the potential for integration into the child's context, into his personal frame of reference.

Hollis and Hollis (1969) in their book, *Personalizing Information Processes: Educational, Occupational, and Personal-Social,* have presented this point of view as it relates to the use of information with people. Basically, they emphasize the need to fit the information to the individual rather than fitting the individual to the information as so often has been the case. They also point out the essential aspects of communication in the process of presenting information.

More specifically, personalizing information involves presenting it in ways and methods which are useful and appropriate to the child. Whether we are talking about information gained from resource people, reading materials, audiovisual aids, or observations, to be useful to the child it must be geared to his language facility, his degree of sophistication with concepts, his world as he experiences it.

Relevant to the Times

As implied earlier, children tend to be "here-and-now" oriented. Research has shown that it is more difficult for children to delay gratification of needs and desires than it is for those who are older and more mature. We are also experiencing a current trend in our adolescent and young adult populations which suggests that the "here-and-now" orientation to life is becoming increasingly popular; hence, there seems to be little reason to expect children to move toward a future-oriented informational outlook.

With these thoughts in mind, and with the idea of making information fit the needs of children in the moment of need, it becomes evident that information provided to children must deal with life as it is today. How it was to us as children or how we think it will be in the future has little relevance to the "here-and-now" existence of today's child. The "cramming" of information down the throats of children because that's the way it happened to us or because "someday you'll need to know this" are rationales without valid bases. Moreover, they are distasteful to children and tend to be avoided if children are left to their own choosing.

Reality Orientation

We have some conflict about what to say here. On the one hand we want to strongly affirm that the real potentials of men are well beyond our current awareness and understanding; hence, for the counselor to say "Harry, you'll just never make it through high school" is at best discouraging for Harry and perhaps very naïve of the counselor. All of us have been fortunate enough to know Harrys who from all the evidence didn't have a fighting chance for success—yet, somehow, someway, they did make it. Not only did they make it, but they made those of us publicly sitting on the sideline waiting to say "I told you so" eat crow even though we may have been privately rejoicing.

On the other hand, however, we feel that it is only fair and appropriate to help the child avoid the overwhelming discouragement which can come from "hitching one's wagon to a star" only to discover later that one's expectations could not be realized. Information, then, "realistically" and sensitively presented to the child for his consideration can help prevent that discouragement which can come from overaspiring.

Our experience suggests that there are many more children who "undershoot" their potentials than those who "overshoot" these potentials. Information fed into the phenomenal world of such children can be encouraging to them and can result in a higher realization of potentials and capacities.

Tentativeness of Information

Once men operated from the assumption that the earth was the center of the universe. For hundreds of years man "believed" that the world was flat. More recently science "knew" that the atom was the smallest bit of matter. In the light of new knowledge, our natural tendency is "pooh pooh these silly ideas" and to think that what we now know is "truth." History has continually proved us wrong, and much of what we now "know" will be laughed at by future generations.

It was not long ago that we "knew" that if a person's heart quit beating he would surely die. However, we don't "know" that anymore. Although we "know" now that human beings must die, someday we may not even "know" that. Perhaps there are even alternatives to that long held inevitability. Our knowledge will change as new discoveries emerge.

As a consquence of new discoveries and new "truth," our perceptions of our choices and values will also change. This in turn will change the meaningfulness of information. Information must be dispensed in terms of "This is what is today" and must be used in terms of "This is how it fits and what it means for today." Tentativeness and changeability must be emphasized if information is to be presented in a manner that will be most helpful to the child.

TYPES OF INFORMATION

Traditionally, the types of information provided through the guidance service have been social, educational, and vocational in nature (Norris, Zeran, and Hatch, 1960). Such information dissemination we believe to be a valid and necessary function of the child counselor. If the counselor is to maximally facilitate the child's decision-making processes and development, relevant informational input is essential. We hasten to add, however, that we are not advocating that the counselor become a vast reservoir of facts, for the counselor's contribution is much more crucial than that of being a data bank. Moreover, modern computer technology is capable of much more rapid and accurate fact storage and retrieval than is the human mind; hence, the counselor who chooses to become a repository of information will be an anachronism in future decades. The primary counselor contribution, we submit, is to help the child make effective use of the information which can be brought to bear on the choosing process.

Social Information

Social information is defined by Norris, Zeran, and Hatch (1960) as

. . . valid and useable data about opportunities and influences of the human and physical environment which bear on personal and interpersonal relations. It is information about human beings which will help a student to understand himself better and to improve his relations with others. . . . (p. 23)

Although quite broad, this definition suggests that knowledge of how other people behave, how they get along with others, and how they deal with personal concerns can be of significance in helping a child learn new ways of behaving and coping.

Havighurst's developmental tasks of early and middle childhood suggest some of those child learnings which are concerned with self and self-other relationships. These include learning sex differences and sexual modesty; learning to relate oneself emotionally to parents, siblings, peers, and others; learning to distinguish right from wrong; building healthy attitudes toward self; learning to appropriate male or female social roles; developing a value system; achieving personal independence; and developing attitudes toward social groups and institutions.

Quite obviously, these learnings are not the exclusive province of the child counselor. They are the province of the total educational enterprise. The use of such information is, consequently, within the jurisdiction of all educational personnel. The counselor can, however, be instrumental in helping other school personnel aid children in the assimilation of such information even though his chief function still remains that of working directly with the child and those who comprise the child's world.

Educational Information

Much of what has been said about social information is also valid when we consider educational information and its dissemination. Again the information must be valid and useable by the child regardless of its source. Educational information during the lower elementary grades is relatively limited and will pertain mostly to questions of school policy and school programs. Here, the counselor may be instrumental in interpreting programs, especially innovative programs, to parents. Such might be the case where the function of the school is reassessed and children are given much greater freedom and responsibility for their own learning. The counselor might find himself not only helping children make the transition from the "old" to the "new" system, but he also might be helping parents to understand the goals, procedures, and expected outcomes of the "new" system.

In the later grades, information relative to the programs and policies of the junior high school or middle school may be helpful to children. As they prepare to move from the self-centered classroom to a departmentalized school structure, from a fixed course of study to a school program having course electives, from the small local community elementary school to the larger central junior high, questions and concerns of a variety of natures are likely to arise. Again, the strategic presentation of relevant information to the child may aid him in making such a transition in a reasonably graceful way.

Vocational Information

Certainly a vast amount of information is available regarding vocations. But as Arbuckle has suggested, ". . . we can assume that occupational information per se has as little personal meaning as the vast majority of information which is poured, shoved, and ground into a child during his years of formal education." (Koplitz, 1968, p. 109) Although this is what Arbuckle sees, occupational information does not have to be that unreal and irrelevant to the child of elementary school age. It has a legitimate place in the elementary school curriculum just as any other body of information. Like all other information, however, it is only important if the child can use it to further his learning.

Typically, vocational information has been collected and disseminated to older children in order to acquaint them with specifics of certain jobs or to broaden their perspective of the world of work in general. Consider for a moment the relevance of the former practice with the elementary school child. Tommy, a twelve-year-old sixth grader, is being pushed to choose a vocational path by his upward-bound parents and their adult friends. "What are you going to be when you grow up?" "What track are you going to follow in junior high and high school?" "Have you thought about what you'll study in college?" All of these are innocent enough questions in themselves but constitute a glimpse of the kind of pressures Tommy is confronted with. Let us further suppose that regardless of the course of study and vocation that Tommy chooses, he will not actually enter the job market until age twenty-two. Now consider the changes which have occurred during the past ten years. How many thousands of new jobs have emerged and how many thousands of old jobs have disappeared? At the end of the next ten years, what will the occupations situation look like? Will the vocational path chosen now be a meaningful or even existing opportunity ten years hence? Who can tell? Most assuredly a twelve-year-old Tommy is ill-prepared for such fortune-telling, but is he any less prepared than the rest of us?

We can predict, for instance, that today's elementary school child will change his type of occupation (not just locations or employers) on the average of at least five times during his working lifetime. How can specific vocational information help prepare children for the rapidly accelerating changes which are an inevitable part of their futures? It can't. What is relevant and essential, however, is the need to help children prepare to meet the challenges of change with which they will be confronted. As is implied in Barry and Wolf's *An Epitaph for Vocational Guidance* (1962), the role of the counselor is one of helping people learn to adjust to their personal situation and the situation of society rather than to strive toward specific occupational goals.

One other problem seems worthy of mention in connection with choosing vocations. Part of our middle-class ethic says, "Work is good. Those who work are good. Those who do not are bad." By the time that today's elementary school child is ready to enter the labor force, however, it is predicted that there will be many more available workers than there are available jobs. As a result, large numbers of prospective workers will be unemployed, or they will be employed on a much more limited scale than we now know. This prediction certainly may be fallacious, for who knows what tomorrow may bring. If it is not fallacious, the consequences for our culture will be far-reaching and profound. Leisure-time expenditure will become an increasingly difficult problem, and unemployment as well. If we as counselors are going to look to the future and see ourselves as facilitators in meeting the needs of the children whom we serve, we are going to have to assume some leadership in modifying the notion that one must work in order to be an acceptable member of our society. Changing times dictate the need to reexamine and redefine values.

Is there any justification, then, for the use of occupational information with children? Yes, but with a process orientation. Occupational exploration in the early grades is just as relevant (provided that such a task has meaning for the child) as exploration in any of area of learning and education. Information should only be a vehicle or means for the exploration process—that process involving critical thinking which ends in personalized understanding.

VOCATIONAL DEVELOPMENT THEORIES

As was suggested in chapter 1, historically a major thrust of psychology and more specifically counseling and guidance has always been the process of vocational choosing. Consequently a number of theorists have attempted to formulate hypotheses designed to help explain the process by which vocational choice is made.

Although our experience suggests that factors of "vocational chance" may be a more fruitful area of study than those of vocational choice, we feel some obligation to briefly sketch some of the more prominent existing vocational development theories for the reader. We would like to stress, however, that these are theories. They have not been proven empirically. Again we suggest that the reader use the following discussion to examine his own experience. Perhaps by so doing, additional clarification and direction can be brought to the area of vocational development and choice.

Ginzberg and Choices

Ginzberg (1951) views vocational decision-making as a process which extends from childhood into young adulthood. He postulates that the individual goes through three periods as he evolves an occupational choice: a "fantasy" choice period; a period of "tentative" choice beginning on the average at about age eleven; and a "realistic" choice period normally beginning at about seventeen years of age. He further suggests that this developmental process is irreversible and that it often involves compromising between interest, abilities, and opportunities.

Generally speaking, the choosing process can only be optimally effective if the individual evolves his choices as a result of the normal unfolding of these age stages; hence, it becomes crucial to the "tentative" and "realistic" stages that the child have adequate opportunity and encouragement for developing "fantasy" choices. In the absence of such opportunities and encouragements, the total process becomes less than optimal.

Roe and Needs

Roe's theory (1956) is based in part on Maslow's higher-order needs in his hierarchical ordering system; that is, her primary emphasis is on how a vocation meets the individual's needs to belong, to have status, and to self-actualize.

According to Roe, early childhood experience with parents is critical to the vocational choice that the child as adult will make. Her theorizing suggests, for instance, that parent-child relationships characterized by a lack of praise of the child will result in certain needs being met in the relationship and others unmet. This may create a thrust in the individual who is choosing a vocation to choose jobs which will meet those unmet needs. That is, he may choose occupations which put him in the limelight and make him visible for praise.

Generally speaking, then, Roe suggests that the chosen vocation of the adult is in large part a result of the way needs were satisfied in the parent-child relationship. As the child matures, these need-gratification patterns evolve into the development of special interests and abilities which later become expressed in an occupational choice.

Super and Self-Concept

From Super's perspective (1957), the vocational choice results from a developmental process which seeks to implement the individual's self-concept. He hypothesizes two major life stages in vocational development: the Exploratory stage and the Establishment stage. The Exploratory stage, which is subdivided into fantasy, tentative and realistic substages, is that period of one's life when the occupation which will implement the self-concept is sought. The Establishment stage, again subdivided into trial and stable phases, involves the individual's actual introduction into a career which provides him with identity and adequate outlets for expression of his interests and abilities. He stabilizes this choice by behaviors which promote success in that career.

Early childhood experiences are also an important aspect of Super's theory since the self-concept of the child is evolving from the moment of birth. His stages and substages of vocational development further help clarify the type of help (information) which should be available to the child at the different developmental stages.

Tiedeman and Decision-Making

Central to Tiedeman's theory (1961) is the idea that vocational development is a function of decisions that are made and implemented in the life of the individual. In other words, choosing an occupation results from the decision-making process—that process which is basic to all learning operations. He has conceived of decision-making as being comprised of two stages: the anticipation stage and the implementation stage.

The first stage, anticipation, is characterized by involvement in random activities and the organizing of relevant considerations into alternatives. These alternatives then are weighed and a decision made which when ready to be acted upon concludes this phase of the process.

Stage two, implementation, follows on the anticipation stage and includes the actual introduction into the occupation, the worker's integration into the occupation and working environment, and the establishment of his occupational equilibrium. At all phases of this two-stage development, the decision-making process is brought to bear as alternatives are clarified and choices are made and acted out.

Holland and Synthesis

Holland (1959) has attempted to integrate and synthesize knowledge of vocational choice theories. His theory assumes that the person, at the time of vocational choosing, is the product of the interaction of his unique heredity with the multiplicity of environmental influences including peers, parents, other significant adults, social class and pressures, American culture, and his physical world. From his experiences, the individual develops a hierarchy of preferred methods of coping with his environmental tasks which constitutes his "life style." This "life style" then determines the major direction of choice in that the chooser "searches" for situations (occupational environments) which satisfy his hierarchy of preferred coping behaviors.

In its essence, then, Holland's theory suggests that vocational choice results from an interaction of occupational environments and the "whole" person. Certainly, this is a comprehensive theory for it takes into consideration all that possibly can be considered in decision-making behavior. Herein, however, is its major liability. How does one make it practicable when it "covers the waterfront"?

The implications of this theory as it relates to children seem obvious. The "life style" of the chooser directs his choices. But "life style" is a product of the interplay of hereditary and environmental influences and is begun at birth and developed through childhood. Change in the hereditary and environmental determinants of "life style," therefore, modifies choices. But what changes influence in what ways? This is a question surely in need of research.

Vocational Theories—A Final Comment

It is hardly profound to state that much of western man's identity is wrapped up in his work and job title. Asked to spontaneously comment on who they are, most people will first state their name and then what they do for a living. Similarly, a child asked to identify his father is likely to state the father's occupation; hence, it seems important and relevant to study vocational development behavior and the method by which people and occupations correlate.

The major theories which exist are broad and general. Moreover, the empirical evidence attesting to their validity is lacking. Often the evidence which emerges from experimental work refutes and contradicts the hypotheses derived from the aforementioned theories. What does this suggest? Perhaps it suggests a need to reexamine and rethink our assumptive underpinnings of vocational development theories. The assumptions upon which the existing theories are based tend to deterministically view man as a creature of destiny acted on by internal and external forces beyond his control. How different vocational choice theory might be if it were based on a belief in man's potential to create his destiny as he actively involves himself in the actualization of his human potentials.

It seems that most of the previous discussion regarding theories of vocational choice relate specifically to adults or young adults rather than to children. Perhaps the best rationale for our discussion in this chapter is that children will become adults and that many children will be members of the labor force in a matter of years. If vocational choice does take place, it would seem that it is a developmental process that occurs over a long period of time. Such considerations as "life styles," needs, self-concepts, and decision-making are products of the total life experience of all human beings.

SOURCES AND USES OF INFORMATION

Information can be gained from a wide variety of sources for use in a wide variety of ways. Many of these sources and uses are quite evident and therefore will not be discussed in any detail. Those less obvious sources and uses will receive our primary focus of attention.

Printed Materials

The most common sources of information available to children which pertains to social, educational, and vocational questions are printed materials and audiovisual aids. The printed materials range from charts and posters which provide some "message," to written job descriptions, to career fiction, to autobiographical and biographical materials. Similarly, information is provided through the audio and visual media of tapes, filmstrips, slides, films, photographs, and others.

Assessment Data

Inventories, tests, and other assessment devices have been devised to evaluate the child's educational strengths and weaknesses, academic capacities and aptitudes, personal concerns and problems, and preferences. These instruments and assessment techniques have, when used properly, been used to provide children with feedback about themselves in social, educational, and vocational areas. Unfortunately, much of the information which has been amassed relative to particular children has not been used to the maximum benefit of these children. We contend that there is little purpose in assessing Billy's reading ability if the assessment data is not going to be used to "individualize" Billy's reading development experiences. Evaluation of various skills and abilities are only legitimate when the data obtained are used to help the child actualize his potentials.

Resource Persons

Another common source of information is through direct experience with resource people. Although the counselor can be, and often is, such a source of information, he may not be the most knowledgeable person available to help children become informed. Information which can be presented firsthand is invested with feelings and meanings which are absent in "talking about" experiences from a distance. In other words, the child who has been the resident of a juvenile detention home may be better able to provide relevant information to other children about such homes than an adult who knows about detention homes only as an observer. Moreover, the child resource person may be much more acceptable to other children in such a capacity than an informed adult.

It should be stressed that we are not advocating the exclusive use of peers as resource people. Rather we are advocating the use of whatever resources that exist and can best aid the child in getting that information which he needs and wants. It seems only logical that the child can gain the most real understandings of another "world" by exposure to and involvement with that "world" and the people who inhabit it. What better way is there to learn and know how it is to live and work in the ghetto than to be there and experience it firsthand?

Modeling Information

"Do as I say, not as I do" is a common admonition which children receive from adults. It has never been an effective method of teaching-learning, however. As we have already stated, we learn by doing and by watching others do; hence, the behavior of adult models (parents, teachers, counselors, and others) is critical to the learning of children with whom they work. The adult models are continually modeling information about "acceptable," "appropriate," and "good" behavior. Perhaps the following illustration will help clarify this point.

A nine-year-old boy, G., had been in play therapy for some time. However, he seemed to be making little progress in being able to deal effectively with his anger. During one of the play sessions, G. and his therapist were needlessly interrupted, resulting in the therapist's becoming angry. He stormed to the main desk and vented his displeasure, then returned to the playroom. At this point, G. began to express his pent-up feelings of anger. This marked an important change in G.'s ability to express feelings. The therapist (model) had dealt directly and positively with his own angry feelings which allowed G. to realize that "properly used goal directed anger can be appropriate and effective." (Alexander, 1967, p. 164)

Information, then, can be transmitted to children by deed as well as word. Modeling of skills, social proprieties, vocational competencies, and a host of other considerations is a valid and effective means of disseminating information.

Small Group Experience

A significant current trend in education is the investigation of the learning potentials of the "intensive small group experience." Although the major thrust of these investigations has been directed at adult and adolescent populations, there is some evidence that the "intensive small group experience" is a powerful learning experience for children as well as adults, and for children in combination with adults.

In the most common kind of "intensive small group experience," people learn to modify methods of relating and expressing themselves in a surprisingly short period of time. A major reason for this is that individual participants are provided the opportunity of getting honest feedback (information) about themselves from their fellow participants—a novel and significant experience for most. In the safety of the group, masks, defenses, and devious ways of being can be abandoned and alternative ways of being which are more in keeping with the "real" person of the participant can be experimented with.

But, you say, that's impractical or impossible with children and especially so with groups composed of children and adults. To this, we can only say it has been done and is currently being done (Bessell, 1968; Rogers, 1969). It most certainly is a challenge to many of our existing practices having to do with the acquisition of knowledge—to our dogmas about teaching and learning; hence, it will require courage and commitment to explore the potentials of the "intensive small group experience" in an open fashion.

THE COUNSELOR'S RESPONSIBILITY

Throughout our discussion we have tried to emphasize that the child counselor is much more than a repository of information relating to social, educational, and vocational matters. It is that "more than" quality which accounts for his effectiveness as a counselor; and yet, he should be expected by children to be helpful to them with their questions about information. It is not a matter of "how much" or "what" the counselor knows, it is rather his willingness to share his knowledge in a way that is useful to the child which is crucial. This involves (1) providing information when he is able and when the child is needy; (2) being able to direct children to other sources when that is appropriate; and (3) being willing to help the child use the information gained in a personally meaningful way.

COMMENT

Information and its use is a necessary part of the counseling process. To be maximally worthwhile to the child, it must be needed, meaningful, relevant to the times, reality-oriented, and tentative.

Information is accessible from a wide variety of sources ranging from printed materials to intensive human encounters. All are valid sources. All can be useful to the individual as he strives to make wise social, educational, and vocational decisions.

Work is an important aspect of western man's identity. Various investigations have attempted to describe the processes by which people wind up in various occupations. To date, these theories seem vague and of little practical value in explaining those processes. Additional investigation is needed.

The counselor is not a data bank where vast accumulations of social, educational, and occupational information are stored. He is rather an agent who (1) helps the child get the information he needs and (2) helps him derive personally relevant meaning from that information.

REFERENCES

ALEXANDER, J. F. "The Therapist as a Model—and as Himself." *Psychotherapy: Theory, Research and Practice* 4 (1967):164–165.

BARRY, RUTH E., AND WOLF, BEVERLY. *An Epitaph for Vocational Guidance.* New York: Columbia Teachers' College Press, 1962.

BESSELL, H. "The Content is the Medium: The Confidence is the Message." *Psychology Today* 1 (1968):32–35.

GINZBERG, E.; GINSBURG, S. W.; AXELRAD, S.; AND HERMA, J. L. *Occupational Choice: An Approach to a General Theory.* New York: Columbia University Press, 1951.

HOLLAND, J. L. "A Theory of Vocational Choice." *Journal of Counseling Psychology* 6 (1959):35–44.

HOLLIS, J., AND HOLLIS, LUCILLE. *Personalizing Information Processes: Educational, Occupational, and Personal-Social.* New York: The Macmillan Company, 1969.

KOPLITZ, E. D., ed. *Guidance in the Elementary School: Theory, Research and Practice.* Dubuque, Ia.: William C. Brown Company Publishers, 1968.

NORRIS, WILLA; ZERAN, F. R.; AND HATCH, R. N. *The Information Service in Guidance.* Chicago: Rand McNally & Co., 1960.

ROE, ANNE. *The Psychology of Occupations.* New York: John Wiley & Sons, Inc., 1956.

ROGERS, C. R. *Freedom to Learn.* Columbus, Ohio: Charles E. Merrill Publishing Co., 1969.

SUPER, D. E. *The Psychology of Careers.* New York: Harper and Bros., 1957.

TIEDEMAN, D. V. "Decision and Vocational Development: A Paradigm and Its Implications." *Personnel and Guidance Journal* 40 (1961):15–21.

SELECTED ADDITIONAL READINGS

APPLETON, G. M., AND HANSEN, J. C. "Parent-Child Relations, Need-Nurturance, and Vocational Mentation." *Personnel and Guidance Journal* 47 (1969):794–799.

BOROW, H., ed. *Man in a World at Work.* Boston: Houghton Mifflin Company, 1964.

DAVIS, D. A.; HAGEN, NELLIE; AND STROUF, JUDIE. "Occupational Choice of Twelve-year-Olds." *Personnel and Guidance Journal* 40 (1962):628–629.

GOLDMAN, L. *Using Tests in Counseling.* New York: Appleton-Century-Crofts, 1961.

GRIGG, A. E. "Childhood Experiences and Parental Attitudes: A Test of Roe's Hypothesis." *Journal of Counseling Psychology* 6 (1959):153–155.

HAGEN, D. "Careers and Family Atmospheres: An Empirical Test of Roe's Theory." *Journal of Counseling Psychology* 7 (1960):251–256.

HANSEN, J. C., AND STEVIC, R. R. *Elementary School Guidance.* New York: The Macmillan Company, 1969.

HOLLAND, J. L. *The Psychology of Vocational Choice.* Waltham, Mass.: Blaisdell Publishing Co., 1966.

HOPPOCK, R. *Occupational Information.* New York: McGraw-Hill, Inc., 1957.

KAYE, JANET. "Fourth Graders Meet Up With Occupations." *Vocational Guidance Quarterly* 8 (1960):150–152.

OSIPOW, S. H. *Theories of Career Development.* New York: Appleton-Century-Crofts, 1968.

PETERS, H. J.; RICCIO, A. C.; AND QUARANTA, J. J. *Guidance in the Elementary School.* New York: The Macmillan Company, 1963.

UTTON, A. C. "Recalled Parent-Child Relations as Determinants of Vocational Choice." *Journal of Counseling Psychology* 9 (1962):49–53.

WILLIAMSON, E. G. *Vocational Counseling: Some Historical, Philosophical, and Theoretical Perspectives.* New York: McGraw-Hill, Inc., 1965.

11

Developing a Counseling Program Unique to the Elementary School

The major function of the school is educational. Guidance services, including counseling, are designed to facilitate this end. It is from this frame of reference that the development of a counseling program must evolve.

For this chapter to be of ultimate value, it would have to develop a program unique to every elementary school based upon those conditions which prevail there. Such an approach is obviously impossible, and the alternative we have chosen in our presentation can only be a guideline for the elementary school counselor in developing a unique school counseling program.

We have tried to make counseling with children rather than counseling in the elementary school the emphasis of this text. Because of the nature of this chapter, however, the child counselor working in a setting other than the elementary school will need to modify what we have presented in order to fit his setting. In any case, modification must take place.

In this chapter we shall discuss what we consider to be some basic considerations in the development of an elementary school counseling program. Next we shall present our notions of how such a program would feel—that is to say, what would be the environmental climate of a school that was truly affected by an elementary school counseling program. We have tried to implement the reader's understanding of this climate by presenting as an example aspects of an elementary school in which one of the authors worked several years ago. Hopefully, this will also lend to the reader's belief that such a climate does and can exist. Finally, we shall discuss as specifically as possible methods which can be applied directly in the development of a unique elementary school counseling program.

BASIC CONSIDERATIONS

Although the major emphasis of counseling is service to the child, it need not always take the form of direct service. Evidence has been presented (Satir, 1966) which indicates that a child's stability or psychological "healthiness" is, in large part, dependent upon the psychological climate of the relationship between the child's parents. Such a point of view gives rise to several considerations: (1) If the climate of the home is of such great importance, the climate of the school may also be of great importance in the psychological development and well-being of the child; and (2) Counseling with the parents and/or family of the child would seem to be one of the most beneficial means of aiding the child.

From our perspective, we believe that one of the major functions of the elementary school counselor is the facilitation of healthy, growth-producing school and home environments. To accomplish this end we predict that the child counselor's role will become increasingly one of fostering such environments through family counseling and environmental approaches in the school and community.

If counseling is a justifiable part of the educational system designed to help the child grow and learn, then it must be hypothesized that *freeing the child to learn* is one of the basic goals of counseling. If such an hypothesis holds, it would follow that *freeing the teacher to teach* would also be of benefit to the child.

Drawing from the materials presented in chapters 5 and 6 regarding the characteristics of the facilitative person and the positive effects of the relationship of the child with facilitative people, it would seem to be important for the counselor to work toward the development of facilitative characteristics in those people with whom the child associates.

A legitimate role of the counselor in his work to be of service to the child, then, would be counseling with teachers.

The School

Schools, on the whole, function in a very conservative and tradition-bound manner. Efficient and logical operation often gives way to custom and habit when innovation and constructive change are attempted in the school setting. It is easier to maintain a homeostatic situation rather than to risk change, for change involves threat. To illustrate, a little quick mathematics indicates that the average public school is open for business approximately one-eighth of the hours in a year. When one stops to realize that education has been given the responsibility of preparing for the future our most important natural resource, our children, it is distressing that so little is being done to take maximum advantage of that time. Moreover, it seems like a vast waste of resources that the school facility is used so little.

Lest the reader misconstrue our point, we hasten to add that we are not necessarily advocating a longer school day or school year. Nor are we suggesting that the current amount of "time spent" is inappropriate. Rather, we are advocating that schools become responsive to the changing needs of children and the culture at large. Moreover, we are proposing that schools become community educational centers where the adults of the community as well as the children come to learn and broaden their life experiences.

The Community

If the school is to become the hub of educational activity, then the families of the community must become the spokes of the educational wheel.

Communities, like children, schools, and families, are different. The counseling program in the school should be a reflection of the uniqueness of the community. For example, the elementary school counselor's role in some communities could very legitimately include participation in parent study groups in homes in the community. Very little besides tradition dictates the counselor's hours as being eight to four, or that his work need be done within the confines of the school building.

Some communities have a high population of college graduates, and the vast majority of the children in the community may be college-bound. Other communities may have very few students who will attend college. The school counseling program should reflect such differences.

The political climate of the community, the existing religious traditions, the community customs, and a host of other unique differences which exist make communities differ. All such factors should be taken into account in the development of an effective elementary school counseling program.

The Administrator

Froehlich (1961) in a speech entitled "If I Were . . . " says, "Well, the first thing I would do is try to get things square with my principal. I'd reach certain understandings with him."

Many elementary school counseling programs are characterized by conflict between counselors and administrators. It seems to us that counselors have often fallen short, particularly in two dimensions that have contributed to such conflicts.

The first of these has to do with role expectations. We feel it is the obligation of the counselor to educate his administration regarding the role of the counselor. The principal of the building deserves a meaningful answer to the question, "What does a counselor do?" If such an answer is not forthcoming, it is most understandable that the principal will define a role for the counselor. As is often the case, this role may not be to the counselor's liking nor will it make the most effective use of the counselor's skills.

In addition, the principal should know how he can tell if the counselor is being effective in fulfilling his role. We feel that this, too, is within the province of the counselor's responsibilities. In other words, the principal is charged with evaluating the counselor and the counseling program. If realistic criteria for these evaluations are not supplied to the principal by the counselor, then the counselor should be prepared to accept whatever evaluative criteria are used by the principal.

Conflicts which lead to the detriment of the program and ultimately to the detriment of the child need not exist between counselors and principals. Such conflicts usually seem to arise from philosophical differences, personal differences, misunderstandings, and miscommunications.

The principal and counselor most often are working toward the same ends. It is our experience that open communication which provides for honest differences tends to minimize conflict and maximize effectiveness.

We suggest a "position paper contract" between the principal and counselor. In other words, we recommend that the counselor put down in black and white what he intends to do, how he intends to do it, and how others will know how well he has done it. With the principal also listing his ideas of what and how the counselor should do his job, an agreement regarding role can usually be reached. Counselors and principals, just as other people, can do a better job of what they do when they know what is expected. The counselor must also keep in mind, however, that the ultimate responsibility for the school, the children in the school, and the programs of the school falls on the principal's shoulders.

Teachers

The teacher is the backbone of the elementary school. If the counseling program has teacher approval and acceptance, it will be functional. If such acceptance and approval do not exist, then an effective counseling program will not exist.

One consideration which seems to have some bearing upon teacher acceptance of the counselor is the counselor's experience in elementary schools. Although we do not agree that effective counselors are in need of elementary school teaching experience (Huff, 1965), we do suggest that the child counselor know the environment of the school, have an understanding of the problems teachers face, and possess an appreciation of the teachers' skills, roles, and responsibilities. If the counselor is to be regarded as "one of us" by teachers, these understandings are critical.

Teamwork is a word so overworked in education that it has lost much of its meaning. Teamwork is, however, the key to the development of a counselor-teacher relationship that will facilitate the most advantageous counseling program for the benefit of the child. There are many ways that such a relationship can be developed. If the counselor can "pick up a shovel" when shoveling is needed and if he is not afraid to "gets his hands dirty" when the work of the school requires it, then acceptance by the teacher will usually result. The counselor who is willing to deviate from his specific role definition when a need arises will be more readily acceptable to those with whom he works—teachers, administrators, and fellow counselors.

It is the obligation of the counselor who wants to develop a fully-functioning child counseling program to educate the teaching faculty in the role of the counselor and the counseling program. If the counselor is effective, what he does will normally sell itself to the teachers. If the counselor is ineffective, no amount of public relations will do the job of selling the program.

Many counselor training classes hasten to warn counselors of all the things in the school they should not do. It seems to us that if a cooperative attitude can be developed within the school where the counselor sees himself as one of a team working toward the development of the child, such discussions are superfluous. For example, counselor trainers often warn the prospective counselor about the importance of defining and maintaining clear lines of demarcation between the counselor's role and the teacher's. Following such advice to its ultimate conclusion could find the counselor unwilling to ever involve himself in any classroom activity regardless of the situation. Such an orientation will undoubtedly not endear the counselor to the heart of the teacher who, due to illness, must leave school unexpectedly but cannot do so because of the counselor's unwillingness to include in his definition of his role the serving as a substitute teacher when needed. Simply stated, our point is this: The counselor as a "helping person" must be helpful to teachers as well as children and must be willing to cooperate if he expects to be considered a member of the staff. It has been our experience that such a counselor attitude is much more critical to his acceptance than the issue of teaching experience or his attempts to convince others as to his usefulness.

The Child

Acceptance of the counselor and of the counseling program seems to come from four primary sources: (1) Children refer children through an informal communication network, a "grapevine." (2) Teachers and administrators refer children. (3) Parents refer children. (4) The counselor can promote himself by formally and informally letting children and adults know about his services. Good experiences with the counselor and firsthand recommendations by those children, teachers, administrators, and parents who have had these positive experiences are the best advertising available for an evolving counseling program.

Children need to know the counselor, what he does, how he does it, and how his services might become of value to them individually. It is the obligation of the counselor to provide such information to them in ways that they can readily understand. Specific suggestions for fulfilling this obligation are presented later in this chapter.

From our discussion to this point, we have tried to emphasize that counseling programs should reflect the specific needs of individual elementary school situations; that is, they must take into account the needs of the individual children, the expectancies of the community, the competencies of the faculty, and also the uniqueness of the counselor. The definition of the counselor's role, then, becomes a function of a particular, unique situation in combination with a person having unique skills and competencies to offer.

THE COUNSELING PROGRAM

It has been our impression from reading discussions of counseling programs that such discussions often tend to emphasize "ideal" programs or specifics such as counselor-client ratios, ways of indexing information, and so forth. In the former cases, the reader can be left with the idea that the whole discussion is "pie in the sky" and in the latter cases that the stated specifics have little to do with the reader's unique situation. In the discussion which follows, we have tried to present a compromise between these extremes. We have tried to document our ideas with real experiences which we have had in a real elementary school setting. Our primary purpose is to show the prospective counselor how a growth-promoting elementary school environment might look and what he, the counselor, could do to facilitate such an environment.

Cutler and McNeil (1962) have voiced quite cleverly some of the major objections to a kind of counseling program in the elementary school. They say:

The transplanting of the clinical design within the public schools cannot be over-stressed as a factor which has brought us to our present state of despair. . . . Among its consequences have been: (1) a continuing allegiance to what Redl has called "pressure chamber treatment," in which the child is removed from his classroom habitat, subjected to a special kind of laying on of hands (termed "being seen"), and then returned (repaired?) to the classroom for another go at it; (2) the perpetuation of established clinical jargon as a means of describing and understanding children, in a setting where the jargon has little real (or even translatable) meaning; (3) the establishment of empires for the management of the "whole child"; (4) the cultivation of interprofessional enmity, and the development of various levels of citizenship among professionals dealing with children in the schools; (5) the increased fragmentation of the child and the taking away from the classroom teacher of an additional opportunity for feeling competent to deal with her charges; (6) the domination of mental health professionals, with consequently little attention to the basic educational issues raised by the programs and by dealing with individual children; and (7) a stultification of effort to develop programs and treatment designs which would meet the unique problems of the moderately disturbed child in the school. (pp. 16–17)

With the above indictments of elementary school counseling in mind, we continue to propose an environmental climate that would be conducive to the growth of all persons in that environment. We do not, however, suggest imposing the clinic model upon the school. As White (1965) has pointed out, the little red schoolhouse is not going to give way to the little white clinic without a fight.

We propose to take a page from psychology's work in milieu therapy, a chapter from what educators have learned about the essentials of a learning atmosphere, and a paragraph or two from those aspects of counseling that have shown their positive impact on human behavior: a combination of these becomes the facilitating environment of the elementary school as we see it.

A Warm Environment

Schools have unique personalities. One way of looking at the personality dynamics of a particular school is to view it in terms of those characteristics which it has in common with the facilitative person.

A school can be thought of as being warm, a place where children and adults like to be, a place where learning becomes fun. Unfortunately, the experiences of many children have confirmed to them that school learning is onerous and distasteful. As a result there is often considerable resistance exhibited by children regarding their school attendance and work. Again, from our experience, we are convinced that school does not have to be this way.

In our example school, one of the biggest problems faced by the school officials was keeping children who were sick *out* of school. The atmosphere and the happenings of the school were so important to the children that they hated to miss school; hence, the school nurse often had to insist that such children go home so that the danger of contagion was reduced and the well-being of the child safeguarded.

The following anecdote from the experiences of one of the authors (referred to here as Teacher X) will hopefully give the reader a clearer picture of the atmosphere of warmth and fun which prevailed in that school.

On the third day that I was in the school, which was also the third day of my teaching career, I went to the teachers' lounge for a short break between classes. (You must remember that as a new college graduate, I was filled with all those typical notions about maintaining discipline, developing respect, and so forth). In my absence from the class, the teacher who occupied the classroom adjacent to mine and who had taught for some twelve years in that school had come into my room. He proceeded to conspire with the class: "When Mr. X comes back in here, I want you to make as much noise as possible. Jump up and down, scream, run. Don't be quiet no matter what until I come back in and raise my hand. Then return to your seats and be perfectly quiet."

Some few minutes later I returned to my classroom to find it in complete chaos. Quickly and resourcefully, I began calling upon one and then another of those disciplinary measures that I had been taught in college. But nothing worked. I began to grow panicky. What were my fellow colleagues in this school going to think of me with all this noise and confusion? When I was about to throw up my hands in despair, in walked the culprit.

"What's going on in here?" he asked. I replied that I was completely baffled and discouraged by it all.

"Well, there is no way I can teach my class next door with this kind of noise. Can't you control your class?"

"I guess not," I replied dejectedly. With my admission, he raised his hand and to my amazement, utter silence prevailed.

"Class, take your seats," he said, and they did. Then confidently walking out the door, he patted me on my bewildered head and said, "If you new teachers need any more help, let me know."

What purpose did this episode serve? One very important purpose was that the children saw their teachers as real people, people who could have fun in school with each other and with children without detriment to anyone. Although the school year was not spent as a series of practical jokes, everyone in the school—teachers, students and support personnel—knew that fun was a part of their learning and their school experience.

An Honest Environment

Authenticity has been discussed as a characteristic of the facilitative person. We also view it as a characteristic of the learning atmosphere. Basic to an optimal learning environment are honest and open transactions between and among teachers, students, administrators, parents, and combinations thereof. School should be a place where all the participants can feel free to express themselves without having to resort to pretenses, cover-ups, and charades.

From time to time, all of us have had the "blahs" and have wished to be relieved of our responsibilities for a time. Yet such wishes usually go unfulfilled and we wind up having to "fake it." In our example school, however, such was not necessary. When teachers or children alike felt down in the dumps, they were encouraged to say so. Recognition of these feelings was made and the usual expectations for the teacher or the child were abandoned, or at least reduced, until that person was able to function well again. In the case of the teacher, this might involve the counselor, the principal, another teacher, or a group of older children volunteering to take over the classroom responsibilities until the teacher was back on his feet. As Teacher X states, "The children let me be a real person with them. They encouraged me to tell them how I felt and then compensated for me as I was at that time. They did this in such a way that I felt obligated to be honest and open with them. Such was the climate for me and for the others in the school, teachers or students."

A Mutually Respectful Environment

The preceding example also illustrates the mutual respect factor of a facilitative learning environment. So often adults demand respect from children without being responsive to the children's demands for respect. Similarly, persons of higher status demand respect from those of lower status without some reciprocal right being afforded the person of lower status. From our perspective, respect must be mutual for it to be facilitative to a productive learning atmosphere. Children must choose to respect the adults in the school setting and those adults must choose to respect the children before a healthy school climate can be attained.

In our example school there was a custodian named John who was quite knowledgeable about the stock market. Consequently, when students became interested in learning about stocks and bonds and other related financial matters, teachers would use him as a consultant in their classes. This in turn made John an important and respected member of the school team. Out of this respect, children would intentionally see to it that the school did not get any dirtier than necessary so that John would be able to spend more time with them talking about the daily closing averages.

The height of this mutual respect was demonstrated on John's birthday. The children knew that John would not be coming to work on that day until 3:30 in the afternoon. Through previous arrangement with the principal and their teachers, the upper elementary grades took it upon themselves to scrub and clean the school building as soon as the lower grades were dismissed from school at 2:30. When John arrived at school that day, the only task left for him to do was to erase the "Happy Birthday John" from each chalkboard in the building. When he left to spend the remainder of the day with his family, he was serenaded by more than a hundred children singing "Happy Birthday, Dear John." The tears in John's eyes as he drove from the school attested to the real meaning of mutual respect.

An Understanding Environment

Another atmospheric quality that the facilitative elementary school possesses is that of understanding those persons who make up the staff and student body. Children and adults need to feel understood from their own personal frames of reference. Another anecdote from the personal experience of Teacher X captures the essence of this quality.

In mid-year I had my new car badly wrecked. By the end of the school year it was repaired and I was set to leave on vacation the day after school was out. Just two days before the end of school, however, I discovered that the garage repairman had not satisfactorily fixed the trunk lid and it leaked. I called the repairman and asked if he could fix the trunk lid before vacation. He said he would call me back.

Like many public schools, the next to last day of the school year was a day for teachers to put finishing touches on report cards and other details, and the children remained home. According to policy, however, teachers were to be at school regardless of whether or not their work was complete. The district administration had underscored this policy by further stating that any teacher leaving the building between 8:00 A.M. and 4:00 P.M. would not be paid for that day.

I was sitting in the teachers' room with the rest of the teachers who had completed their work when the school secretary came in and informed me I had a phone call. Our school, not being a new and fancy structure, had but one telephone and it was in the principal's office. I walked into my principal's office and who should be sitting there with her but the district superintendent. I gulped and picked up the phone to be told by the garageman that if I could get my car downtown immediately, they would be able to fix it. I stammered a little, then asked if they would fix it if I got there after four. At that point, my principal, realizing my plight, said, "Say, Mr. X, since you are done with your work, could you go downtown right away and pick up the awards for tomorrow's awards assembly?"

I nodded my willingness, informed the garageman that I would be at the garage shortly, and left the office. Once outside, my principal caught up with me and said, "Those awards won't be ready until tomorrow morning, but you might honk on the way by."

This serves as an example of an atmosphere where people tried to see things from the other person's point of view. Moreover, effort was extended to the other person to meet his needs in the easiest and most reasonable way possible.

A Cooperative Environment

A facilitative learning environment is also characterized by emphasis on cooperation rather than competition. This is not to say that competition has no place in the learning environment. Hopefully, the following example of the cooperative environment that existed within our model school will help to illustrate a way in which competition can be used to facilitate cooperation rather than inhibit it. Teacher X tells it this way:

The upper two grades at our elementary school were departmentalized. I taught seventh- and eighth-grade science and had a homeroom of eighth graders. There was also another eighth-grade homeroom sponsored by the math teacher. Toward the end of the school year I decided to give my science classes a test over everything we had studied during the year. I announced a competition between my eighth-grade classes.

"The day after the exam," I said, "we'll have a party. Each person in the class with the lowest average on the exam will buy two bottles of pop, one for himself and one for a member of the other class. The homeroom teacher of the class with the lowest average will also bake a cake for the party."

I gave the students in both classes ten days to review all the concepts and ideas covered and told them I would help them in any way they wanted me to.

The first day there was almost complete silence in the classroom as each child began reviewing the past year's work in science. By the second day the class had divided into clusters. I noticed particularly one cluster that was comprised of the three girls in the class who had consistently made the highest grade averages during the year and the boy with the lowest grade average in the total class.

I questioned one of the girls after class regarding what had been happening. She said, "We've decided if we studied and studied for these ten days we probably would get 147 instead of 145 out of the possible 150 points. But if we help Jerry learn, he might get 70 or 80 instead of the 30 he would get without us. In that way, our class might win."

On the day of the test, after school was out, both sections crowded into my room. I stacked the papers in two groups, one stack for each section. I scored one paper from one section and then one from the other. After each exam was graded I put the score on the board to a chorus of cheers and moans.

When I finished grading Jerry's paper and reported his score to the two sections by marking an 86 on the board under section one, a deafening cheer erupted in the room. Jerry was lifted to the shoulders of his classmates and paraded around the room. Jerry, with the help of his classmates, had done better than he had ever done before. Now, as a result of this special circumstance and the cooperative climate, Jerry was being rewarded for his effort.

When the last test was graded, it became evident that my homeroom had been narrowly defeated. Yet, it was with a great deal of pleasure that I baked that cake for the party the next day.

Expecting Responsible Behavior

People generally seem to do that which is expected of them. In a school climate that expects children to be responsible, children learn to behave responsibly.

The first teachers' meeting held in our example school might serve as an illustration of an atmosphere that expected every citizen in the school community to behave responsibly. Again, Teacher X states:

I was standing in front of my seventh-grade science class talking about something of great significance, such as the reproduction of the starfish, when a knock came at my door.

I went to the door and found my principal standing there. She announced, "I had the cooks bake up some goodies and all the teachers are going to get together to talk."

"Now?" I exclaimed. She nodded her head in assent.

"But I am right in the midst of lecturing to my class. I can't leave now!" Patiently she reminded me that my students had been left since they were in the first grade and that they could get along well without me. So, after some hesitation, I decided if I could leave the door open and watch, it might be all right. As I walked out, I saw one of the students move to the head of the class and say, "I'd like to tell you about an interesting article I read the other night in *Scientific American* . . ."

When I finally returned to the class, I found a group actively engaged in an experiment, another group playing an adaptation of the TV game, "College Bowl," using science-oriented questions, and still another group trying to struggle with the concept of valence and chemical elements. Two children were working on the next day's English assignment.

Several months later I called my principal in the morning to report I was sick and not coming to school. From this experience and others, it was not a surprise when she asked if I wanted her to get a substitute for me. Obviously, she was not fearful that the children could not learn without an adult teacher being present.

The Total Climate

Certainly our example school was not without problems. The faculty were not always striving to create a better environment for children. Sometimes they didn't care. The children were not always responsible in their actions. Sometimes they didn't care. But on the whole, the school climate was one of care, trust, openness, honesty, warmth, understanding, mutual respect, and cooperation between and among the children and the adults who comprised the school staff. There was also a spirit of fun and playfulness which usually pervaded the total learning environment.

But what, you ask, does this have to do with the major school function of educating children? Does the climate really make a difference? Do children really learn as much in such an environment? Again the results from this single school situation are a strong affirmation of the approach. The achievement of the children from this school as measured by standardized achievement test scores and subsequent high school grades was markedly superior to that of students from other elementary schools in the same district. We submit that the atmosphere was largely responsible for those differences.

COUNSELOR'S ROLE IN FOSTERING A FACILITATIVE LEARNING CLIMATE

As we have stated earlier, we consider the counselor to have a major responsibility for the fostering of a facilitative learning climate in the school community. We recognize that few, if any, school environments are the products of a single person's efforts, imagination, and goals. Such an environment is best accomplished through collective goals and through cooperative efforts between and among counselors, teachers, administrators, parents and, most importantly, children. If, however, the competent child counselor can bring his personal wholeness, his attitudes of wanting to be helpful, to all participants in the school environment, his specialized knowledge and skills, and an open-mindedness, he will be well on the way to developing an effective elementary school counseling program.

Specific considerations in the evolution of such a program include the counselor's willingness to show his wares, to present himself as a model to be extended beyond the boundaries of the school building and the school day, and to communicate his services to those in need.

Showing His Wares

In keeping with our emphasis on experiential learning, we submit that one effective way for the counselor to promote a counseling program which can foster a facilitative school climate is to demonstrate what counseling is and what potentials there are for it. This suggestion reminds us of some lines from the children's game "New Orleans." You may remember that selected lines of the game say, "What's your trade?" "Lemonade." "Show us then if you're not afraid." The counselor must be willing to "show us then," otherwise his acceptance by children, teachers, parents, and other interested persons will be inhibited.

From our perspective there are a number of ways that the counselor may show his wares. For students and teachers, the counselor can go into the classroom and talk with students about counseling. He can present slides or movies exploring the counseling sessions. He can use audio and video tapes of group and individual counseling experiences; but, whatever approach he uses, he must keep in mind that the purpose of the various approaches is to give children and teachers the opportunity to make choices relative to the potential benefit that they may reap from the counseling service.

Many of the same approaches also have direct application for use with extraschool groups like PTA groups and community agencies. From our experience, demonstrations such as role-playing a counseling interview provide a fine vehicle to help interested persons learn about the counseling service. Such demonstrations are often followed by lively discussion and comment.

The Counselor as a Model

We have suggested in various other places in this work that modeling is an effective method of promoting learning. When the school staff, the children, and the larger community are able to see the consistency between what the counselor says and what he does, the counselor is well underway in his efforts to foster a facilitative learning environment. In other words, the counselor must be a warm, genuine, open, cooperative, caring, trustworthy, and understanding person to those with whom he comes in contact. By being such a person with consistency, the threat of his presence will be minimized.

The counselor who is willing to unstintingly share himself with others and who is willing to let himself be known is one who can foster similar behaviors in others by his own behavior. He is most effective in being a model when these aforementioned attitudes and commitments are deeply entrenched in his life style; that is, his caring for individual human beings must be in evidence in his contacts with children, parents, teachers, administrators, and all others with whom he has relationships, no matter what the setting or the time. Again, counseling is a way of life.

The Counselor as a Teacher

In contrast to the impact that the counselor can have on people through his actions, we would now like to turn to the impact that he may have through formal and informal teaching. It is important to note that we see no qualitative differences between quality teaching and effective counseling. Both activities deal with the promotion of learning, and if different, are only different in degree.

Teacher and parent study groups conducted by the counselor are ways that the counselor can directly and indirectly affect the total climate of the school and the individual home environments in which children live. Such groups often aid the participants in their understanding of themselves and children by providing new ways of looking at and coping with the behaviors of children. From these understandings all are able to benefit.

Advertising the Services

It is highly probable that the effective counselor will have little need to "sell" his services after he has once established an atmosphere of trust and confidence with the children, teachers, and parents in the school setting. Our experience again suggests that "grapevine" communication will do the job.

Even so, we also suggest that the counselor consider the distribution of brochures to community patrons of the school. Brochures might describe the services available and also give a progress report of the development of the service. By doing so, the counselor sets a tone of wanting to keep his service before the public and to keep the public informed.

Other ways of making the services of the counselor known are abundant. Interviews of the counselor on radio and television, programs designed to have the counselor respond to telephone questions, talks with service club groups, all are legitimate ways of communicating the service afforded by the counselor, of eliciting support for the services, and ultimately of affecting the nature of the school environment in a positive way.

In the final analysis, however, it will be the actual accomplishment of the counselor in his daily work with children, parents, teachers, and others which will determine his acceptance over the long haul. No amount of public relations work and salesmanship can substitute for those changes he can foster in the lives of children and in those adults who comprise the worlds of the children.

COMMENT

In this chapter we have discussed the application of our counseling philosophy to an elementary school setting. We have attempted to show that such a philosophy in use promotes a school climate which in turn fosters high-level learning and behavior on the part of children. In discussing specific qualities of the learning environment, we have drawn upon personal experiences to illustrate and support our beliefs.

We have also suggested that the counselor has a major responsibility for the fostering of a facilitative learning environment in schools. His chief tool and asset is himself and his ability to consistently model and promote those attitudes and convictions which enhance an environment in which children, teachers, administrators, and parents cooperate toward the well-being and advancement of all.

REFERENCES

CUTLER, R. L., AND MCNEIL, E. B. *Mental Health Consultation in the Schools: A Research Analysis.* Michigan Society for Mental Health, 1962.

FROEHLICH, C. P. "If I Were . . ." Paper read at San Joaquin Valley Guidance Association and Region 3 of California Association of Secondary School Administrations, Calif., 1961.

HUFF, V. E. "The Millstone of Teaching Experience." *Personnel and Guidance Journal* 44 (1965):192–194.

SATIR, VIRGINIA. *Conjoint Family Therapy*. Palo Alto: Science & Behavior Books, Inc., 1966.

WHITE, M. A. "The Little Red Schoolhouse and the Little White Clinic." *Teachers College Record* 67 (1965):188–200.

SELECTED ADDITIONAL READINGS

ALSCHULER, A. S. "Psychological Education." *Journal of Humanistic Psychology* 9 (1969):1–16.

BECK, C. E., ed. *Guidelines for Guidance*. Dubuque, Ia.: William C. Brown Company Publishers, 1967.

BERMON, LOUISE M. *New Priorities in the Curriculum*. Columbus, Ohio: Charles E. Merrill Publishing Co., 1968.

DINKMEYER, D. C., ed. *Guidance and Counseling in the Elementary School*. New York: Holt, Rinehart & Winston, Inc., 1968.

DREWS, ELIZABETH M. "Beyond Curriculum." *Journal of Humanistic Psychology* 8 (1968):97–112.

———. "Fernwood, A Free School." *Journal of Humanistic Psychology* 8 (1968):113–122.

FOX, R.; LUSZKI, MARGARET B.; AND SCHMUCK, R. *Diagnosing Classroom Learning Environments*. Chicago: Science Research Associates, Inc., 1966.

GLASSER, W. *Schools Without Failure*. New York: Harper & Row, Publishers, 1969.

KOPLITZ, E. D., ed. *Guidance in the Elementary School: Theory, Research and Practice*. Dubuque, Ia.: William C. Brown Company Publishers, 1968.

KOWITZ, G. T., AND KOWITZ, NORMA G. *Operating Guidance Services for the Modern School*. New York: Holt, Rinehart & Winston, Inc., 1968.

LEONARD, G. B. *Education and Ecstasy*. New York: The Delacorte Press, 1968.

MEEKS, ANNA R. *Guidance in Elementary Education*. New York: The Ronald Press Company, 1968.

MOGAR, R. E. "Toward a Psychological Theory of Education." *Journal of Humanistic Psychology* 9 (1969):17–52.

MOUSTAKAS, C. E. *The Authentic Teacher*. Cambridge, Mass.: H. A. Doyle, 1966.

MURPHY, G. *Freeing Intelligence Through Teaching: A Dialectic of the Rational and the Personal*. New York: Harper & Row, Publishers, 1961.

NEILL, A. S. *Summerhill*. New York: Hart Publishing Co., Inc., 1960.

OHLSEN, M. M. *Guidance Services in the Modern School*. New York: Harcourt, Brace & World, Inc., 1964.

RENFIELD, R. *If Teachers Were Free*. Washington: Acropolis Books, 1969.

VON HILSHEIMER, G. *Green Valley: A Democratic Approach to Education*. Washington: American Society for Humanistic Education, 1964.

12

Counseling Trends and a Training Approach

COUNSELING TRENDS

The field of professional child counseling in this country is largely a development of the last three decades. As is true in most newly emerging fields of study, child counseling has experienced many different directions and focuses during this period. For us, this dynamic, influxive, changing, and emerging area is an exciting one in which to be involved. There is so little known and, consequently, so much to be discovered.

In this chapter we have endeavored to provide the reader with a sense of this dynamic quality. By discussing trends which we see in the area and by the development of a training model, we hope the reader will be challenged to also become a pioneer and help expand the understandings and knowledge of this fledgling discipline.

Beyond Schoolism

The brief history of the "helping professions" has been one characterized by the development of a number of different helping approaches (Harper, 1959). These approaches have most often been derived from the unique therapeutic experiences of individual helping persons. Regrettably, the personal effectiveness of such practitioners has prompted immediate and blind discipleship and "band wagoning" of an approach before sufficient investigation could be conducted into the effectiveness of the approach when employed by one of the disciples. As Parker (1968) has said:

The profession might be better characterized by its rapid "theory seizures" than by its hard evidence of value. Unfortunately, the original effectiveness of the leader is seldom transmitted to his followers. The messianic hopes dwindle as the disciples imitate their leader without possessing the spirit that inspired him. (p. 2)

Even though considerable controversy and debate still exist relative to the merits of various theoretical orientations, there is a movement toward the transcendence of "schoolism" to an empirical search for those variables which promote positive therapeutic outcomes.

This movement seems apparent in the recent literature of counseling. Works by Ford and Urban (1963), who have provided a systematic analysis of divergent theories and have attempted to convert the different theories into a common language scheme; Stieper and Wiener (1965), who have attempted an identification of fundamental therapeutic variables; Berenson and Carkhuff (1967), who have examined the sources of gain in effective therapeutic approaches; Kell and Mueller (1966), who have discussed the primary conditions of quality counseling experiences; Brammer and Shostrom (1968), who have formulated a systematic eclectic counseling model; Guerney (1969), who has presented evidence of positive counseling outcomes outside of theoretical bias; and others, all seem to point toward an increasing maturity and desire to go beyond "schoolism" in the area.

The Medical Model

Much has been written in the literature of psychology and the "helping professions" about the inadequacy of the medical model of "sickness and wellness" when applied to counseling. Szasz (1960), a psychiatrist, has created considerable controversy in professional circles with his rejection of the medical model in the treatment of mental problems. Seeing emotional problems as disorders in learning, he views treatment as a learning-relearning process. Farnsworth (1965), Glasser (1965), and Perls (Shostrom, 1967), although medically trained, similarly express disillusionment with the medical model. They too have developed alternative treatment approaches based on learning and educational principles.

Even though the challenges to the mental illness concept are increasing, the helping professions still rely heavily on that model. We believe that an alternative model for the purposes of understanding and treating emotional disturbance is evolving. This model is becoming based on empirically validated psychological principles, an advance which will bring a new stage of maturity to the helping professions.

New Directions for Man

A popular cry among a concerned segment of our society is that modern technology is enslaving and dehumanizing man. Quite obviously, such is not the case, for technology per se has no potential apart from the way it is used by man. It is man who is enslaving and dehumanizing man.

In recent years humanistic psychology has emerged as a force to counter this dehumanizing trend and to act as an alternative to the behavioristic and

Freudian approaches to human behavior. Fundamental to this new third force psychology is a focus on man's higher level needs, aspirations, ultimate values, peak experiences, awareness, transcendence of self, life meanings, and related concepts. From its birth as a small protest movement in the late 1950s, the third force has now become a many-faceted, thriving, independent, and organized movement concerned with the extension of the humanistic orientation in psychology, education, and related fields.

In contrast to behavioral psychology which considers man as if he were an object or a thing to be studied "scientifically" and controlled, and Freudian psychology which deterministically treats man as merely a biological animal, humanistic psychology attempts an orientation to man which goes beyond these considerations. It seeks to view man's higher potentials as human rights. As Maslow (1969) has so aptly stated, "The need for dignity, for example, can be seen as a fundamental human right in the same sense that it is a human right to have enough calcium or enough vitamins to be healthy. If these needs are not fulfilled, pathology results." (p. 3) Such a view of man obviously necessitates new ways of conceiving of human research and measurement. It also denies the concept of statistical normality as *the* criterion for judging the quality and appropriateness of man's behavior.

In furthering this approach to man, modern technology can become a useful tool in service to man. For example, computers and learning programs can be used to free man for the study and development of his human potentials. The teacher or counselor who can disseminate needed information through the use of computer technology can free himself for more creative human functions—those functions which are beyond the scope and province of technological advances.

Knowledge and Change

Knowledge in all fields and especially the behavioral sciences is changing at an ever-increasing rate. This is a condition which has been identified as one of the greatest problems facing modern man. Questions arise such as: How much change can a human being accept? How rapidly can he accept it? Can he abandon his tradition of using static concepts and means in order to adopt process-oriented concepts and means? Can man survive apart from the use of process-oriented concepts and means?

Certainly these are challenging questions. They imply the need for new ways of life—new governmental methods, new societal standards, new religious commitments, and new educational practices. From our perspective, educational programs designed to prepare counselors to help people cope with the changing world must anticipate an increasing rate of obsolescence for knowledge. Moreover, they must explore bold new approaches and processes keyed to the formulation of attitudes and values which encourage the individual to engage in the life-long process of educating and reeducating himself. In this regard, it seems critical to "hook" the individual on his own process of learning rather than on its products. Such an individual will be better able to flow with the changingness of knowledge and practices. He will be better able to tentatively commit himself to the best knowledge and practice of that time, but he will also be prepared to move to new tentative commitments when the data so indicates.

The Intensive Small Group

The rapidly spreading phenomenon of the intensive small group experience (sensitivity training, T-grouping, human relations workshops, basic encounter grouping, laboratory training, and so forth) in our society has been cited as potentially the most important social innovation of this century (Rogers, 1968). Designed to improve the learnings and abilities of participants in interpersonal communications and understandings, to aid them in coping with change as a way of life, and to foster change in organizational environments, the intensive small group would seem to have great potential for application to a wide variety of settings serving diverse populations.

Rogers (1969) has outlined the hypotheses which underlie the process of the intensive small group experience as follows:

A facilitator can develop, in a group which meets intensively, a psychological climate of safety in which freedom of expression and reduction of defensiveness gradually occur.

In such a psychological climate, many of the immediate feeling reactions of each member toward others, and toward himself, tend to be expressed.

A climate of mutual trust develops out of this mutual freedom to express real feelings, positive and negative. Each member moves toward greater acceptance of his total being—his emotional, intellectual, and physical being, as it is.

With individuals less inhibited by defensive rigidity, the possibility of change—in personal attitudes and behaviors, in teaching methods, in administrative methods—becomes less threatening.

With a reduction of defensive rigidity, individuals can hear each other, can learn from each other, to a greater extent.

There is a development of feedback from one person to another, such that each individual learns how he appears to others, and what impact he has in interpersonal relationships.

As individuals hear each other more accurately, an organization tends to become a relationship of persons with common goals, rather than a formal hierarchical structure.

With this greater freedom and improved communication, new ideas, new concepts, new directions emerge. Innovation becomes a desirable rather than a threatening possibility.

These learnings in the group experience tend to carry over, temporarily or more permanently, into the relationships with peers, students, subordinates, and even to superiors, following the group experience. (pp. 306–307)

Although the intensive small group process has been used extensively in industry, its acceptance and applicability in schools and other cultural institutions have only recently begun. As Rogers (1968) has noted, however, the movement is picking up momentum and is becoming a "grass roots" movement as well as a professional movement. In some ways, portions of the movement have become cultish, and the purposes and processes of the small group have been abused. These abuses have led some qualified and responsible leaders in the movement (Shostrom, 1969) to caution the unsophisticated consumer about becoming involved in such groups.

At either the "grass roots" or the more professional levels, it would seem important for the child counselor to be informed and qualified to advise and perhaps conduct groups of this nature. If the movement extends to the public schools, as is predicted, such activity may become a primary responsibility of the counselor.

Focus on Children

An emerging trend in the field of mental health is the development of programs focusing on the prevention of childhood disorders and problems and the investigation of normal patterns of child development (Hobbs, 1964). This focus has resulted from the realization that the most effective way to make substantial changes in the mental health of the future generation is to concentrate on the children of today. With this idea in mind, Hobbs (1964) has advocated that at least 75 percent of our resources be directed toward the study and treatment of the mental health problems of children. The remaining 25 percent would be used to "hold the line" on current adult mental health problems.

With such an emphasis, the function of the child counselor will potentially take on added importance and scope. He may be called upon to be a major leader in the resolution of mental health issues and problems of the future.

Family Counseling

Numerous studies have shown that the family behaves as if it were a unit in which relationships are in some sort of balance (Jackson, 1957; Masserman, 1959; Ackerman, 1962). Moreover, when one person in a family shows symptoms of disturbance, all family members are affected in some way. From this evidence it is becoming apparent to increasing numbers of counseling practitioners that treatment of a disturbed family member is best accomplished by treatment of the family unit (Dreikurs, 1969). This is true regardless of the age or position of the family member, for attempts to change only the disturbed family member's way of operating in effect places the total burden for changing the homeostasis of the family unit on that disturbed member's shoulders. In the case of a disturbed child, he not only has to work toward change in his own personal way of doing things, but he also has to combat the forces in the family unit which are directed toward the maintenance of a static family condition. In other words, the child is trapped between the expectations held for him by the family unit and his own desire and need to change (Satir, 1966).

In family counseling where all members of the family unit are involved, the burden of responsibility for change rests upon all members of the family unit. With such a sharing of responsibility, family relationships and interactions can be examined and redefined so that a new homeostasis can be arrived at in the family. This new homeostasis in turn can support the disturbed child as he works out new and more adaptive behaviors.

From our perspective, such an approach to effecting the behavior of children is most legitimate for the child counselor. The exclusive treatment of the child would appear to be at best a less productive approach. As child counseling evolves and continues to seek an identity, the use of family unit approaches will undoubtedly become more accepted and utilized.

Subprofessionals

Another movement in the "helping professions" which is seeking acceptance is the utilization of persons who are ". . . naturally significant to those in need of help, or who can be made to be significant as intermediaries, as aides, or as agents of the professionals" (Guerney, 1969, p. iii; Dimick, Huff, and Ricksecker, in press). The pioneering work of Rioch (1963) who used carefully selected mature housewives to do counseling under supervision has opened up the door for other investigators to consider the use of subprofessionals as mental health specialists.

More recent studies have reported the use of "naturally helpful" college students in working with disturbed elementary school children (Cowen, Zax, and Laird, 1966), in play therapy (Stollak, 1968), and as group therapy leaders with hospitalized chronic male schizophrenic patients (Poser, 1966). At least one study reports the use of high school students as mental hospital workers (Fellows and Wolpin, 1966). Still other reported investigations suggest the use of parents (Shah, 1967; Walder, et al., 1967; Wahler, et al., 1965), foster grandparents (Johnston, 1967); peers (Buehler, Patterson, and Furniss, 1966); teachers (Harris, Wolf, and Baer, 1964); and lay persons (Carkhuff and Truax, 1965) as therapeutic agents in working with disturbed children and adults.

It seems clear that the prospective supply of professional mental health personnel will never meet the needs and demands of the future for services; hence, the use of subprofessional personnel is indicated. Moreover, the evidence to date suggests that there is a vast untapped reservoir of persons who are "naturally helpful" to those in need; that is, there are "untrained" persons who produce positive results. As Bergin (1963) has concluded, such persons are "those who have certain personal qualities and ways of responding to others rather than a well-trained armamentarium of techniques." (p. 248) By tapping this "untrained" reservoir, we may be more adequately able to meet the demands for future mental health services.

Use of Professionals

In addition to the increased use of subprofessionals as therapeutic agents, it is becoming more and more evident that we must also train the professional person in ways to multiply his effectiveness. Hobbs (1964) has suggested that the professional person be used to guide the work of carefully selected persons with limited training. Although he is speaking primarily about the extensively trained mental health specialist (psychiatrist, psychologist, social worker, and others), his suggestion also has merit for the counselor as he works with children. It may be that the child counselor could serve a legitimate and important function by having selected parents or high school and college young people to work as therapeutic agents with young children under the supervision of the counselor. Certainly there is ample data of a tentative nature to prompt investigation into the efficacy of such a practice.

In any event, the future will undoubtedly demand that the highly-trained professional therapist function more as a supervisor and consultant to the less-trained mental health worker than has been the case to date. In so doing, he can multiply his effectiveness by developing means of working through other people.

The Counselor in the Community

Another predicted mental health direction which has implications for the child counselor is that of community psychology (Ricks, 1969). As our understandings from research evolve, new methods for educational intervention into the development of children whose lives become warped by poverty, unhealthy family environments, and social discrimination will emerge and undoubtedly will change the nature of the child counselor's role.

It is conceivable that the work of the counselor will become much less chair-bound and more oriented toward active involvement and intervention where the action is. Not only will the counselor become more actively involved with children in need, but he will also become an instrument of environmental change and modification.

Unless current trends change, the public faith and professional mysticism which have surrounded the activity of the counselor and psychotherapist will be increasingly challenged. Counselors will be required to produce results as the public becomes a more sophisticated and knowledgeable consumer of the counselor's services. Theoretically biased and idiosyncratic counselor practices will give way to pragmatically demonstrable methods of fostering change in behavior. Job security will become dependent upon professional competence rather than job title or job tenure, and the effective child counselor will potentially become a key individual in the shaping of the community.

THE TRAINING OF COUNSELORS

Although there is a recognized shortage of competent counseling specialists to meet the increasing needs and demands of society, the current trend is toward increasing the amount of training needed for licensing or certification as a professional counselor. Provided that such added training increases the counselor's competence to effectively discharge his obligations, then that training is justified. However, the factors of time spent in training and in achieving familiarity with specific content may have little to do with the development of counselor competence. It is the quality of the experiences afforded prospective counselors which is of major consequence.

In an attempt to provide a training program which would develop highly qualified counseling practitioners, we have discussed in the following pages those considerations which we believe to be basic to a quality training program. We recognize that these concepts and practices have not been subjected to rigorous evaluation. They are tentative and somewhat speculative, and yet our experience attests to their usefulness. We feel certain that a two-year graduate program designed on the model which we present could graduate counselors who would be very productive practitioners.

Selecting the Learner

This section, which discusses the process of selecting counselor trainees, may seem inordinately long and detailed. If so, perhaps a word of explanation regarding the rationale for the discussion will help clarify its purpose.

We believe that selection is a very critical step in the total training process. If the student is to benefit maximally from his training to go on to become a creative practitioner, then rigorous selection procedures based on requisite attitudes, skills, and personal characteristics must be used.

Moreover, it is our contention that once the trainee is accepted to a program on the basis of such a rigorous selection procedure, ideally, he should not be dropped or dismissed except for very unusual circumstances. Once the student is accepted as possessing the requisite attitudes, skills, and personal qualities for admission, it becomes the responsibility of the program's staff to facilitate the trainee's growth to that of a highly competent individual. As Rogers (1969) has suggested, student failures in such a system are failures which are reflections on both the staff and the student.

It should be pointed out that from a hypothetical point of view, we believe all persons have the potential to develop into effective counselors, given sufficient amounts of time and facilitating conditions. Practically, however, it seems most useful to identify and select those persons who at the time of selection possess relatively higher levels of those qualities leading to success. By helping these persons to function at even higher levels, we can more readily bridge the gap between the demand and availability of counseling services.

The discussion which follows, then, is an attempt to suggest criteria and procedures for selecting counselor-trainees which more adequately identify trainees who will benefit most from training.

Selection Criteria

The literature of counseling is replete with discussions of the importance of the counselor's personality in relation to his success. Rogers (1951, 1954, 1961, 1962) has written extensively about the personal counselor qualities that promote positive client change. Kemp (1967) has discussed what he calls counselor intangibles which have a direct impact on the outcomes of counseling. Their work as counselors and counselor trainers has led Kell and Mueller (1966) to conclude that effective counselors help their clients most by being human. From an analytic point of view, Bordin (1968) sees counselor warmth as a key personality characteristic in effecting client change. Moreover, pages could be filled with similar statements about the importance of counselor maturity, care, love, faith, and a host of other personal qualities cited as crucial to positive counseling outcomes.

From an empirical perspective, findings are also pointing to the importance of the counselor's personality. Bergin (1966) suggests that therapeutic progress varies as a function of counselor warmth, empathy, adjustment, and experience. From his findings, he suggests that selection and training of counselors need to use these qualities as basic criteria. Allen (1967) has concluded that effectiveness in counseling is related to the counselor's openness to his own feelings and not to his academic background. The extensive work of Truax and Carkhuff (1967) and their disciples also continues to emphasize from an empirical base the significance of the counselor's accurate empathy, self-congruence, and warmth in the effective therapeutic relationship. In addition to these works, numerous other studies could be cited which give emphasis to the impact of various counselor personality characteristics on the outcomes of counseling.

Nevertheless, in spite of the expert opinion and the supportive research emphasizing the importance of the counselor's personality in counseling, most training institutions still rely primarily on selection procedures based on undergraduate grades and standardized abilities tests (American Psychological Association, 1954). Although such criteria may not be totally irrelevant, we contend that other criteria which attempt to focus more on the personality of the prospective counselor are needed. In the discussion which follows, we have identified some of the personal qualities which we feel are important in the selection of counselor candidates.

RELATIONSHIP QUALITIES

Included in these personal qualities would be the degree to which the candidate is able to effectively communicate with children and adults. Rogers (1969) has more tightly defined this characteristic as empathic ability. Stating that empathic understanding is one of the best indices of psychological maturity, he suggests that only the individual who is reasonably secure in his own personal identity is able to permit the other person to be or become his unique self—a goal of counseling. Although satisfactory instruments are as yet unavailable for assessing this quality, other means can be used. We suggest that prime sources of data relative to this quality are children and adults with whom the candidate has had previous relationships.

It is conceivable that much could be learned about the candidate's ability to effectively communicate with others by depth interviews with his close associates, colleagues, subordinates, and others from his environment. Yet another process for consideration could be to have trained raters observe and judge the candidate's abilities along the prescribed dimensions in an ongoing T-group setting. In this way, firsthand knowledge of the candidate's level of functioning as well as his growth potential could be assessed.

From our experiences with children we have become increasingly aware of the child's ability to "read" adults directly; that is, children being less cognitively and verbally oriented and more affectively oriented are better able to directly feel the "real person" of adults. They are better able to accurately perceive incongruencies, deceits, appearances, facades, and pretenses than are adults. Consequently, we believe that a group of healthy children could be used as a screening procedure for counselor candidates. Specifically, the candidate would be asked to spend a couple of hours with a group of five-year-old children in a play therapy room or some similar setting. At the end of this time, the children would be asked to provide feedback relative to their feelings about the candidate. Such an experience would give others (faculty, fellow students) the opportunity of observing and further assessing the candidate's potential.

CURIOSITY AND ORIGINALITY

Another criterion of selection which seems useful to us is an assessment of the candidate's degree of curiosity and his ability to generate original responses. Again, as Rogers (1969) has pointed out, the individual who is genuinely curious and eager to find knowledge in the world about him is the individual who will probably aid maximally in the discovery of new knowledge, new devices for doing things, and new approaches to problems.

Certainly at this point in the development of our knowledge, our methods for assessing such qualities are gross and in need of refinement. Even so, the validity of the approach does not seem subject to serious question. We currently have tests for creativity which can be used as one way of assessing these qualities. Other procedures need to be developed which can tap the imaginative and wide-ranging curiosity and the ability to be unafraid to express tentative and unique ideas in the prospective student.

COGNITIVE FLEXIBILITY AND PSYCHOLOGICAL OPENNESS

Closely related to curiosity and originality are cognitive flexibility and psychological openness. From a review of the literature that indicates that misperceptions of oneself promote misperceptions of others, Allen and Whiteley (1968) evolved studies to assess the effect of cognitive flexibility and psychological openness on the selection, training, and effectiveness of counselor trainees. Using a combination of projective tests, objective tests, simulated counseling situations, and rating scales, Allen and Whiteley were able to conclude that both constructs are highly related to effectiveness in counseling and in counselor training.

These findings are supported by the work of Kemp (1962) who compared the responses of relatively open- and closed-minded counselor trainees on paper-and-pencil hypothetical situations and in actual counseling situations. The open-minded candidates were able to respond consistently to both situations with understanding and supportive responses. The more close-minded trainees, on the other hand, were able to respond with understanding and supportive responses to the paper-and-pencil hypothetical situations, but in the actual counseling situation they gave more evaluative, interpretative, probing, and diagnostic responses. In the actual counseling situation which evoked considerable threat and anxiety in the close-minded group, the counselor-trainees had to narrow and distort their responses. There was no opportunity to review and choose the "appropriate" response when the situation demanded immediate response.

From the limited evidence available, it would seem appropriate to consider the degree of candidate cognitive flexibility and psychological openness in the selection process. Such a focus seems indicative of a worthwhile direction even though the supporting research evidence is not extensive.

OTHER VARIABLES

Independent studies by Bergin and Solomon (1963) and Truax, Silber and Wargo (1966) using widely differing student populations and training approaches have identified some additional variables for consideration in the selection of counselor trainees. In investigating a number of correlates of empathic ability, Bergin and Solomon found that there was a nonsignificant negative correlation with verbal intelligence and a similar nonsignificant negative correlation with the "psychologist" subscale of the graduate record exam. They also found that certain measures of psychological disturbance (Psychoasthenia and Depression Scales of the MMPI) were negatively correlated with empathic ability, while selected measure of personal strength (autonomy, dominance, and adaptability to change) were positively related to empathic ability. Moreover, empathic ability also seemed to be negatively correlated with needs of order, abasement, and a cognitive counselor orientation.

Using scales designed to measure the actual ability of counselor trainees to communicate accurate empathy, warmth, and self-congruence, Truax, Silber, and Wargo (1966) compared these measured abilities with a number of personality variables. Their findings suggested that those students developing a lower need for order, a higher adaptability to change, a lower need for abasement, a higher need for autonomy, and a decrease in defensiveness were more successful in developing therapeutic skill.

The findings of these studies are suggestive rather than definitive. They do, however, provide additional ways of looking at the problem of selecting those counselor trainees who will benefit maximally from training.

A Model for Training

Throughout this volume we have touched time and time again on aspects of the learning process which relate to child behavior change. We have stressed the necessity for that which is being learned to have real meaning and personal relevance to the learner. We have implied that significant learning only results from a self-initiated basis and that involvement and experiencing by the learner are essential. Such learning is pervasive, changing the individual in both his cognitive and affective aspects. It involves a personal appropriation of the concept in question; a making of it his very own. It is then that he *really* learns, *really* understands, and *really* knows. This is the kind of learning that we believe to be essential in the education of effective child counselors. That is to say, those conditions and human qualities which promote growth, development, and wholeness in the child client are fundamentally the same conditions and human qualities which promote growth, development, and wholeness in the prospective child counselor.

Training Purpose

The fundamental purpose of the program which will be described is to establish a learning environment in which trainees and faculty cooperate to enhance the learning process of all participants. Although such a goal may sound simple and parallel to that of most other training programs, in actuality it becomes a rather distinct departure from the majority of existing training approaches. As specifics are discussed, these departures will become clarified.

One basic aim of the program would be the focus on real problems needing real solutions. In other words, the trainee would be encouraged to pursue his own interests and to become involved in his own search for resolutions to personal concerns of emotional, intellectual, or professional natures.

Second, the program would provide the learner with a variety of resources including books and journals, programmed materials, informed human beings with whom to interact, opportunities for observation of experienced counselors and follow-up discussions with them, audio-video tape libraries of experienced counselors at work, laboratory facilities for role-playing, and psychodramatic sessions.

A third basic thrust of the program would be to engage the individual student in the development of the total training program. As was implied earlier, this process of evolving a program unique to the individual's needs and desires would be a cooperative venture between the student and the faculty, with neither being cast as the final authority.

A fourth focus would be toward the development of counselor-trainee effectiveness through the medium of face-to-face interaction between real people—trainees and clients. Opportunities would be provided for trainees to work individually and in groups with children, parents, and other significant people in the child's life. Family counseling opportunities would also be provided. Trainees would be encouraged to involve themselves in the community in working with human problems as they exist in their natural context.

A final emphasis would be in the development of flexibility and adaptability to changingness. As was stated earlier, a primary characteristic of our modern society is its rapid rate of change. Trainees would be encouraged and aided in becoming increasingly involved in their own life-long educational process so that they would be able to flow with change rather than become threatened and resistant to it.

THE BASIC GROWTH GROUP

Counselor training programs have benefitted in a number of ways from federal support and sponsorship during the past decade. One fundamental benefit has been the development of the "institute" approach to training. Basically, this approach has involved the careful selection of a number of participants (usually about thirty) and the potential for an intensive educational experience for those selected. From our experience as enrollees and faculty in institute programs, we conclude that the opportunity for maximal learning is afforded when faculty and enrollees cooperate to further each other's learnings.

From this "institute" approach precedent, we suggest that the learning context be comprised of basic growth groups—groups of from ten to fifteen persons. These groups would preferably consist of a balance between males and females and a diversity of socioeconomic and cultural backgrounds. Each group would be assigned a faculty member who would function chiefly as a resource person and facilitator of growth experiences.

The fundamental purpose of the basic growth group would be to foster and promote the personal growth and development of the individual participants. Gibb (1968) has suggested that the goals of such a group would be to develop a high degree of membership, trust, affection, openness, cooperation, interdependence, and self-realization within, between, and among group members. In such a primary identification group, trainees would be able to increase their effectiveness in interpersonal relationships and be able to learn new ways of behaving with the support and encouragement of the basic group. More specifically, the hoped-for outcomes of the basic growth group would be as follows:

1. Greater trust. With a high quality experience, the trainee would come to trust in himself, in his own impulses and capabilities and in those of others.
2. Greater capacity to love and accept love. The trainee would come to care more deeply for himself and others and to express such feelings openly.
3. Greater empathy. The trainee would learn to take in stimulation from his outside world with reduced distortion and would be able to understand more accurately the feelings and thoughts of others.
4. Greater congruence. The trainee would learn to communicate his thoughts and feelings with minimal distortion. His verbal and nonverbal messages would be clear and consistent with each other.

5. Greater interdependence. The intensive group experience would provide the trainee with intense personal relationships—relationships in which each person can interdepend on the other. In other words, the individual trainee can learn to be autonomous and dependent as his needs and the needs of situations require (Gibb, 1968).

COMPLEMENTARY PERSONAL GROWTH EXPERIENCES

In addition to the experiences of personal growth which result from the intensive growth group, there are other sources and means for personal growth which complement the group experience. Moustakas (1968) identifies man's personal dialogue with himself and man's intimate encounter with another human being as additional pathways to the evolution of one's self-growth and one's growth in human relations.

In discussing man's need to "get in touch" with his inner experience and to tap his own senses, Moustakas (1968) emphasizes man's need for isolation, self-absorption, and solitude. The condition of being alone but not lonely is often fundamental to this development, "Discovery, preference, interest, and value coming through the confirmation of one's own senses are radically different realities from commitment and awareness that is shaped by the facilitation or intervention of others. There is no substitute for personal knowledge or for sensitivity and feeling that come from self-communion." (Moustakas, 1968, p. 34)

Other authors have also directed attention to self-learning that results from self-dialogue. Progoff (1963), a pioneering researcher in the theory and practice of human development, has evolved systematic procedures for helping the individual become aware of his own inner life experiences (dreams, fantasies, and so forth) as a source of self-knowledge and growth.

The writings of Farrow (1942), Horney (1942), and Shor (1955), among others, have emphasized the usefulness of self-analysis in developing increased understanding of one's behaviors and motives. In such a situation, the individual becomes a "participant–subject" and his own therapist as he searches for new meanings and insights into his self.

More recently, films as well as audio and video tape recordings have been used as self-learning devices. For example, Kagan, Krathwahl, and Miller (1963), Holmes (1964), and Huff (1966) have reported the use of reviewing and relistening procedures with clients and counselors-in-training. In general, they have concluded that the individual who reexperiences himself on tape has the potential for gaining increased self-understanding and knowledge through this process. In short, the value of self-learning seems to be not only supported in theory but also through empirical investigation.

Personal growth experiences also derive from one-to-one relationships where each person comes to know the other apart from facades and pretenses.

Such knowledge can only result from an intense interhuman relationship in which mutuality, trust, and deep understanding occur.

Certainly, it is the experience of us all that meaningful relationships are sometimes very complicated to foster and maintain. We have all known the struggle which results from trying to remain true to one's own commitments while trying to understand and respect the feelings of others at the same time. Such experiences, although difficult, are also profoundly important, for they provide opportunity for us to stretch for reaches beyond the known, to quest for mutuality beyond discord, and to search for deeper dimensions of one's self. As Moustakas (1968) has pointed out, the real benefit in such circumstances can only be derived when the two individuals in the relationship are willing to stay with the conflict until a meeting between I and Thou results at a newer and more significant level.

For the individual who is committed to furthering the well-being of others, such private and person-to-person experiences would seem to be of great benefit. Only inasmuch as the prospective counselor is willing to continue evolving who he is will he be able to engage in growth-promoting experiences for others.

PROFESSIONAL GROWTH EXPERIENCES

Ideally, professional and personal growth experiences interrelate and integrate to form experiences which lead toward the development of a competent, whole human being. For the sake of discussion, however, we have divided personal from professional growth experiences. We caution the reader to keep this consideration in mind as he involves himself in the following discussion.

Fundamental to the acquisition of professional competence as a counselor is the notion that learning is facilitated when the learner actively and responsibly participates in his learning process. Moreover, the most significant learnings are those derived from self-initiated bases—bases which confront the whole learner with real problems needing solutions. The key to effective learning is the involvement of the learner with matters which are perceived by the learner to have relevance and meaning to him.

Such an orientation necessitates that the counselor trainee would be largely responsible for the formulation of his own training program. Not only would he be responsible for involving himself in experiences which would promote his learning, but he would also be largely responsible for presenting evidence of his growth and development; that is, he would become knowledgeable about evaluation by being involved in his own self-evaluation processes.

To a very large degree, then, the faculty member in a program of this design would be a person who had a major responsibility for promoting an optimal climate and environment for learning to happen. Such a climate would be characterized by a high degree of trust in the trainees as persons with high motivation to invest themselves significantly in self-initiated learning. Additionally, the faculty member would be a resource person willing and able to discuss issues and theoretical positions with trainees, to demonstrate and discuss his own counseling style and process, to provide feedback to trainees relative to the trainee's growth as a facilitative human being, and to provide new experiences for trainees. Since we believe it is of importance for trainees to have experience with a variety of counselor styles and modes, it would be necessary to involve trainees with expert outside consultants who could complement the expertise of the regular faculty.

Again we emphasize that an atmosphere of cooperation and interdependence between and among faculty and trainees would be encouraged. Small discussion groups would be basic vehicles for helping trainees evaluate, understand, and integrate new ideas presented to them from readings, lectures, programmed materials, films, demonstrations, simulations, and other sources. In addition, opportunities would be available for trainees to work jointly as junior partners with faculty members engaged in research, community development projects, and so forth. Through an apprenticeship-type experience, the trainees would acquire understandings, skills, and methods for accomplishing his own creative projects as he evolves through his training.

Most assuredly, a key emphasis in any effective program designed to prepare counselors would be the practical application emphasis. Trainees need extensive experience in working with clients who express a wide variety of psychological states, coping mechanisms, cultural differences, and ways of expressing themselves. Moreover, trainees need the experience of being a counselor in a variety of helping modes such as play therapy, individual interviews, group sessions, family counseling with children, adolescents, and adults if they are able to function most adequately in helping relationships. Such experiences should pervade the entire duration of the training program.

In addition to the direct experience of counseling, trainees also need opportunities to function in consultative capacities. As was suggested earlier in this work, consultation with the minimally trained "natural helper" may be the major function of the professional counselor of the future. If so, then the provision of opportunity for trainees to have direct consultation with community agencies, organizations, institutions, and groups is a critical aspect of their learning experience. At this point we would like to underscore our conviction that consultation is not qualitatively different from counseling. The personal qualities and skills that have been discussed as applying to the effective counselor also apply to the effective consultant.

It has been our observation that counselors from differing work situations have difficulties in understanding and working effectively with administrative personnel; hence, we propose that the counselor trainee have the opportunity to function in administrative capacities. From such an experience the trainee would become more aware of management theory and application and of the problems faced by the administrator. In turn he would be able to discharge his duties as an agency counselor with understandings of the total agency function.

Earlier in this discussion we noted that one profitable way of learning to do research was through the trainee apprenticing himself as a junior partner to a faculty member actively involved in ongoing research. Similarly, we believe that competence in counseling, consulting, and administrative management may be acquired by the modifications of the junior partner approach.

Van Atta (1969) has discussed the co-counselor approach to the learning and supervision of counseling practice with counselor trainees. He suggests, as have others (Gibb, 1968; Corsini, 1964), that the trainee work in a co-counselor capacity with an experienced counselor. Such an approach has the advantage of allowing the trainee to observe the experienced counselor at work, to work with complex cases which go beyond his level of competence, and to stretch himself to his fullest with the realization that his experienced co-counselor is available for support and for "bailing him out" if the need should arise. In many situations we believe that a similar process could be adapted to consultative and administrative roles. When the trainees are afforded the opportunity to deal with real problems while maintaining the assurance that there is an "expert" to fall back on if needed, then they can invest themselves to their fullest capacities in the experiences which are provided.

Throughout this work we have placed considerable emphasis on certain fundamental therapeutic qualities which research and numerous practicing counselors have found to be critical to client growth. We have discussed experiential approaches to the fostering of higher levels of these conditions in prospective counselors through the use of self-dialogue learnings and through other activities and experiences designed to promote "wholeness" in the trainee. Since, however, empathy, warmth, and self-congruence are such central ingredients in the growth-promoting relationships, we would like to present one additional method for trainees to use in developing higher levels of these qualities. Truax and Carkhuff (1967) in their book *Toward Effective Counseling and Psychotherapy: Training and Practice* have discussed specific procedures that they have used to promote higher expressed levels of empathy, warmth, and genuineness in trainee functioning. Basically, they advocate that the inexperienced counselor be exposed to sample recordings of experienced counselors providing very high levels of these therapeutic conditions. From these samples the trainee can become aware of what should be done in the therapeutic relationship. In addition, such recordings can provide

the trainee with some familiarity with client problems, dynamics, and relationship variables.

From listening to positive examples of therapeutic skill, the trainees
can move to role-playing situations where they successively assume the role
of counselor and client. These interactions are recorded and subsequently
rated, using the scales for assessing levels of the three facilitative conditions
which have been devised by Truax and Carkhuff (1967). Experienced
counselors would help the trainees become proficient in the use of the rating
scales while also encouraging them to experiment with new modes of behaviors which would reflect higher levels of counselor-offered conditions.

Building upon such experiences in role-played and simulated situations,
the trainee would then move into counseling contacts with live clients. The
counseling sessions would be recorded and evaluated using the rating scales.
From these ratings, the trainee would get direct and immediate feedback
regarding the quality of his relationship with his clients. In turn, this feedback
could be used for new learning and for the furthered growth of the trainee.

EVALUATION

Traditionally, counselor training programs have focused on grades of
trainees in academic content areas and supervisor judgments of competence
in counseling skills and methods. Unfortunately, neither of these criteria has
proven to be highly correlated with the counselor's ability as a therapeutic
person; hence, alternative evaluation procedures are needed.

As was mentioned earlier in this chapter, one criterion of evaluation
which is relevant to the training program outlined is self-evaluation. As the
trainee learns to be self-disciplined and self-directing, he will learn to evaluate
his own work and contributions from the basis of his own purposes. When
the trainee is free to pursue his own goals, he will work toward the realization
of these goals rather than for the approval of others.

Another evaluation procedure which would be fundamental to this
program would be continuous feedback from peers and faculty members. It
would be helpful for the trainee to receive direct verbal and nonverbal feedback from those with whom he is associated in the program so that he would
be able to assess the effects of his behavior upon others. From such feedback
he could continuously reassess his growth and development in personal and
professional areas. This type of feedback process would be more unique to
the intensive small group experience but would certainly not be exclusive to
it.

A third source of evaluative feedback could come from clients, parents,
friends of clients, and others who might be significant persons in the lives of
clients. Our own counseling experiences have led us to conclude that these
sources of feedback are indeed important sources. Moreover, they are sources

which are seldom used in judging counselor competence. It profits little if the counselor is the only one who thinks he is accomplishing positive outcomes. If these same positive outcomes are not reportable by the client and by those who intimately share the client's world, they may be only counselor illusions.

Rogers (1969) has suggested another procedure which would seem to have considerable merit in demonstrating trainee competence. He advocates that the trainee establish a cumulative folder of the work which he has accomplished during his training. This folder might include reports of projects in which the trainee was involved, papers written exploring certain ideas, record of his own self-evaluations, case reports, research ideas and studies conducted, publications, types of interviews, and other evidences of growth and accomplishment. Similar to the professional artist's use of a portfolio, the counselor trainee would be able to submit his collected work to faculty and peer evaluators and to prospective employers.

As we have discussed these various evaluation procedures, we have tried to focus on the relevance of evaluation as a stimulus for trainee growth. Evaluation is only useful to the trainee when it gives him some idea of where he stands at a moment in time relative to some sought-after goal. Evaluation has little meaning if it does not promote the redirection and refocusing of trainee goals. Learning is advanced through the cycle of trying something and getting feedback about its effect. In an atmosphere of freedom and acceptance, the feedback can be positive or negative with learning being the result; that is, the individual is not evaluated as a "good" or "bad" person on the basis of his experiment. He learns what he can glean from the experience and moves on. This process is critical to optimal growth.

It should also be noted that multiple and diverse evaluation procedures are potentially more profitable to the learner than singular ones. In other words, feedback from a wide variety of sources accomplished in a variety of ways provides the trainee with a much broader and more solid basis for further growth; hence, we advocate that the trainee avail himself of feedback from peers, colleagues, clients, students, supervisors, teachers, and others who are capable of providing it. Moreover, we suggest that a variety of methods be used to accomplish the task.

ADDITIONAL CONSIDERATIONS

The program which we have outlined in the preceding pages is one which would be very intense and demanding for trainees, their spouses, and their children. In more traditional programs with which we have been involved, we have often observed growing distance between trainees and their families as a result of the training experience. A primary complaint seems to revolve around the spouse's not being able to understand and appreciate the growth experiences of the trainee; hence, conflicts emerge and promote dissention in family units as well as provide inhibition to trainee growth.

In order to combat such problems, we have been able to provide experiences for the spouses of trainees to become involved directly in experiences of a comparable nature to that of the trainees, but on a limited scale. In some instances this has meant having couples T-groups and providing sensory awareness experiences. In others it has involved observations of counseling sessions and the supervisory process. In others it has meant participation in role-playing and simulation games. In still others it has involved attendance at lectures and special presentations.

The results of these spouse experiences have been gratifying indeed. Not only does the inclusion of the spouse reduce the potential for family conflict due to the spouse's increased understanding of the trainee's educational experiences, but it also in many cases has provided the incentive for spouses to become strongly and actively supportive of the trainees' efforts. Consequently, we believe that quality counselor training programs need to consider not only experiences which will benefit the trainee but ones which will also encourage spouse involvement and support.

Another consideration which seems worthy of comment is our contention that trainees involved in intensive training experiences of the kind which we have discussed also need the opportunity to periodically "get away." Although a training program need not involve the trainee in so much work that he "becomes a dull boy," such a potential does exist; hence, it seems important that trainees would be able to retreat from the rigors of the training experience for brief periods of time for the purpose of refreshing themselves in nonprofessional surroundings and activities.

In our own graduate training we discovered the importance of having a "home base." By "home base" we mean a central room location set aside for informal contacts between and among trainees, faculty, and consultants. It was important for us as trainees to know that this was our place simply to be together, to evolve ideas over coffee, to review tapes, to talk about baseball, or whatever. Moreover, we always knew there would be at least one of our peers or instructors there with whom to share experiences.

Since we have gone on to become counselor trainers, we have observed the same need in our students. The opportunity for sharing and learning or just sitting in an informal "home base" setting seems to be fundamental to the well-being of trainees. When such a need is recognized, respected, and acted upon by faculty, benefits occur both to the trainees and their mentors.

COMMENT

In this chapter we have discussed what we believe to be the emerging directions of mental health programs with special emphasis on child counseling. We have attempted to provide the reader with some sense of the dynamic and zestful nature of the areas as it seeks to evolve into a mature discipline. In addition, we have developed what we believe to be an innovative child counselor training model. We have field-tested many of the ideas contained in this model and have found them to be important aspects of training to our students. Other ideas which we have presented reflect practical applications of our overarching philosophy.

In general, we have tried to emphasize that training is a process leading toward the development of "whole" people. Such a process, of necessity, then, needs to focus on both the affective and the cognitive needs of the trainee. Although for discussion purposes we have separated the more affective domain from the cognitive, we recognize that training must be integrative for the individual. Certainly, all experiences have both affective and cognitive dimensions. Training should recognize and effectively exploit this knowledge.

REFERENCES

ACKERMAN, N. W. "Adolescent Problems: A Symptom of Family Disturbance." *Family Process* 1 (1962):202–213.

ALLEN, T. W. "Effectiveness of Counselor Trainees as a Function of Psychological Openness." *Journal of Counseling Psychology* 14 (1967):35–40.

———, AND WHITELEY, J. M. *Dimensions of Effective Counseling*. Columbus, Ohio: Charles E. Merrill Publishing Co., 1968.

BERENSON, B. G., AND CARKHUFF, R. R., eds. *Sources of Gain in Counseling and Psychotherapy*. New York: Holt, Rinehart & Winston, Inc., 1967.

BERGIN, A. E. "The Effects of Psychotherapy: Negative Results Revisited." *Journal of Counseling Psychology* 10 (1963):244–249.

———. "Some Implications of Psychotherapy Research for Therapeutic Practice." *Journal of Abnormal Psychology* 71 (1966):235–246.

———, AND SOLOMON, SANDRA. "Personality and Performance Correlates of Empathic Understanding in Psychotherapy." *American Psychologist* 18 (1963):393.

BORDIN, E. S. *Psychological Counseling*. New York: Appleton-Century-Crofts, 1968.

BOSZORMENYI-NAGY, I., AND FRAMO, J. L., eds. *Intensive Family Therapy*. New York: Harper & Row, Publishers, 1965.

BRAMMER, L. M., AND SHOSTROM, E. L. *Therapeutic Psychology*. Englewood Cliffs, N.J.: Prentice-Hall, Inc., 1968.

BUEHLER, R. E.; PATTERSON, G. R.; AND FURNISS, JEAN M. "The Reinforcement of Behavior in Institutional Settings." *Behavior Research and Therapy* 4 (1966):157–167.

CARKHUFF, R. R., AND BERENSON, B. G. *Beyond Counseling and Therapy*. New York: Holt, Rinehart & Winston, Inc., 1967.

———, and TRUAX, C. B. "Lay Mental Health Counseling: The Effects of Lay Group Counseling." *Journal of Consulting Psychology* 29 (1965): 426–431.

CORSINI, R. *Methods of Group Psychotherapy*. Chicago: William James Press, 1964.

COWEN, E. L.; ZAX, M.; AND LAIRD, J. D. "A College Student Volunteer Program in the Elementary School Setting." *Community Mental Health Journal* 2 (1966):319–328.

DIMICK, K. M.; HUFF, V. E.; AND RICKSECKER, E. L. "Training for Humanness: An Approach." *Journal of Employment Counseling,* in press.

DREIKURS, R. *Understanding Your Children.* Burlington, Vt.; University of Vermont Press, 1969.

FARNSWORTH, D. *Psychiatry, Education and the Young Adult.* Springfield, Ill.: Charles C Thomas, Publisher, 1965.

FARROW, E. P. *Psychoanalyze Yourself.* New York: International Universities Press, 1942.

FELLOWS, L., AND WOLPIN, M. "High School Psychology Trainees in a Mental Hospital." Paper read at California State Psychology Association, January, 1966.

FORD, D. H., AND URBAN, H. B. *Systems of Psychotherapy.* New York: John Wiley & Sons, Inc., 1963.

GIBB, J. R. "The Counselor as a Role-Free Agent." In *Counseling Theories and Counselor Education,* edited by C. A. Parker. Boston: Houghton Mifflin Company, 1968.

GLASSER, W. *Reality Therapy.* New York: Harper & Row, Publishers, 1965.

GUERNEY, B. G., ed. *Psychotherapeutic Agents.* New York: Holt, Rinehart & Winston, Inc., 1969.

HARPER, R. A. *Psychotherapy: 36 Systems.* Englewood Cliffs, N.J.: Prentice-Hall, Inc., 1959.

HARRIS, FLORENCE R.; WOLF, M. M.; AND BAER, D. M. Effects of Adult Social Reinforcement on Child Behavior." *Young Children* 20 (1964):8–17.

HOBBS, N. "Mental Health's Third Revolution." *American Journal of Orthopsychiatry* 34 (1964): 822–833.

HOLMES, JUNE E. "Counselee Listening: Another Dimension of the Counseling Process." *Counselor Education and Supervision* 3 (1964):153–157.

HORNEY, KAREN. *Self Analysis.* New York: W. W. Norton & Company, Inc., 1942

HUFF, V. E. "The Effect of Interview Replay on Client Movement Toward Psychological Health." Unpublished doctoral dissertation, University of Arizona, 1966.

JACKSON, D. D. "The Question of Family Homeostasis." *Psychiatric Quarterly Supplement* 31 (1957):79–90.

JOHNSTON, RUTH. "Some Casework Aspects of Using Foster Grandparents for Emotionally Disturbed Children." *Children* 14 (1967):46–52.

KAGAN, N.; KRATHWAHL, D. R.; AND MILLER, R. "Stimulated Recall in Therapy Using Video-Tapes: A Case Study." *Journal of Counseling Psychology* 10 (1963):237–243.

KELL, B. L., AND MUELLER, W. J. *Impact and Change: A Study of Counseling Relationships.* New York: Appleton-Century-Crofts, 1966.

KEMP, C. G. "Influence of Dogmatism on the Training of Counselors." *Journal of Counseling Psychology* 9 (1962):155–157.

―――. *Intangibles in Counseling.* Boston: Houghton Mifflin Company, 1967.

MASLOW, A. H. "The Farther Reaches of Human Nature." *Journal of Transpersonal Psychology* 1 (1969):1–9.

MASSERMAN, J. H., ed. *Individual and Familial Dynamics.* New York: Grune & Stratton, Inc., 1959.

MOUSTAKAS, C. E. *Individuality and Encounter.* Cambridge, Mass.: Howard A. Doyle Publishing Co., 1968.

PARKER, C. E., ed. *Counseling Theories and Counselor Education*. New York: Houghton Mifflin Company, 1968.

PERLS, F. Foreword in E. L. Shostrom, *Man The Manipulator*. Nashville: Abingdon Press, 1967.

POSER, E. G. "The Effect of Therapists' Training on Group Therapeutic Outcome." *Journal of Consulting Psychology* 30 (1966):283–289.

PROGOFF, I. *The Symbolic and the Real*. New York: Julian Press, Inc., 1963.

RICKS, D. F. "Counseling and Psychotherapy Tomorrow: Forecasts and Questions." In *Explorations in Sociology and Counseling,* edited by D. A. Hansen. Boston: Houghton Mifflin Company, 1969.

RIOCH, MARGARET J.; ELKES, E.; FLINT, A. A.; USDANSKY, B. S.; NEWAN, R. G.; AND SILBER, E. "National Institute of Mental Health Pilot Study in Training Mental Health Counselors." *American Journal of Orthopsychiatry* 33 (1963): 678–689.

ROGERS, C. R. *Client-centered Therapy*. Boston: Houghton Mifflin Company, 1951.

———. *On Becoming A Person*. Boston: Houghton Mifflin Company, 1961.

———. "The Therapeutic Relationship: The Core of Guidance." *Harvard Educational Review* 32 (1962):416–429.

———. *Freedom To Learn*. Columbus, Ohio: Charles E. Merrill Publishing Co., 1969.

———. "Interpersonal Relationships: USA 2000." *Journal of Applied Behavioral Science* 4 (1968):265–280.

———, AND DYMOND, ROSALIND, eds. *Psychotherapy and Personality Change*. Chicago: University of Chicago Press, 1954.

SATIR, VIRGINIA. *Conjoint Family Therapy*. Palo Alto: Science & Behavior Books, Inc., 1966.

SHAH, S. A. "Training and Utilizing a Mother as the Therapist for Her Child." Paper read at Eastern Psychology Association, Boston, 1967.

SHOR, R. E. "Recorder Self-Therapy: A Technique." *Journal of Counseling Psychology* 2 (1955):150–151.

SHOSTROM, E. L. "Group Therapy: Let the Buyer Beware." *Psychology Today* 2 (1969):36–40.

STIEPER, D. R., AND WIENER, D. N. *Dimensions of Psychotherapy*. Chicago: Aldine Publishing Company, 1965.

STOLLAK, G. E. "The Experimental Effects of Training College Students as Play Therapists." *Psychotherapy: Theory, Research and Practice* 5 (1968):77–80.

SUBCOMMITTEE ON COUNSELOR TRAINEE SELECTION. *Journal of Counseling Psychology* 1 (1954):174–179.

SZASZ, T. S. "The Myth of Mental Illness." *American Psychologist* 15 (1960): 113–118.

TRUAX, C. B., AND CARKHUFF, R. R. *Toward Effective Counseling and Psychotherapy: Training and Practice*. Chicago: Aldine Publishing Company, 1967.

———; SILBER, L. D.; AND WARGO, D. G. "Training and Change in Psychotherapeutic Skills." Unpublished manuscript, University of Arkansas, 1966.

VAN ATTA, R. E. "Co-Therapy as a Supervisory Process." *Psychotherapy: Theory, Research and Practice* 6 (1969):137–139.

WAHLER, R. G.; WINKEL, G. H.; PATTERSON, R. F.; AND MORRISON, D. C. "Mothers as Behavior Therapists for Their Own Children." *Behavior Research and Therapy* 3 (1965):113–124.

WALDER, L. O.; COHEN, S. I.; BREITER, D. E.; DASTON, P. G.; HIRSCH, I. S.; AND LIEBOWITZ, J. M. "Teaching Behavioral Principles to Parents of Disturbed Children." Paper read at Eastern Psychology Association, Boston, 1967.

SELECTED ADDITIONAL READINGS

ATKINSON, R. C. "Beverly: The Computer is a Tutor." *Psychology Today* 1 (1968):36–39, 57–60.

FROMM, E. *The Revolution of Hope: Toward A Humanized Technology.* New York: Harper & Row, Inc., 1968.

GUNTHER, B. *Sense Relaxation Below Your Mind.* New York: P. F. Collier, Inc., 1968.

HIRSCH, W. Z., ed. *Inventing Education for the Future.* San Francisco: Chandler Publishing Co., 1967.

JOURARD, S. M., AND OVERLADE, D. C., eds. *Reconciliation: A Theory of Man Transcending.* New York: D. Van Nostrand Co., Inc., 1966.

LAING, R. D. *The Politics of Experience.* New York: Ballantine Books, Inc., 1967.

MALTZ, M. *Psycho-Cybernetics.* Englewood Cliffs, N. J.: Prentice-Hall, Inc., 1960.

MURPHY, G. *Human Potentialities.* New York: Basic Books, Inc., Publisher, 1958.

OTTO, H. A., ed. *Explorations in Human Potentials.* Springfield, Ill.: Charles C Thomas, Publisher, 1966.

PERLS, F. S.; HEFFERLINE, R. F.; AND GOODMAN, P. *Gestalt Therapy.* New York: Julian Press, 1951.

ROYCE, J. R. *The Encapsulated Man.* Princeton: D. Van Nostrand Co., Inc., 1964.

SHOSTROM, E. L. *Man the Manipulator.* New York: Abingdon Press, 1967.

SMITH, A. *The Body.* New York: Avon Books, 1968.

WETZEL, R. "Use of Behavioral Techniques in a Case of Compulsive Stealing." *Journal of Consulting Psychology* 30 (1966):367–374.

WIENER, N. *The Human Use of Human Beings.* Garden City, N. Y.: Doubleday & Company, Inc., 1954.

13

Summary of Concepts

This, the final chapter, has as its purpose more than a restating of what the preceding chapters have presented. We like to think of this chapter as highlighting the concepts of our thinking with regard to child counseling and the child counselor.

Originally it was our plan to make the final chapter a prediction of the future of child counseling. Our idea was to contact leaders from the counseling, educational, political, and social scenes and summarize what they projected the future of child counseling to be.

The major response to our request was basically twofold: (1) Several of the individuals we contacted felt they knew so little about child counseling that they were unwilling to guess at its future; and (2) Others reported that they were so deeply involved in their own projects that they lacked the time or interest to involve themselves in guessing at the future of child counseling.

We did, however, receive a number of responses to our request. Some of what was communicated to us by this means has affected our thinking throughout the text. Several of the letters we received included statements which we have quoted in the body of this chapter where they seemed to integrate and state a concept particularly well. Following are the highlights of our presentation as we perceive them.

CHILDREN ARE PEOPLE

Throughout this writing we have emphasized the concept that children are people. As such they are fully deserving of respect and trust. This point is well made in personal correspondence received from Jack Gibb, a nationally prominent human relations theorist and practitioner. Gibb says,

Our theory of trust relationships is particularly suited to work with children, of course. Our theory is that a personal, open, allowing, and interdependent relationship is therapeutic and growth-inducing. This kind of relationship can be established in the home, in the school, in the classroom, and in the counseling group. The primary problem is to learn to trust children. Most counselors and teachers and parents with whom we work have so many fears and distrusts of children that counseling is very difficult for them. The problem is not the children but the teachers and parents. Learning to counsel children is a process of adult learning—adults learning to lose their fears and distrusts of children.[1]

THE WORLD IS NOT BLACK AND WHITE

Our language has forced us to communicate and sometimes to even live as though the world were composed of black-and-white issues. Throughout our discussion we have tried to continually emphasize that such is not the case. The world is not dichotomous. Rather, it is composed of issues, concepts, ideas, beliefs, life stages, relationships, all of which exist somewhere between the polar extremes of black and white.

The recognition of the dilemma between the dichotomous nature of language and the continuous nature of the real world is to us a significant recognition. The child counselor who understands is one who is aware of the nuances of meanings surrounding single concepts. He must be able to abandon dichotomous ways of approaching the world so that the unique meanings of the client can be deeply understood.

LEARNING AND EXPERIENCE

Learning is a process leading to knowledge which in turn is reflected in behavior. For learning to be most meaningful, to effect behavior change, it must be personally relevant to the individual learner. Moreover, this learner must become involved in his own learning process through the pursuit of his own private interest and needs. From our observations and experiences and the reported experiences of others, significant learning is also a function of direct experience; that is, behavior seems to be most significantly affected when the learner is engaged in experiences from which the total organism learns.

This approach is contrasted to the "learning about" approach which is more characteristic of lecturers and books presenting information to a prospective learner on the assumption that information changes behavior. Although we value the contribution of lectures, books, and other information media, we believe that such sources are peripheral to direct learning opportunities.

THE HUMANISTIC PHILOSOPHY

From the preceding chapters, it should be apparent that our emphasis on child counseling stems from a humanistic philosophy. Fundamental to

1. J. R. Gibb. Personal communication, 1969.

this philosophy is a belief in the dignity and worth of the individual human being and in his right to freedom and to the realization of his total humanness. As you have read, you may have become aware of an apparent contradiction in our philosophy, namely that on the one hand we advocate freeing children to believe and behave as they choose, and on the other, we strongly advocate that child counselors operate from a humanistic orientation.

We feel we have superseded the "I can't accept people who can't accept people" contradiction. We do believe in freedom of choice for the individual. We further believe, however, that the individual can choose most wisely when he has the fullest information about the alternatives from which his choices must come.

We have made our presentation of the development of a humanistic philosophy for the child counselor as an alternative that may be chosen by the child counselor. It has been our experience that such a philosophy is an effective way of working with people toward their growth and development. We feel strongly that the adoption of such a philosophy on the part of the child counselor, the teacher, the parent, and the child is a step toward a better world in which to live.

A letter that we received from Barry Stevens, co-author of the book *Person to Person,* seemed to capture our thinking regarding the development of a humanistic philosophy. She states,

> Essentially there are two views of man. One of them is that man has to be pushed around, filled with information, molded, manipulated, made to behave. This becomes internalized and I also push myself around, etc. The other concept of man—a more religious one, in my view—is that we are born with the ability to find our own way, make our own discoveries, choose for ourselves. This is not a *new* view. It keeps being re-discovered.
>
> The other view says that you must do what others want you to. When I was a small child, this view threw me into chaos and despair. I had seen a globe, and knew the world was round. When people said that I (or someone else) must do what others wanted me to, I "saw" this world, with people sticking out of it all over, like hairs growing out of a head, and each person was bowing to another person, doing what the *other* wanted him to do. In such a world *everybody* was left out. This world was not for me. I was blackness shot with pain. I wanted to die rather than go on with it. I behaved badly and I knew this, and I couldn't stop. Then my mother—a very gentle person who loved children—expressed her own despair saying, "I don't know what's *wrong* with you!"
>
> There was nothing in the world around me, or in the language that I knew, to make it possible for me to express what was going on in me. I could only take from my mother's statement that there was something wrong with me, and that it was so awful that even a grownup didn't know what it was. I went looking for it, and in the process lost touch with *what was going on in me.* My own answer was there—or here—in me. It always is. When I lose my way, I need someone to help me find it, not tell me what it is, for that, they can never know. "Counseling" means "giving advice." I would like us all to give up this notion that any one of

us can advise another. I don't know a word for helping people to find their own answers, but at least this is happening. More and more of us are working to break up our own giving of advice and telling people what to do, wishing to break up our interference in other people's lives in the name of "responsibility." If you make yourself responsible for me, how can I become responsible for myself?[2]

HUMAN GROWTH CONDITIONS

The preceding quotation points to the necessity for allowing the individual to assume responsibility for himself, which is, of course, a form of respect. In addition to this important concept, there are a number of other conditions that are equally as important in a growth-producing relationship or atmosphere.

The relationship or atmosphere must allow for authentic interactions between people. It must be one which fosters open communication including feedback to the individual as to how he is perceived. It must be interdependent and allow for cooperation rather than competition. It must be warm and understanding of the individual.

These and other characteristics must be the prime factors in the establishment of a relationship or an environment that fosters the growth and development of the child.

EVOLUTION OF A PERSONAL THEORY

Although, as previously stated, we have hopes of influencing the thinking and actions of child counselors, we do not in any way want to "cram our thinking down anyone's throat." We do feel, however, that the most effective counselor is one who operates from a position of consistency.

One purpose of this book has been to make a presentation and to encourage the reader to filter through his own experience what we have said. Another quotation from the correspondence we have had with Barry Stevens serves to illustrate this point.

A friend of mine has three teen-age daughters, the youngest of whom is blind and has been since birth. She says, "Ugh! I don't like him. He's ugly!" She says, "I hate the color of that dress." She does not know these things. They are not a part of her experience. She has heard her sisters say them. And I thought, "How much of what I say is like that—not a part of my experience at all."[3]

We would encourage the reader to develop, for himself, a consistent philosophy evolved through his own experience—one that is open to change,

2. Barry Stevens. Personal communication, 1969.
3. Ibid.

but that is a reflection of the uniqueness of his individuality. As for the part that this text might play in such a development, we ask the reader to compare his own experience with what we have written and look again at what he believes and how he behaves.

COUNSELING AS A WAY OF LIFE

The effective counselor is a facilitative person, using the tools he possesses to extend himself most effectively to others. We do not feel that counseling, as we have discussed it, can be turned on or off. Counseling is a way of being, a way of behaving, a way of living. The counselor attempts to affect human growth potentials whether inside the counselor's office or on the street corner. The truly facilitative person is facilitative regardless of the setting.

The tools that the counselor possesses can be seen as analogous to the tools of the carpenter. Individual interviews, play therapy, psychodrama, and others are all ways of effecting change in human beings as are the saw and hammer tools for effecting changes in building materials.

The master carpenter has skills in the use of many tools. He inspects a situation and chooses to use the tool or tools that he possesses to best build the building. He takes into consideration not only the tools themselves but the objective to be accomplished and his personal skill with the various tools.

The master counselor also has at his disposal the use of many tools. With experience he becomes more and more skillful with his tools, developing from time to time new ways of using them while also developing skills in the use of new tools.

A further application of the carpenter-counselor analogy is that the carpenter's tools are merely an extension of his arm, his hand, and his fingers. Although it would be difficult, a house could be built by a carpenter with only the use of his hands. The tools help him make a better product, but by themselves they are useless. The significant variable is the counselor and the manner in which he can use the available tools to extend himself most effectively to his clients.

APPLICATION OF CONCEPTS TO SCHOOLS AND COUNSELOR TRAINING PROGRAMS

Most of what we have said regarding the growth and development of the child client has direct or indirect application to the education of the child in the public school and the education of the child counselor. Beliefs in human potentials, the facilitative characteristics of the individual, and the importance of a growth-producing environment are all fundamental considerations which lead to productive learning. From this premise we have developed what we consider to be innovative approaches to the education of children and counselor trainees.

CHILD COUNSELORS WORK WITH CHILDREN AND ADULTS

A number of examples we have used in this book come from our experience in working with adults as well as with children. We would like to point out that the book is written to benefit adults who work with children. Children's attitudes and behaviors will be affected by our writing only as an indirect result.

A more important rationale, however, has to do with what we perceive to be the role of the child counselor. As we envision him, he works with both children and adults. It is our belief that counseling with teachers, counseling with parents, and family counseling will all become methods that the child counselor of the future will need to use professionally.

Child counselors have as their primary responsibility the fostering of the growth and development of the child. This most certainly will take the form of counseling directly with children. However, the child counselor will also work toward his goal of helping foster child development in direct or indirect ways through counseling with the adults in the child's environment.

Ann Dreyfuss, a prominent child and family therapist, seems to underscore this notion of helping children through other than the traditional child-therapist interaction model. In a personal communication to us she writes:

I work with elementary school children in individual counseling, in group counseling, and see the child within his family structure (family therapy). I see each of these areas as important, and it is ideal though rare, when they can all happen together. I believe that children are extremely well able to work within the family system in family therapy and often this seems to be the most productive and forward moving way of approaching counseling. Often therapists say that they are not old enough to understand. Yet I feel that they understand a tremendous amount more than they are given credit for and can be significant in helping work through some of the family problems. It is my belief that the more family counseling can be brought into educational work, the better off we will be![4]

THE GESTALT CONCEPT

Throughout this book we have separated concepts that are, in fact, either inseparable or that are severely weakened by separation. The individual is truly "more than" the sum of his parts. The "more than" aspect comes from the quality that is added by the effect of the combination of the many separate parts.

4. Ann Dreyfuss. Personal communication, 1969.

The strength of a family, for example, is not the sum total of the strengths of each person in the family—it is more. The strength that is inherent in the family from the unitedness of the family is not any one person's doing. Rather, it is a function of the combined individual strengths plus the unitedness of the family.

The individual child and adult should be viewed in the same way. For the sake of discussion, we have fragmented the individual into separate parts. This we have done, not because we view these parts separately, but because we know of no other way to discuss the whole.

The child or adult is, however, much more than these separate parts. In counseling it must be remembered that it is the total being with whom we are working. A preoccupation with any one of the many factors that make up that being causes one to lose track of the more significant total person.

A BELIEF IN PEOPLE'S ABILITY TO CHANGE

On one hand it would seem that a belief in the ability of the individual to change is so basic that it does not warrant discussion. On the other hand, such a belief is so essential to counseling that it deserves a great deal of attention.

We must all believe at some level that people can and do change or such processes as teaching and counseling are nonsense. It is, however, appalling the number of times judgments are made regarding an individual in terms of "that is what he is," allowing for little thought of what he could become.

Briefly, then, it appears to us that intellectually almost everyone connected with the education of children from parent to teacher to counselor to administrator believes in the ability of the child to change. In terms of behavior, however, this concept is often forgotten in favor of simply evaluating and categorizing what a child is.

Our discussion regarding the aspects of the effective counselor might serve as an example for this concept. Let us assume for a moment that you, the reader, could accept what we have stated about the facilitative characteristics of the effective counselor. Was your reaction as you read about these characteristics one of surveying yourself to guess at the quality and quantity you possessed? Was it one of evaluating others in these characteristics? Or was it one of saying to yourself, "How can I increase my abilities along these lines and how can I help others to demonstrate more of these qualities than they presently do?"

We firmly believe in the value and importance of the individual as he is. We further believe that each person can become something more than he presently is. It is toward this end that we have presented our concept of child counseling.

Name Index

245

Neill, A. S., 55, 83, 212
Nelson, R. C., 166, 181
Newan, R. G., 236
Niland, T. M., 165
Nitzschke, D., 10, 11, 12, 21, 22
Norris, W., 185, 195

Ohlsen, M. M., 153, 160, 164, 212
Oldridge, B., 11, 22
Osborn, A. F., 55
Osipow, S. H., 196
Otto, H. A., 161, 164, 237
Otto, H. J., 11, 22
Overlade, D. C., 237

Parker, B., 143
Parker, C., 213, 236
Parsons, F., 6, 7, 22
Patterson, C. H., 11, 57, 85, 86
Patterson, G. R., 218, 234
Patterson, R. F., 236
Paul, G., 86
Pavlov, I., 4, 75
Pepinsky, H. B., 57, 85
Pepinsky, P., 57, 85
Perls, F. S., 86, 214, 236, 237
Peters, H. J., 196
Phillips, B., 55
Piaget, J., 37, 181
Pine, G. J., 79, 84, 122, 143
Pinel, P., 2
Poser, E. G., 218, 236
Progoff, I., 227, 236

Quaranta, J. J., 196

Rabe, P., 85
Rank, O., 79, 85
Redl, F., 55
Reik, T., 144
Renfield, R., 212
Riccio, A. C., 196
Ricks, D. F., 219, 236
Ricksecker, E. R., 218, 235
Rioch, M., 218, 236
Roe, A., 189, 195
Rogers, C., 8, 20, 22, 41, 54, 57, 79–80,
    81, 85, 91, 104, 105, 107, 122, 144,
    162, 164, 171, 177, 181, 194, 195,
    216–217, 221, 222, 223, 232, 236
Rohen, T. M., 165

Rokeach, M., 111, 122
Rothman, E., 55
Rosseau, J. J., 167, 168, 181
Royce, J. R., 237
Ryckoff, I. M., 105

Salter, A., 86
Sangiuliano, I., 122
Satir, V., 165, 197, 212, 218, 239
Schmeding, R. W., 139, 143
Schmidt, L. D., 105
Schmuck, R., 212
Schofield, W., 105, 122
Schutz, W. C., 156, 161, 164
Schwitzgebel, R. L., 78, 85
Scott, L. H., 55
Seeman, J., 151, 164
Shacter, H. S., 55
Shah, S. A., 218, 236
Shapiro, J. C., 105
Shepherd, C. R., 165
Shertzer, B., 86, 122
Shor, R. E., 227, 236
Shostrom, E., 20, 21, 26, 33, 58–59, 68,
    84, 91, 104, 122, 141, 143, 214, 217,
    234, 236, 237
Silber, E., 236
Silber, L. D., 224, 236
Simon, N., 3
Slavson, S. R., 174, 178, 181
Slawson, R. R., 55
Smith, A., 237
Sniffen, A. M., 153–154, 163
Snyder, R., 122
Snyder, W., 105
Solomon, L., 147, 169
Solomon, S., 224, 234
Sonstegard, 150, 164
Spence, K., 29
Stefflre, B., 56, 67, 80, 85
Stevens, B., 240–241
Stevic, R. R., 196
Stieper, D. R., 214, 236
Stollak, G., 218, 236
Stone, S., 86, 122
Stroof, J., 195
Sullivan, H. S., 37, 54, 86
Super, D., 189–190, 195
Sweeny, T. J., 116, 122
Szasz, T. S., 214, 236

Subject Index